The Night Lake

COUNTERPOINT | Berkeley, California

THE
NIGHT
LAKE

A Young Priest Maps the Topography of Grief

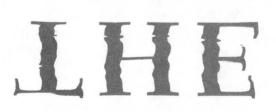

Liz Tichenor

The Night Lake

First hardcover edition: 2021

Works referenced, with gratitude:
Abide with Me: words by Henry Francis Lyte (1793–1847); music is Eventide by William Henry Monk (1823–1889). *If We Live*: text is Romans 14:8, NRSV, with gratitude for the music written by Rolf Vegdahl in *Singing Our Prayer: A Companion to Holden Prayer Around the Cross* © 2009 Augsburg Fortress. *Open My Heart*: reprinted with permission by Ana Hernández, © 2005; www.anahernandez.org. Psalm quotations are taken from the Psalter in the 1979 Book of Common Prayer. Quotations from prayers and anthems are also taken from the 1979 *Book of Common Prayer*. Unless otherwise indicated, all Scripture quotations are from New Revised Standard Version Bible, copyright © 1989 National Council of the Churches of Christ in the United States of America. Used by permission. All rights reserved worldwide. Scripture quotations marked (ESV) are from the ESV® Bible (the Holy Bible, English Standard Version®), copyright © 2001 by Crossway, a publishing ministry of Good News Publishers. Used by permission. All rights reserved. *The Storm*, Copyright © 1994, 1997 by Wendell Berry, from *Entries*. Reprinted by permission of Counterpoint Press. *Within our darkest night* and *Stay with me*: chants written by Jacques Berthier; reprinted with permission from *Songs from Taizé*, copyright © Ateliers et Presses de Taizé, 71250 Taizé, France.

Library of Congress Cataloging-in-Publication Data
Names: Tichenor, Liz, author.
Title: The night lake / Liz Tichenor.
Description: Berkeley, California : Counterpoint Press, 2021.
Identifiers: LCCN 2020012011 | ISBN 9781640094062 (hardcover) |
    ISBN 9781640094079 (ebook)
Subjects: LCSH: Tichenor, Liz—Family. | Episcopal Church—Clergy—Biography. |
    Children—Death—Psychological aspects. | Mothers and sons—California—Berkeley.
Classification: LCC BX5995.T39 A3 2021 | DDC 283.092 [B]—dc23
LC record available at https://lccn.loc.gov/2020012011

Jacket design by Donna Cheng
Book design by Jordan Koluch

COUNTERPOINT
2560 Ninth Street, Suite 318
Berkeley, CA 94710
www.counterpointpress.com

Printed in the United States of America

10 9 8 7 6 5 4 3 2 1

For Alice and Sam

The Storm

We lay in our bed as in a tomb
awakened by thunder to the dark
in which our house was one with night,
and then light came as if the black
roof of the world had cracked open,
as if the night of all time had broken,
and out our window we glimpsed the world
birthwet and shining, as even
the sun at noon had never made it shine.

—WENDELL BERRY

Contents

Contents

Contents

THE NIGHT LAKE

DEATH

DEAIH

Futility

I did not know I could see what was not there. Not yet. But I could hear the absence.

"Jesse, is Fritz breathing?" I could not believe I was asking this question. I answered it myself, before he could: "I don't think he is."

We were lying in bed, our new baby swaddled next to me. He and his sister were both finally asleep. This had taken hours. But—

"Should I wake him?" I asked. "Just to check?"

It's the kind of move that young parents dread. Rule number one: You do not wake a sleeping baby, even one who's been sick, out of sorts. You don't wake them. Period.

I brought my head close to my son's, to listen, to be reassured, but I wasn't. I held my hand over his mouth. The air was still and dry.

"Jesse, I really don't think he's breathing."

I was shaking. I pulled my son to the center of the mattress, the light blue flannel sheet looking suddenly sterile beneath him. I ripped open the Velcro on the mint-green fleece swaddle. I tried to jostle my baby awake. He was motionless.

"Fritz!" Jesse screamed, frantic. "Fritz, Fritz, wake up!"

Was this the moment? When, precisely, did everything change?

We flew into action in our tiny cabin. Jesse began CPR—he was trained for this, trained to train people for this. He directed the summer camp where we lived and worked, he taught and certified lifeguards. My husband had a piece of paper that said he could breathe life back into people who, for some terrible, inexplicable reason, had stopped. How could Fritz have stopped breathing? *Why?* Jesse began pumping this tiny chest, rocking our baby's body, pushing air into his quiet mouth.

It was my job to call 911. Adrenaline was coursing through my body. I felt it everywhere, surging even through my fingertips, but I managed the three numbers, dialing well. I did not fumble. I remembered our address. I spoke clearly. "My son isn't breathing. He's just a little baby, not even six weeks old. The doctor said he was fine, but now he's not breathing. Yes, my husband is doing CPR. Yes, I'll flag down the paramedics, I'll help them find their way to our cabin."

I threw on jeans and a shirt while my husband, naked, kept pumping and then breathing for our son, then pumping again. Grabbing my coat and slipping into my muddy black clogs, I stepped out into the clear January night. The stars were a jumble on the black water of Lake Tahoe, a tenth of a mile down the hill. The bit of snow that remained crunched underfoot as I ran down our gravel driveway, as if my speed would make the paramedics come faster. Where were they? The fire station was right across the highway from our camp. I stayed on the line with the 911 operator, pacing, staring up the dark hill for the lights that would come to solve this absurd problem. That was their job, to fix this. If they would just get here faster, I thought, it will all be fine.

And they did come. I ran farther through the dark to meet the fire truck, so long it stretched the length of the parking lot, end to end. "Please hurry!" I exclaimed as they jumped down. "My son isn't breathing, please, please hurry," I begged, as if they didn't know why they were there, as if otherwise they might think to slow down and take in the breathtaking view.

A tough woman led the men, duffel in hand, moving swiftly up the hill yet refusing to run. She must have known that running, slipping, falling, would not help anyone, but her deliberate pace infuriated me. How could she so carefully *walk* right now?

We burst through the dented metal door and into the cabin. At the other end of the six-foot hallway, we could see straight into the bedroom, finding the same scene I had left minutes earlier: my naked husband, unrelenting, unwavering, trying to coax life back into our motionless, breathtaken son. The two of them filled the room's only open floorspace beside the mattress where I had so recently rocked my son to sleep. Fritz was still snug in his onesie, his cozy fleece pants, his minuscule white socks, and I was coming to see that these perfectly mundane clothes were becoming increasingly irrelevant. In one sweep, the paramedics moved him onto the little patch of open carpet in our cramped cabin's living room, right next to the bedroom. Our cabin's entire space—340 square feet—was not enough to accommodate all this action, or this team of large people, or the pressure of turning this unfathomable night around. But it was what we had: a tiny, lifeless baby at the center of our tiny, packed home.

I sat on our coffee table, my back to the wall and the window and the night just outside. I stayed close, hovering above the action, knees pulled to my chest. I watched, breath held, as if imitating my son. Wires and gauges and meters began to spill out from the duffel bags; the machines should have given us answers, but they could not. Still no pulse, no breath, no anything. When they asked his weight, I said ten pounds. Fritz was huge for being just over a month old, just that afternoon at the urgent care center someone had guessed four months. But for an EMT, ten pounds was very, very small, so they were doing the math, calculating dosages, then filling a syringe with some clear liquid—epinephrine?—magic stuff, the perfect serum that would jolt his heart back to pumping endlessly, effortlessly. There was no rhythm in his heart to jolt, though; the electric paddles were useless. Nothing happened. They tried again, his tiny leg beginning to swell from the injections.

Now, suddenly, it was time to go, they said. I was bewildered.

The cabin was littered with medical wrappers; an ambulance had arrived out of nowhere and impressively maneuvered backward up our narrow, curving gravel drive. The paramedics loaded Fritz onto a six-foot stretcher that must have weighed well more than he did, and carried him into the night. Jesse and I followed, scrambling. Alice was still asleep. Jesse was calling our neighbor Stuart, trying to explain in a sentence or two the entire crashing down of our world—hospital, baby not breathing, kid sleeping, come now, we're leaving. I slipped a nursing bra in one coat pocket, as if propriety might help, and stuffed a water bottle in the other, without knowing why. Stuart hadn't arrived yet from his house down the hill, but already we were going, trying to keep up with the ambulance. I made it out the door, then faltered on our rough wooden steps. I came back inside, grabbed Fritz's car seat, my arm swinging up fast with it empty. I did not expect we would need it on our way home, but heeding this expectation seemed like it could strengthen some downpour of bad luck, like I would be caving to a perverse betrayal of hope.

We caught up to the ambulance quickly, tailing it on the dark highway that clings to the curves of Lake Tahoe. As we headed south, the lake was just to my right. Cold water washed over boulders at the edge, impenetrable, a blackness that I wished would swallow me whole.

The ambulance led with lights flashing, piercing the night, as we wound through the woods without the aid of streetlights. Jesse drove while I fretted, unable to form words, only watching. My eyes were glued to the scene I could just make out through the back windows of the ambulance. The paramedics stood over the gurney, pumping. Their heads were bent down in total focus, their shoulders rising and falling rhythmically, trying without ceasing to coax life back into my son.

But the siren did not scream. They did not break the speed limit. We did not race. Ten minutes ticked by, then twenty on the road, more and more time since Fritz last had been breathing. I knew. Jesse knew. We were both coming to understand that this was a show they were putting on for us, not for Fritz, who was not coming back. If they thought his salvation might be waiting at the hospital, they'd have been flying down the highway, and instead they were choosing to keep the living safe on these icy, treacherous roads. They were trying to show us that everything that could have been done had been done, a feeble gift for us, their excising any room in which we might wonder if they had tried everything.

The bright lights of the rising city were jarring after the wilderness of the eastern shore. We cruised past the casinos and signs for naked dancing girls and bottomless drinks in Stateline, Nevada, and then on into the tourist traps of South Lake Tahoe. Up ahead we saw the light turn red, and the ambulance continued through. Jesse turned to me, unsure. "Go for it," I said. "Fuck the ticket, we're not leaving our son." Soon lights came on behind us—sure enough, as if our luck weren't bad enough (as if this were a matter of luck), a cop had seen our flagrant traffic violation. He followed, lights flashing, then finally a siren sounding, though not from the ambulance ahead, which would have signaled some shred of hope. We continued. After a half mile, the cop slowed and turned onto a side street, quieting his affront to us—perhaps he'd learned over the radio what it was we were following.

The hospital's signs began dotting the landscape of rental homes and Ski-Doo shops. We turned the sharp left and twisted up behind the hospital to the ambulance bay, parking and jumping out. It was freezing outside the car—I realized how much I'd warmed up on the drive—had it been thirty minutes? Forty? Running over packed snow, I was inundated by the sound of the air. It was deafening. I looked up to see a helicopter, its blades spinning fast, perched just above us on the roof of the one-story hospital, at the ready. It was us, I realized, the chopper was waiting for.

Rushing inside, Jesse and I were ushered into the one large room of the small ER. It was the trauma room, and it was ours. I stood in the middle of the room, thrust deeper into the reality of what was unfolding. My son was still not breathing. "What the fuck!" I moaned. "What the fuck is happening? What the fuck!" There was no making sense of what was before me. There was only obscenity. They held me back from the table where Fritz now lay. Someone pushed gently on my shoulders, helping me, cajoling me, to sit down in a chair that had just arrived. Jesse stood behind me, and together we became the solitary audience in the middle of this trauma room, a space far too big for this baby boy.

The paramedics circled the table where Fritz lay still. They explained to the attending doctor what they had found, what they'd tried. The doses given on-site and during the ride. They tried one more, there under the bright fluorescent lights, but without expectation. The doctor was a young woman. She commanded the space, holding charge. She had a no-nonsense air about her, but I saw behind her eyes that she cared. I recognized in her voice her longing for this night to be anything other than what it had become. This was the night she dreaded.

"Does anyone have any other ideas?" she asked the team, calm, but almost pleading. "Is there anything we haven't tried?"

Silence. They had long exhausted the possibility of life returning. It had been almost an hour now. She called out our son Fritz's time of death: 23:31.

It was now official: on January 9, 2014, at 23:31, I became the mother of a dead son.

Claimed

Maybe this was when everything changed. The room certainly did. People cleared out quickly, retreating to relative safety. The doctor approached us, and someone brought another chair for Jesse, though we were now allowed to approach the table, which had been off-limits just moments before. The doctor told us facts we couldn't hear. I asked questions, or not, nothing stuck. Someone pulled the monitors and wires from Fritz's body, then handed him to me. They all left, and we were alone, the three of us.

It was surreal. Silent, except the breath moving through Jesse and me. Until we wailed. Have you heard a grown man wail? It could carve caverns in stone, it could almost pull the dead up from their graves.

I cradled this being who was still of my body, who still fit with me so perfectly. Since his conception, since he had become himself, all the things that had entered Fritz's body had come from me—he was a boy made of my blood and my milk. That had been all until an hour ago, when they pumped six rounds of drugs into his right thigh, swelling his tiny leg, a futile last-ditch effort to pull him back.

Fritz's head rested on my chest as it always had. Even in death his slender fingers curled instinctively around my index finger. I felt his weight thicken as his warmth faded away. He was wearing only a bright green cloth diaper now, and I tugged the hospital's rough white blanket up around him as if he still needed to be kept warm—I couldn't help myself.

Finally, I passed him to Jesse, not wanting to let go but also needing to see this father and son together. Jesse curled down, tender, tracing Fritz's skin, kissing his head, tears streaming down his own face.

Something grabbed me, lurching me forward. "What about organ donation?" I exclaimed, feeling the urgency of another life teetering, some other unknown baby at the brink. "How does it work? How quickly does it have to happen?"

Neither of us knew. I sprang from my chair, pushing out through the heavy double doors. The doctors and nurses were all gathered around the desk just outside our room, holding a quiet vigil, waiting for us. They looked up, surprised.

"Organ donation, how does it work?" I demanded, frantic. "We want to do it. Do we need to do it right now?"

"No," the only male nurse said gently. "You have time. Nothing needs to happen now."

I exhaled and returned. I didn't want the added burden of allowing more death to transpire, even accidentally.

I was rapidly arriving at the realization that I didn't know what I was doing. No one had taught me what to do with a dead baby. This void would come to haunt me. I was an Episcopal priest, someone professionally and academically trained to be present at heartrending times like this. But not as the mom. Cradling a dead son was entirely foreign to me.

I pointed out to Jesse that Fritz's blood was beginning to pool, forming big maroon splotches in his arms. The ventilator tube was still taped into his mouth. His eyes were closed, save for a thin slit revealing black wells, dark as the night lake, death coming to claim him already.

I told Jesse I wanted to baptize him. It was theologically questionable. I didn't believe he needed it—the sacrament was not a ticket you needed to have punched in order to be welcomed into heaven, whatever that beyond might look like. I didn't believe in a God that would reject a baby, dying too young to have made it through this ancient ritual. But I wanted to mark him. Seal him. I reached into my coat pocket to retrieve my water bottle, the one I'd snagged as I ran out of our cabin without knowing why.

It was a Sigg, one of those hip, hardy Swiss-made ones, aluminum, with a clever lid that didn't spill. A sort of pinkish lavender with swooshy fish printed on it, it was the last vessel I would have chosen for a baptism, but it was all we had. I positioned Fritz gently in the crook of my left arm, and tipped the bottle downward, one-handed. I let just a few drops of water fall into my right hand and then clenched the bottle between my knees. Carefully I touched the water to his head. "Fritz, I baptize you in the name of the Father"—I collected a few more drops—"and of the Son"—and the last drops—"and of the Holy Spirit." I set the water bottle on the bright linoleum floor, clutching my boy. "You are claimed as God's own," I promised him. It was barely audible; I could only form a whisper in my choked throat. "You are loved. This is your family, with us, and with God." As death pulled him from our grasp, I had to name that it was God who claimed him first, and claimed him last.

We entered into an in-between time, when everything was done, and yet we lingered. I didn't want to let go, I thought I wanted to take the time to memorize every bit of him again—and yet this dead baby was a terrible sight to behold: his face no longer quite his own, tape blocking my kisses, eyes vacant, slight limbs increasingly leaden.

After some time, I turned to Jesse. "I don't want to remember him like this," I said, maybe already knowing that the image would never leave me. I carried Fritz back to the gurney, laying him down on his back, just as you're supposed to. We tucked the blanket around him, but left his face open, still unable to make ourselves prevent the breath he could not draw. We kissed him, saying, "I love you," and "Goodbye."

The double doors swung shut behind us. I could not bear to look back.

What Follows

Maybe that was the moment—not the discovery of breath stopped, not the ambulance ride, not even the doctor pronouncing the official time of death. I wonder if the moment everything changed was when we left the room. When I walked away from my baby, leaving him alone and now lifeless, gone. Pushing through those double doors, I moved from being a mother in crisis to the mother of a dead baby, becoming the kind of mother people will readily tell you they cannot fathom being.

We stepped into the muted hallway of the ER.

"What happens now?" I asked someone. "We don't even have an insurance card for him yet."

The man—a sheriff?—ushered us around the corner and into a small room. "Not to worry," he said calmly. "We'll take care of all of that." He sat us down.

My nursing bra, stiff from dried milk, was still in my pocket. I didn't know what time it was. Did we have to sign things? Pay things? Apparently not. At first, right then, it was surprisingly simple. Did we want to talk to someone? He had called a chaplain, just in case. She was on her way. This made me smile, just barely, my identity as a priest still a secret. He gave us the name of a funeral home, said to call to make arrangements. Arrangements. What an odd word, *arrangements*—a collection of letters that can set flowers together just so, allowing their colors and textures to pop in contrast, and that can also mean "Please, if you don't mind, could you take my son's body and burn it, crush it? Yes, this week would be ideal." After standing witness to death, you promptly cross over into the land of absurdity and sickening euphemisms.

I was exhausted and numb by the time the chaplain arrived, a woman in her early sixties maybe, weathered in the way that people who have given their lives to the ski slopes and beaches of Tahoe are—all leather, but with the added sparkle of some casino makeup for good measure. She was rocking a tremendous mullet—bright red and blond, curly, gelled spikes on top, slick waves cascading down her back. My ability to refrain from judgment long gone, I gaped. Where the fuck am I? Who is this person, sent to somehow make this better?

She began with the condolences one would expect, but then she quickly turned a sharp corner into the dangerous waters of "God has a plan" and "Everything happens for a reason" and "God doesn't give you more than you can handle."

I was astonished, but too tired to be angry, or maybe so aghast that I didn't want to waste my breath correcting her. She eventually asked if we had a church. Okay, fine, I thought. Here we go. Jesse and I looked at each other, and laughed. Real laughter, if muted, which felt strangely, profoundly good.

I started in. "Yes, we do have a church. Actually, I'm an Episcopal priest."

"Oh!" the chaplain exclaimed. Light flooded her face. She grinned, palpably relieved. "I'm so glad! This will be so much easier because you are believers!"

Physical revulsion burned in my chest. "I think it's time for you to go," I heard myself tell her.

She prayed some gooey, inflammatory prayer, patted me pityingly on the shoulder, and at last left. The door closed. Jesse and I looked at each other and again coughed out laughter. What the fuck just happened?

We were still unclear on how one goes about having a dead baby, practically or otherwise, so it took some time for us to ascertain from the sheriff—why was he still there?—that there was nothing more for us to do. The authorities would find us later—good Lord, would they ever—so we were free to go now. I stopped to pee, suddenly realizing that I was still very much in my own body, and that my body was catching up to me, my breasts already growing hard, swollen with milk.

We thanked the nurses in the forlorn way that comes with thanking someone for attempting something they could not accomplish. But they'd been kind to us, and they had tried, and we were grateful. We stepped out into the night, and the parking lot was quiet. The unnecessary helicopter was silent, tucked away again, out of sight.

It was just the two of us now, Jesse and me, and the empty car seat.

Going Home Empty

It was a quiet drive home. What was there to say? Without answers to guide us, we sat together as Jesse took the curves slowly along the lake, the half-hour drive stretching past forty minutes in the cold dark. There were no flashing lights to lead us this time, no ambulance to follow, just the occasional slivering silver light cutting off the lake.

As soon as we pulled up to our cabin, Stuart was out the front door, hanging on to the pine railing, anxious for good news, his tousled auburn hair caught in the stark white of the porch light. He had still been living in possibility, hoping for the best.

Empty-handed, Jesse rose first, stepped out, hugged Stuart. I watched as my husband's shoulders sloped heavily, saw how he worked to raise his head to look up into Stuart's eyes. He was now shouldering the truth for me, offering some explanation I could not hear. It took all my strength to rise from the car. I stumbled into Stuart's hug, silent, his rough, unshaven jaw bristling against my temple. We turned then and trudged up our steps and into our warm, hollow home to find our daughter, Alice, not yet two and a half years old, still fast asleep. She'd slept through the whole nightmare.

Sleep didn't come easily, no matter that I was beyond exhausted. With the adrenaline still coursing through me, my mind raced. I knew soon that I couldn't sleep alone. When Fritz had arrived the month before, Jesse and I had begun a divide-and-conquer approach to sleep: in one of our cabin's two cramped bedrooms, Jesse and Alice shared the big bed; in the other, Fritz and I shared the smaller bed. I couldn't sleep there without him, so I crawled up and around into the cave of a bed where Alice lay cozy, dreaming, as yet untouched by the tragedy that now enveloped her parents. I wove myself around her, desperate to feel her heartbeat, to feel her breath. She wriggled, annoyed, but eventually nuzzled in with me.

Hours passed. I stared at the black of the ceiling a few feet above me, and at the weak glow of the snow through the crack around the curtains. I didn't know this new existence. My body didn't know how to live in this place, how to follow the most basic rhythms of sleeping in the dark, preparing to rise again for the next day. Jesse, too, struggled to find sleep, his body also overtaken by adrenaline. I saw his chest rise and fall, agitated, ready to fight, as if it were his own chest being pummeled now, pressed to live again. The image flashed before my eyes, there in the dark, remembering Jesse pumping on Fritz's heart.

He left the cabin to try to run off the chemical mix of adrenaline and cortisol, going down and racing the length of the beach, all out, back and forth again and again, he'd later tell me, until his body could do no more.

Eventually, my body finally gave way to exhaustion, against the protest of my brain and heart. I couldn't sleep with Alice's wiggles, though, and slumped back to my mattress in the other room, collapsing into a few hours of sleep, the bed now mine alone.

I awoke to Alice crawling on top of me, the morning light bright and unforgiving in its assertion that life continued.

"Where's baby Fritz?" my daughter demanded immediately.

"Oh, sweet love." I sighed, already crying. I was not ready for this. I didn't know how to do any of this.

Jesse had followed Alice and crawled into bed with us, reaching across her to rest his hand on my shoulder. He squeezed me tight, both of us already shaking with tears.

At least we could be together in this place of not knowing the first thing about how to do this grief.

"Sweet love, your brother died last night. He got very sick, and he stopped breathing. Our bodies can't live without breathing." I was weeping at this point, struggling to form words and push them out of my mouth. They were garbled. "The ambulance came, and they took him to the hospital, and they tried everything they could, but they couldn't bring him back."

Alice was perplexed. "Why? Where is he? Why did you leave him there? When is he coming back?"

We answered her questions.

She paused. She bounced tentatively on the bed, curious but not shaken.

Then, "Where's baby Fritz?"

Then, "Why?"

Sweet Jesus, I thought. This is going to take every single thing I've got.

Alice sat up between us, looking first at one parent, then the other. She paused, then smiled, relaxed. "I see that you are sad," she chirped. "But I'm not sad! Let's play!"

I slowly rose to follow her out of the bedroom, both grateful and bewildered: this child was only two years and three months old.

Spreading Story

There is a kind of reality that begins to set in only when others know of it. For the time being, Jesse and I were still inside a bubble of privacy, a secret world of sorts. The doctors and nurses and paramedics, the sheriff, and that awful chaplain—these were not our people. For everyone else, life was going on as normal, because they did not yet know. For them, Fritz was still alive. All was well. But already that was crumbling into a harsh new reality.

Jesse had called his parents from that little waiting room in the hospital—John and Cheri had then tried to sleep a few more hours before setting out to drive to us, heading over the twisting mountain passes still in the dark. They arrived at dawn and were settled into another cabin.

It's a small compound, Camp Galilee, built into the side of the hill sloping down from the four lanes of US Highway 50 to the eastern shore of Lake Tahoe. I never would have guessed I would live in Nevada, but then I never could have imagined any of this. I'd finished seminary in Berkeley the year before, and Jesse and I decided to move to the lake, where we'd spent several summers already. I was twenty-eight years old now, and I'd been a priest for just over a year, the life I'd been reaching for since I was a teenager. We had set it up so that I was splitting my time between a parish an hour away in Reno and this Episcopal camp where we lived, while Jesse worked here as the camp's program director.

The camp is just eight acres, covered with a high ceiling of pine trees and dotted with buildings rather shabby from long-deferred maintenance, money always being tight. Two long bunkhouses stick out of the hill on the north end of the property, ideal for summer campers but rustic, primitive any other time of the year, with chilly concrete floors and feebly spitting showers. A small stone church stands in the camp's center. Closer to our side, the cinder-block dining hall and kitchen edge into the hillside, claw marks from hungry bears' prying visible on the trim around its main door. Then three small cabins stained shades of brown to blend into the grass and scrub: the one that was our home, and two for guests, set along a gravel drive. To the south are two more houses: one up the hill for Laurie, the camp chef, and one down closer to the lake for our friend Stuart, who is the executive director, and his family.

Right, I realized. Stuart. Stuart knows. He is our people. This nightmare was real, even here, even at camp, even at home.

Jesse and I numbly dressed ourselves and zipped a winter coat over Alice's footie pajamas. We walked across the ambulance's tracks in the snow to knock on my in-laws' door, to face this truth. Alice was exuberant at discovering the surprise visit from her grandparents, unconcerned by our labored movement, our raw emotions.

I sat on the lone chair in their cabin, Jesse stood, letting me lean into his side. We told them the little we knew, the story frustrating in its concision. Why had he died? No idea. There was no reason, really. Nobody knew. This was a story that would grow, crafted by uttering it again and again throughout the day, on into the days to come. But here at the beginning of the first day, we had not yet pieced any of it together.

Fritz had been sick, we told them. But we weren't really sure why, or with what. He had just been crying so much. So very, very much. Inconsolably, through the night, through the day, through another night and another day. And this was not in the way of *oh, babies cry, don't worry*; this was different. Nothing helped. His spit-up that first night, Tuesday into Wednesday, was odd—a strange dark color. Bile, I thought. Not milky like the other umpteen times a day he'd spit up on me. And still he cried. On Thursday, he spit up this bile-ish stuff again, with tiny threads of blood lacing through it. It scared me. I knew it wasn't right, but he was still eating, still peeing, and he did not have a fever.

We debated what would help the most. Finally, I decided to take him in, to forgo the nap for me and for him that we both needed badly. I drove with him south to the urgent care center in Stateline, just below our beloved community center, just up from the preschool Alice loathed. Stepping forward to the receptionist, I explained that Fritz didn't have an insurance card, that I didn't know his social security number, that he was too little.

The waiting room was filled; I sighed at the sight, the likely contamination, the wait ahead of us. But before I could finish scrawling out his forms, we were called. With a newborn, it seemed, you could jump the line.

The nurse took Fritz's oxygen level, clasping his fingertip, then his temperature. Both normal. The doctor came into our small room. Fritz was still asleep in his car seat, even in the harsh, bright lights. I explained the bile, the traces of blood, the inconsolable crying. It is surprisingly difficult to communicate to a doctor that something is mysteriously very, very wrong, even to one who had—as he told me—worked in family medicine for many years.

The doctor was kind, but his quietly furrowed brow suggested maybe I was just an overtired mother of a newborn, that I did not understand that babies cry, a lot, for no apparent reason. I couldn't seem to offer anything that led him to my level of concern. He offered ideas of tests we could do at the hospital the next day, felt around Fritz's abdomen till Fritz woke screaming, and pronounced him perfectly healthy. Was I what the doctor thought I was—an overreacting, hypervigilant new mother? Me? Even though I already had another child?

"But what did I know?" I said to my in-laws. The doctor told me he was fine. I stopped for gas, drove home, let Fritz sleep. When he finally woke, he started wailing again, inconsolable. Nothing helped: not milk, not fresh diapers, not walking or singing or anything. I simply held him while he tried to climb my chest, kicking and clawing at whatever invisible thing was tormenting him, unable to shake the misery hidden within.

He calmed down only by virtue of sheer exhaustion. As Jesse and I changed him again, late in the evening, he lay limp in our arms. It wasn't right. Jesse and I looked at each other with confusion and worry.

I searched Jesse's eyes, needing guidance. "But the doctor said he was fine," I said, trying to convince us both. "He told me Fritz is fine. They'll check more things out tomorrow."

And so we continued. I swaddled him, nursed him, and rocked him in bed for a long time. I sang to him, the same lullabies over and over and over again. His breathing was funny, but maybe that was because he'd been wailing for hours and was exhausted but still angry. I was exhausted, too. It had been an endless two days. And then, finally, he was asleep. I held him longer, until he was really clearly asleep, then laid him gently on the mattress next to me and slowly flopped back. By ten o'clock, the house was silent.

I made it through, I thought. We did this day, and now they're both asleep, Alice and Fritz.

And they were, until they weren't. Until he wasn't asleep, but no longer breathing. When had it happened? Somewhere in those moments, those few mysterious minutes between when I rocked him to sleep, when I laid him next to me, and when I somehow simply knew.

This is what we told Jesse's parents, the story starting to take form. My mother-in-law pulled Jesse to her side, leading him to sit down on the bed next to her. Cheri held her son as my father-in-law wept. I sat, watching, now silent.

We couldn't stay in this early, raw place for long. Alice was alive and very much her energetic self. She was on the move, demanding food, attention, fun, a bizarre commingling of spirits with our own. My in-laws took her, ran with her, while Jesse and I went home and began to get our wits about us, to figure out what the hell you do when you've awakened to find that you are still newly the parents of a dead baby.

Early in the morning, before I began making those dreaded calls that would extend this reality, there was a gentle knock on the door. I opened it. Laurie was standing on the top step. Our next-door neighbor, the chef who lives just a minute's walk up the trail through the sage. Pulled by gravity, the weight of it all, I fell into her arms, slumping there against her old camp sweatshirt for a long time.

"Oh, love," she said. "Oh, my love."

I didn't have to explain anything—she knew.

I let go and stumbled down the few feet of the hall to my bedroom. Laurie followed, ready to catch me. We sat down hard on the mattress, and I crumpled into her lap. I collapsed there in her softness as if she were my own mother, the one who had also died, who had so recently left me.

But Laurie isn't my mother; she is actually nothing like her. She is my age, my friend, and knew I needed someone to hold me. Laurie could do that for me. She clutched me into her soft belly, nestled under her chest. Her long brown hair fell thick around us, hiding us, sheltering me from everything beyond us. She took her worn hands, callused from all the meals she cooked for this camp, and stroked my hair as I wept, as I fell into wailing, my whole body shaking.

Laurie is sturdy, the sort who comes knocking, unafraid. Stuart told her that morning that Fritz had died—this was all she knew. Laurie sat on the edge of the mattress with me, the covers still a tangle from the death that had twisted them in the night. She held me until I had released all the anguish I could into that moment, until I could speak again, could tell her the story. I told her all we didn't know, pulling her into the midst of this confused misery with me. I did not know what I needed yet, but I could tell that Laurie would be the one to show up with much of it. Not offering solutions or distractions, she was one of the brave ones, there to offer companionship as I spiraled into the depths.

Sacrosanct

After Laurie left, I began making the phone calls. I was quickly learning the importance of clear, careful diction, coupled with patient repetition: people simply could not comprehend the news I was sharing.

"Who died? What? Wait, what! How? Oh my God. Oh my God, Liz."

It was worse when it took a couple of tries to explain. I learned to be more cautiously articulate.

"I have to share some terrible news with you." There: framing the situation, setting expectations. "This one is really bad," I added, my voice quaking. That meant something, coming from me, having had to make calls like this just sixteen months before, after my mother's suicide. "My son, my baby Fritz"—(Do you understand who I'm talking about? Is this clear? Our *newborn*?)—"died suddenly last night. They did everything they could, but they could not save him."

People gasped, fumbled. Guttural noises. Long silences. Lots of questions, few had answers.

Then came the "Why?" It is an awful question. It seeps in, it floods all reason, and all we had by way of answer was the "We do not know."

I took breaks in between calls. Telling people your baby is dead is exhausting, soul-crushing. No one is ever ready for this news. I was half a day ahead of them in letting this reality sink in; the shock of the cold call was terrible to hear over and over—even as they so wanted to offer me care, it was I who had to walk them into this place, orient them, think of their feelings here. Yet I did not want to take care of anyone, not now.

When I couldn't make any more of those calls, I retreated to the back bedroom, closing the door. It was a cave-like room, but slightly bigger than the one I shared with Fritz, big enough for a makeshift closet in one corner, clothing racks and shelves suspended from the walls. The closet half of the room was packed floor to ceiling with our things, leaving just enough space to stand on the floor to change; still, it was better than the other bedroom, where you had to stand on the mattress. I crawled up onto the fort of a bed. There was barely enough room to sit up straight beneath the sloping eaves. We had built the bed frame as tall as we could, to make room for more storage underneath, knowing we'd have to be clever to make this cramped space work as a family of four.

The cabin was empty now. I didn't know where everyone was, but I was grateful for the silence, grateful for some bit of privacy on the other side of these rattly, paper-thin walls. I breathed, chattering not from the cold but from grief, for a minute, two, three. I tried to close my eyes. I could not sit still for long, though. I could not be alone. Leaning against the pale green wall, I pulled the blanket up around me, a soft fleece one my mother had made for me, had sent to me in college. I raised my phone. It was a cheap smartphone that I'd put into a sturdy life-proof case made of thick plastic—that's what they called it, *life-proof.* Great for water and sand, but of no help for these awful conversations.

It was Friday. Phil's day off, Friday is sacrosanct. Phil: my friend, ten years my senior, my mentor, also my priest. Jesse and I had only just moved from California to Nevada at the start of the previous summer, barely seven months before, and I hadn't found anyone to mentor me yet, hadn't settled in enough that someone here could step into that role for me. So it would have to be Phil I now called. I had studied under his direction as an intern in my field education placement, spending three of my last four years of seminary with him at All Souls Episcopal Parish, back in Berkeley. I was vaguely amused to be interrupting his day off again—it had also been a Friday when I'd called him last year to say my mom had killed herself. Of course today would be a Friday, too.

He answered promptly, knowing I wouldn't call on a Friday without good reason. "Hello, Liz Tichenor!"

I did not have the energy for the prologue. "Phil, Fritz died last night." The words were gravel in my mouth, but Phil understood them on the first try—it is his job as a priest to listen well.

"Oh, Liz," he said shakily, echoing Laurie. "Oh my God."

I heard the horror in his voice, not just for me but also for himself, as he took on my pain. It is also his job to practice compassion. *Com + passion,* to "suffer with" another. I could tell that Phil did ache with me, that he did not shy from the pain. He did not ask me to take care of him, though. There was nothing to be done yet, but it was clear that he would walk with us, even from a four-hour drive away, that I was still one of the family.

I hung up as Alice pounded on the door, excited. She had found the massive bubble wand and was looking for the fruit leather I'd hidden out of reach, and could I please read to her again? We hadn't read *The Little Engine That Could* at all today, Mommy. Please?

I emerged, dragging out of my phone call, buoyed up only slightly by this tether to my people in Berkeley. It held me back from hurtling further into the depths, helped me step slowly again toward my daughter, who was already racing to the living room, clutching her book.

Enough

Late in the afternoon, on that first day after Fritz died, I stood in the dining area of our cabin's biggest room: five paces to my left, along the west wall of the room, was our kitchen—several cupboards, a sink, an oven, a few square feet of counter space. Three paces to my right the floor shifted from linoleum to carpet. Bookshelves lined the south wall, and the couch occupied the entirety of the east wall: our living room. But where I was standing, in arm's reach of the three-quarter-size fridge behind me and the folding wooden table from Ikea in front of me, I was squarely in the dining room, such as it was. Our lives in this cabin were compact, with all existence layering in on itself, again and again, no one activity escapable from another.

I reached up to the pine shelf above our table where a small glass bottle was nestled in next to our plates. I had set the bottle on that shelf a month before Fritz was born, and there it had remained until now. It was no more than two inches tall, clear glass hinting green, its body an angular oval shape. I carried it back into what had been my bedroom—and his— retreating. Closing the hollow door and sitting down on the mattress, I slid my pinkie inside the bottle, stretching carefully to retrieve a folded piece of paper. Slowly unfolding the note, no larger than Fritz's footprint, I ran the pad of my index finger across the paper. Green leaves were pressed into the pulp's weave. Each partly hidden, they left the hint of green hearts just under the paper's surface. I turned the paper over. On it was written: *You are enough in every moment.*

I closed my eyes, sinking back into the extra pillows I'd needed while nursing just yesterday. I was quickly learning how completely inadequate I felt for the task of grieving. Was grief a task? That seemed like a paltry description of this new land into which I'd been deposited. I could not yet comprehend its vastness, I could not make out a map of the terrain, its demands, could not plot my way forward into the menacing future. Grief, even the grief so steeped in the shock of these first days and thus somehow numbly buffered, was far more than I suspected I could survive. The days further ahead would be worse—when the flood of support began to wane, and the bodily armor of shock began to dissipate, and the plodding on of time forced me and my family to begin constructing a new normal. But even now, just one day's resident in this foreign place, I felt that the note stood in contradiction to a profound fear I had not questioned. I knew one thing: the days ahead would be worse. I did not know that I would be enough.

The gently looping handwriting on the note was, in itself, encouraging. I couldn't decipher whose hand had written it, though. Laurie's, maybe, but it could just as easily have been my mother-in-law's, or one of my other neighbor's. My mind filtered back to that night—the evening of All Souls' Day, incredibly, the feast day on November 2, when we remember all the saints and all the souls we love but see no longer. On that night two months before, I'd gathered with a small circle of women and girls whom I loved, and who loved me, as I prepared for the baby who was due in nine days. How fitting, I thought back—preparing for him on All Souls', this baby who would die so early.

We didn't need a baby shower for Fritz. We already owned the essentials, just a little worn. We had no qualms about dressing him in the pink onesies and pajamas we had tried to avoid with Alice but had accumulated anyway. We had cleared one of the shelves in the small bedroom, the room that was to be his and mine, and lined it with onesies and hats and miniature fleece jackets, then carefully stacked blankets and burp cloths. We rearranged the living room, carving out space on one shelf for cloth diapers, the couch doubling as a changing table. There was no room for anything but the basic necessities.

A traditional baby shower seemed superfluous. But these women thought we should still do something to mark the passage. "A Blessing Way," Monica had suggested. She was a marriage and family therapist, and Stuart's wife. They lived just a one-minute walk down a steep trail of gravel and sand from our cabin, sage always grabbing at my ankles with its spiny, angular branches and its sweet smell.

Monica was both practical and thoughtful, and had read somewhere about the Blessing Way, a Navajo rite held to prepare for a baby's arrival. I probably squirmed—who were we to appropriate some other culture's celebration?—but Monica explained that we were only borrowing the general sense of coming together for feast and blessing, while leaving behind our Western obsession with gifts. Sure, I'd said. In that case, I was game.

The November night was simple. Just six of us: Laurie; my mother-in-law, Cheri; Monica and her two daughters; and me, with my massive taut belly. We turned out the men and met in Monica and Stuart's home, an old lake house at the edge of camp that they had slowly fixed up, bit by bit, until it was comfortable not just in the summer but also year-round. The sun was already down, the wall of windows looking out to the night lake offering only the outline of black mountains on the other side, their bases speckled with faint lights.

I settled into the deep leather couch while the others sprawled on the rug in front of the fireplace, all of us relaxing in the time to eat good food, to talk excitedly, to wonder about this person who was soon to join us. Monica's girls, Gracie and Ava, then nine and eleven, scrubbed my feet, lathered them with thick lotion, and painted my toenails. They strung together a bracelet for me, each choosing and adding beads. I closed my eyes, resting my hands on my son swimming within.

Each woman and girl wrote a tiny note, folding it and putting it into this wee glass jar. I was supposed to open them during labor when I needed strength and encouragement, notes to help me remember that these women were with me in spirit.

Labor was too fast for that. By the time Fritz was finally, really coming, on December 1, twenty days past his due date, I was so floored by the searing pain and intensity of my contractions that I could not think to reach for a note. I could not have focused my eyes to read one anyway. But now, totally unsure of how I could go forward in grief, I needed them.

I opened my eyes and traced the words again—*You are enough in every moment*—and I hoped desperately that this was true.

I decided now that with the remaining notes, I would open one a day. Never having been one for patience, I wanted to read them all immediately. But I supposed that spreading them out would help me more. I trusted that reading some bit of encouragement each day would help me make it through the first week. Even making it through one entire day no longer seemed a given: nothing was a given anymore, nor ever would be again.

The Coroner's Visit

On the second day, Saturday, the note was pale blue on one side; it could have been painted with watercolors. The raw edge of the paper was soft, forgiving. I read it: *Bless your family, bless your ease, bless your painful struggles.* I read it a second time, puzzled. What would this look like? Where was there ease now? How could our family, permanently rent apart, ever again feel blessed?

We knew the sheriff's coroner was coming, as was apparently routine. He called when he was in the parking lot by the church. Jesse ran down to meet him. I watched them through the window as they retraced the paramedics' steps from the parking lot, up the gravel path, and past the bare picnic tables and dormant flower beds. When I heard them step onto the tile of our narrow entryway, I moved to the couch and sat cross-legged. The faintly yellow walls seemed to close in around me. The coroner walked into our living room, his badge reflecting brightly. Jesse pulled out the rolling desk chair from under the table for our guest, then joined me on the couch, resting his hand on my knee.

"I'm sorry for your loss," the coroner stated; evidently this had to be said. "I'll need to walk through the events of the other night to make sure I have it all straight."

His tone was brusque, but I also sensed that he was nervous, wildly uncomfortable to have been assigned to us. He told us self-consciously that he was new on the job, that he'd been working there for only a few months.

"So I see here that you woke up to find your baby not breathing on Thursday night, is that correct?"

"No, it's not," I said. "I hadn't gone to sleep."

He flipped through the papers on his clipboard. "The report I have from the EMTs reads that you were sleeping in bed with your son when you discovered he wasn't breathing. There are clear risks associated with sharing a bed with an infant, ma'am."

My mouth hung open, heat gathering behind my eyes. What? Was he *blaming* us?

"The EMTs are mistaken," I said flatly. "I never went to sleep."

"Why don't you walk me through it, then," he said, voice chilled.

I recounted the days of crying, the trip to urgent care, the awful evening of endless screaming. "I swaddled him, rocked him in my arms, and sang to him until he fell asleep. I laid him down on the bed next to me. Then Jesse came in, and we leaned against the pillows, talking quietly in the bed. We were awake. It was then that I sensed Fritz wasn't breathing."

"We were both awake," Jesse reiterated, sliding closer to me.

"Please make sure this gets corrected in the file," I said. "It's important. We did not ever fall asleep."

The coroner nodded, furrowing his brow as he scribbled notes on his legal pad. "Were you under the influence of drugs or alcohol?"

"No, absolutely not," I answered, relieved that at least I hadn't sought to dull the sound of my baby's ceaseless wailing with a glass of wine, as I easily might have.

"Were there blankets or covers on him?" the coroner continued, checking his notes. "What's the mattress like? Some mattresses are unsafe for babies, you know."

I sighed, exasperated, shaking my head—it hadn't occurred to me that I'd be defending myself.

"No," I said, trying to remain calm, growing fearful that my anger could be used against me. "No, there were no blankets anywhere near him. He was swaddled, in a swaddle designed for infants. The mattress is firm— you are welcome to feel it yourself."

He rose, the chair spinning away from him. "Yes, I need to examine it."

For what? I wondered. What can this guy possibly know about what mattresses are suitable for babies? He was not an MD, not a medical examiner, but a deputy sheriff now assigned to periodically work as a coroner. But I led him the four feet down the hallway to the bedroom and edged back toward the dresser, gesturing to the mattress on the floor. "This is the bed. This is where my son died."

The coroner knelt down, pushing on the mattress. "Yeah, that seems fine," he said, sounding almost surprised. I wondered if it would be easier for him if there was a reason, if there was clear fault to be assigned, a way he could make this more logical.

We went back to the living room and sat down again. Now in a quieter voice, the interrogation apparently complete, the coroner explained that the autopsy would be happening soon, done by a pediatric coroner down in Sacramento. Someone would tell us when it was happening, and hopefully that would give us more answers.

He abruptly changed gears then, strangely softening his tone. "You know, I have a baby, too, and this kind of thing is just so scary. Last night I came home to find my wife asleep in the La-Z-Boy, with our baby asleep in her arms. I lit into her. 'What are you doing? Do you have any idea how dangerous this is?' I shouldn't have yelled, but come on. I mean, I know it's easier, sleeping like that, but it's just not worth it. I made her promise not to do it again, to make sure she gets the baby into the crib, no matter what."

I stared hard at him, then blinked. I had researched the risks and benefits of co-sleeping, and felt confident in our choice. At this point, I was pretty sure we weren't going to be held legally responsible for Fritz's death—

there'd be no charges. But what I was hearing was that this man sitting in my living room believed mothers to be responsible, that when a baby dies the mother has somehow caused it.

Jesse heard it, too, taking my hand as if to say, No, you are not crazy— this guy is out of line. He let me squeeze his hand, hard, nodding just enough to let me know he understood.

I was done. "Is there anything else you need from us?"

"No, this should do it. We'll be in touch. Call me if I can be of any help," the coroner said, handing me his card.

Rising to his feet, Jesse looked down into my eyes as if to say, I've got this, you stay. I sank back into the couch. Jesse reached out, offering him a handshake. Somehow my husband could remain gentle, even kind, even now.

"Thank you for coming," said Jesse, his voice formal but not harsh, moving the coroner along and out of our house.

I sat there, frozen, tears rolling down my cheeks.

Arrangements

The paper I drew out of the glass jar on Sunday was a faded red, interrupted by big curving shapes of white and green, like a carved block print. *May your son always know laughter and tears.* I exhaled slowly, almost imperceptibly. Would he discover these in the great beyond? Fritz had been so young that tears did not fall when he cried, even when he screamed. He'd heard our laughter but had not yet laughed himself. What would it be like to learn these, to know tears and laughter, each in turn, in whatever life lay past this place? I had not spent my energy on theological questions, yet they were beginning to press in. Generally, I just didn't care about any of this, these not being the theological dilemmas that most grabbed my curiosity, but they forced themselves on me anyway, in people's questions, in their frustrating assertions, and even in this little note from the evening of blessing.

The worst phone call I would ever have to make needed to be done this day: the call to the funeral home. I didn't know if anyone would be there on a Sunday, but I had finally mustered the courage and I needed to try. Annie, my mom's older sister, had arrived by then, sharing with Laurie the mantle of mothering me. My aunt looks enough like my mom to short-circuit my brain sometimes, tricking me into thinking it's Mom herself, the two moving and speaking from the same entangled strands of DNA. Alone with her in our cabin, I told her I needed to make the arrangements.

Sitting with Annie on our couch, blanketed in sun, I dialed, then jumped up to pace in tight circles, then sat again, nervous. A grandfatherly voice answered, and I launched in, my face hot, my words tumbling out in a blur. "My son died, I need him to be cremated, they gave me your name at the hospital, can you help us?"

Ralph, the seasoned director of the funeral home, had plenty of logistical questions: timing, age, cause of death. I could tell he didn't get babies often.

Then: "I'm a grandfather," he told me. "I know how precious these little ones are. Keep trying, make sure you have more. It'll help to have more, have as many as you can."

I was horrified at his presumption, but meekly replied, "All right," having forgotten how—or having lost the will—to fight back.

We moved on to all the fancy urn options, the countless ways I could honor my son by paying this business more money—the same son he believed I should immediately seek to replace.

I refused the high-end urns. "We'll be burying his ashes right away. We want the cheapest, simplest option."

"We have ceramic urns, and burled wooden boxes, and brass ones that you can engrave as a keepsake. There are urns specially made for children, with teddy bears holding them."

I reiterated my insistence on cheap, disposable. "No teddy bears!" I told him firmly.

Finally, he acquiesced, explaining the frugal option.

"A plastic box? Great."

One battle won, I thought, moving on to prices. I was aghast to learn just how expensive cremation could be, even for such a tiny body. For perhaps the first time in my life, I haggled, digging in my heels, pushing back at the absurdity of it.

"We really don't have that much money," I said. "I don't know how we're going to do this; that's just so very much for us."

Ralph said he'd check with a guy, see what he could work out. He finally acknowledged that, yes, in fact the process would take much less work for a baby who'd died at forty days.

I hung up, livid that this man would have the gall to tell me to have more kids while I was asking him to burn the body of this one. I collapsed on the couch, crumpling into my aunt's lap, sobbing. I sobbed and sobbed. I had never, ever imagined making such a phone call.

Later on, Ralph checked back, letting us know the funeral home would give us the cut rate, a sympathy price for a baby's body and a young family just starting out. Maybe it was an empty triumph, beating the funeral home industry; still, I was satisfied to win at least this once.

Milk

The fourth day, I went to open the note even before making coffee.

This note was the sturdiest. Tan, perhaps just tagboard. I opened it:

> *I am strong!*
> *I am powerful!*
> *I am beautiful!*

"God, if only," I muttered. Utterly without control in this grief, I felt none of these things.

The breast pump had arrived that afternoon, the Monday after Fritz died, at the same time as a stout flat-rate box of hand-me-down clothes from my cousin, who I later heard felt horrible about the timing, having mailed the package when Fritz was still alive. I laughed. I was still near the beginning of discovering all the ways the situation might be made worse, but nothing could make me sad *again*—I was already steeped in it.

But oh, the milk. So, so much milk. I'd always had too much milk: it was my superpower. And it was a good superpower, except that it made my babies throw up. When Alice was a newborn, she puked. All the time. Everywhere, massive quantities of milk, sprayed to cover a room, a whole person, at any moment. The standard advice of waiting it out, finding an equilibrium? It made no difference. I was bathed in baby vomit, over and over, every day.

When Alice was six or eight weeks old, a friend asked me if I had tried pumping. I had not. I knew nothing about breast pumps, save that they were supposed to make the problem of too much milk far worse. My friend's kids were bigger, and she offered me her old pump. She brought it to church one Sunday, and we went into the bathroom in the basement. She pulled out tubes and flanges and stoppers, showed me how to connect them to this magic suckling machine. I tried it at home that afternoon, surprised by the full tug, the milk spraying out and rhythmically pounding the back of the bottle contraption. In a few minutes the bottle was full, then overflowing, as my other breast leaked. No wonder Alice is throwing up all the time, I thought—it was a ridiculous amount of milk, and it was jetting out like water from a fire hose.

It was also an absurd amount of extra milk to just have hanging out in our fridge, for this baby who refused bottles. But there was no way I would pour it out. I had heard about milk banks somewhere along the way, and googled with my right hand, holding Alice asleep at my left breast, finally content after being fed a reasonable serving size. Her relentless vomiting ended that day.

Milk sharing, I was finding out, was a thing. Beyond banks, Facebook groups were set up by region. All free, just mamas who had too much milk connecting with those who did not have enough. I was sold. After a few times of passing off my milk through these groups, Nathaniel arrived. He was the newly adopted grandson of Ann, a woman who worked at my seminary, one of the first women to be ordained a priest in the Episcopal Church. Ann had heard I had too much milk. Her daughter Abbie, Nathaniel's mom, was interested. Done. The bags stacked up in our freezer, rectangular but thicker at one side, so they never really stayed in place. I'd pass off full coolers to Ann. That summer, when we were up at Tahoe working at the camp, I sent a full chest cooler down to the Bay with Stuart, who met up with Nathaniel's dad in a hotel parking lot. It felt like we were sending a drug runner across state lines, the great contraband being frozen breast milk.

When Fritz was a couple of weeks old, Abbie had emailed me. She'd heard of Fritz's birth, and we were once again in sync: she and her husband had just welcomed home Ruthie, another newborn. Did I have extra milk again? she wondered. Ruthie would love it.

But Alice was still nursing, too, one of them on each side, my arms full. While they both suckled, Alice would reach to hold hands with Fritz, curving her legs around his body. I didn't have to pump this time around; Alice took care of the extra for me. As I was beginning to think about having to go back to work, though, I was looking toward needing to pump for Fritz's bottles while I was gone in Reno all day. We were going to need to teach him to drink from a bottle soon. I pulled out the old pump, but it was dead. The light turned on, and nothing more—no sound of a motor, no suction. I called the company, grateful for the stellar warranty. A new one would be on its way promptly.

And there it was in the Monday mail, four days after Fritz died.

Alice nursed, lots, but I had far more milk than she needed. I began to pump again, remembering the feel, the strange wobble of the plastic bags, barely holding their structural integrity under the weight of my warm milk. I wrote to Abbie again, saying that I did have milk for Ruthie after all. It was awful to pump, but worse to hold it in. I tried to slowly dial back my production, but still my breasts were massive, aching, engorged. Even as the mechanical hum of the pump was heartbreaking, it gave me some relief. At least my body could help keep some other person going, growing, living. Once again brick-like bags of frozen milk began to stack up in our freezer, though it was small enough that I had to periodically move them—well labeled—to the camp's walk-in freezer behind the kitchen.

The next day's note came with different handwriting and as a much-needed complement to the previous day's suggested mantra. It was another faded red note, a diagonal stripe of green cutting across the bottom corner, just overlapping the red: *May you be blessed with patience.*

Right, I thought. It did not need to all happen, all be healed, all be solved today. But I did not come with patience. Not naturally. If there would be any patience, it would arrive as a blessing. It would be a gift of grace to let this road in exile simply be: slow, plodding, forward.

Sorry

Wednesday. Parenting both a dead child and a living one is onerous work, as I was quickly learning—it was late in the afternoon before I remembered the jar. I had been juggling calls and arrangements and funeral decisions, and telling Alice "The Story of Fritz Died," as she called it, a story she demanded constantly. She was finally napping, though, the house otherwise empty, when I reached for a note. Unfolding it, I saw islands of red and gray, surrounded by a swirling lake of yellow, a map of this foreign land I'd entered.

> *May you breathe*
> *in this moment*
> *and let it be*
> *as it is, right now.*

I might not be able to do anything else. I might not be able to let anything be as it was. But I could breathe, and I would hope that this might be enough. For now, I would just breathe. I breathed once, then again.

Fritz had not been dead for even forty-eight hours when our friend Catherine emailed us her itinerary. "Erik and I are coming this week," she wrote, then caught herself. "But you have absolute veto power."

No, I would not veto their visit. It was what we needed. Catherine and Erik, exactly them, them with us, now.

They made their way to Tahoe as soon as they could, flying from Indiana to Oakland, on two separate days, and each then renting a car for the drive up to Camp Galilee. Work was complicated for them both; this was the quickest way a trip could be arranged.

They had been Jesse's friends first. He and Erik lived together early in college, in a rambling old New England house at the edge of Hanover, New Hampshire, where we were all in school at Dartmouth. The house held six or eight young men at a time, new housemates cycling through quarter by quarter as students came and went from study abroad programs. They all knew each other from the Navigators, Navs for short, a Christian student group. Someone along the way had named the house the HPZ—the Heavy Petting Zoo—perhaps as a testament to the complicated sexual ethics taught by this particular evangelistic ministry.

The four of us had come to know one another at the Episcopal Campus Ministry, though, also there at Dartmouth. The Episcopal student house was called The Edge, short for the wealthy patron who initially bankrolled the house, Mr. Edgerton, but perhaps more aptly because we stood at the other end of the Christian line, edgy and progressive, a place where people rooted in the evangelical tradition often came to reside more freely, finding a second home there.

My friendship with Erik and Catherine was a kind that I hadn't seen before, mostly for how it took root and deepened well after college. My bond with them grew not by sharing daily college life so much as by annual visits in the years that followed. Our love for one another was more solid than would be expected, given the space that had separated us. But we had been in each other's weddings: they had both stood up with us, and Jesse was Erik's best man in the summer that my belly was round with Alice, in the only decent maternity bridesmaid's dress I could find, fuchsia and drapey, but still stretched tight around my middle. And now we were here, and Catherine and Erik were the sort of friends who showed up, who didn't need to ask, who simply came.

We had barely twenty-four hours with Erik—it was all he could swing as a new tenure-track professor just beginning to earn his keep; Catherine could come earlier and stay longer.

"Are there things that you want to make sure we do together?" she asked her first morning as we breathed in the steam rising from our coffee. "I mean, if there are things that you have to do that you want my help with, let's plan for that."

I sat cross-legged in the nursing glider, considering the invitation. I loved her for it—I also felt nauseated, imagining the horror of all that still needed to be done.

Fritz had been dead only a week. But maybe if I asked now, Catherine could enact her help later in the trip, somehow dulling the ache of my needing it in the first place.

"Will you help me pack his clothes?" I asked, my voice tentative. "I don't think I can do it by myself." I didn't want to do it at all, but I was also terrified of becoming that grieving mother who leaves her dead kid's room exactly the same, undisturbed for years to come.

Our time with Catherine and Erik passed quickly, even in the fog of grief. There was nothing to do, and everything. No work, but preparations, Alice to entertain, the impossible task of remembering to eat. We hiked, the four of us, leaving Alice back at camp with friends, climbing up to the ridge far above the lake. It was glorious. The whole sweep of the Tahoe basin was stunning, beauty so strong it made my mind spin.

The lake was formed by faulting in the earth's crust some 24 million years ago, when the Carson Range to the east and the Sierra Nevada to the west were thrust up from the earth. It wasn't until just 2 million years ago, though, that the north shore was stopped up by a flow of lava from Mount Pluto. Finally, around 160,000 years ago, and then again just 20,000 years ago, glaciers slowly pushed their way through this place, carving out Emerald Bay and some of the most striking features of the south end of the lake. It was all here, and had been for so many millennia, intersecting with this one brief moment of ours on top of the ridge, with me unsure of even how I might make my way through this single day. I still felt hollow, but I loved being with these friends, burrowing into their warm sides on the outcropping of boulders, cold and high, now more than 7,000 feet above sea level, the air seemingly even thinner than back at our cabin. I looked down into the sheet of the blue lake below us, the patterns of wind and the trails of boats swirling the water, in precise curves from our vantage point. I tried to conceive of the bottom of the lake, 1,644 feet down at its deepest, so far lost beneath this decorated surface.

On her last afternoon with us, Catherine came to remind me. "You had said you wanted me to help you pack up his things—can we do that? It's probably time now."

I hated having made this request in the first place, as if that were the reason we would now have to do this awful task. Jesse nodded, though. We would do it together. Jesse snuck into the back bedroom where Alice was napping and dug out an assortment of zippered vinyl bags, the kind that sheets come in, dropping them on the mattress in the small bedroom. Clear afternoon light fell on the pale lavender walls, this paint new, one of the several shades we'd chosen to try to make the cabin feel like home. I scooped up an armful of Fritz's clothes from the shelf and set them in one pile on the mattress, then a second. I sat down in the place on the bed where he had died, leaning heavy against the wall. I'd nursed him, right there, I thought, looking at the bed. Right there. The room felt absolutely vacant. Catherine and Jesse joined on either side of me, all of us staring at the heap of jumbled colors, obsolete, useless.

I reached forward, hesitating, then picked up a pair of pajamas, pinching them between my index fingers and thumbs, holding them up as if inspecting a work of art. Gray, newborn size, embroidered with fire trucks. Snaps, reaching from the left foot up to the chin. Who puts snaps on newborn clothes anyway? Zippers are much easier. I tried to fold them in half, top to bottom, but instead I fell over, clutching them, pushing them down, kneading them into the bed. One sob escaped through my lips, then another.

Jesse placed his hand on my thigh. I couldn't see his hand clearly as waves of tears crashed in front of my eyes, but I could feel him shaking with his own tears, even as he remained with me. I sat, bent over, holding on to these ill-conceived jammies as if they would keep my boy from leaving. Minutes passed. Jesse and I wept; Catherine was weeping, too.

I pulled myself upright, still awash in tears, and turned to Jesse. "I'm sorry," I blurted out. "I'm so sorry." These new words stuck awkwardly in my mouth.

He looked up at me, confused. "What? You have nothing to apologize for," he said, now crying harder, shaking.

"I'm sorry," I stammered again. "I'm sorry I let our son die." The words tumbled out. "I'm so sorry."

His eyes opened wider, electric, bluer than ever beneath the tears. "Liz, this isn't your fault. You didn't do anything wrong, you did everything you could have done. We both did."

"I'm so sorry," I sobbed again, choking. "I'm just so sorry."

He looked up, finally hearing me. He stopped fighting. "I'm sorry, too," he said, softly. Then again, more confident, "I'm so sorry."

I leaned into him, my teeth chattering. I laid my head on his chest. His brown-and-silver beard, now wet, brushed my forehead. I held on to his arm, tight, and we wept. My grief had been so solitary in this wilderness, it was hard to even see Jesse, to see his grief, too. For the first time in days I understood that I wasn't alone, that he and I were in this together.

Catherine scooted in closer, resting her head on my shoulder. She reached around my back to hold Jesse as we all seemed to dissolve into one another. Some part of me hovered above, watching us, even as I lived it. It struck me as a grim scene to bear witness to, a couple apologizing to each other for allowing their son to die, though neither was at fault. And yet it was the sort of thing that needed a witness—Catherine, someone to place her hands on us like a flying buttress and say, Yes, I will enter into this mess, I will help you stay upright, I will hold you even as you crumble.

Still sandwiched between their weight, tears still rolling down my face, I carefully folded the pajamas I had been clutching. In half, neck to toes, and then side to side. I set them down on the mattress and reached for another pair. Cornflower blue with yellow elephants, and a zipper, his best PJs, the ones I always took first from the pile of clean laundry. I ran my thumb across the fabric, reverencing the holiness it contained beyond its mass-produced quality. After all, this fabric had once contained our *son*, Fritz. I folded the pajamas in half, smoothing out the footies, then in half again, and set them on top of the fire trucks. Jesse picked up a pair. So did Catherine. Slowly, carefully, we began to fold each again. It was unnecessary; they had been folded on the shelf. But each piece needed to be handled once more, picked up, made just so, set down, put away. The piles grew: onesies, pajamas, tiny fleece pants, jackets, a mound of socks, many hats. We quietly worked together, as it had become that—work, a job that needed to be done, labor knit of our dual needs for order and catharsis.

Jesse crawled across the mattress to reach the vinyl bags. He picked one up and pulled back a flap, holding it wide. "You ready?" he asked.

"No," I answered, "but here we are." I picked up the first stack of onesies, sliding it into place, into the space of waiting again, while he held it open. Then another stack, and another. A second bag, filled. A third, now packed with the bright piles of FuzziBunz cloth diapers, carefully stacked with the snaps matching all at the same end. Teal and lime green and purple and orange and red and blue and yellow and pink. One bright green diaper was missing, I knew. We had left it on him in the hospital when we turned and walked out the door.

Jesse rearranged a stack in the final packed bag, making sure the piles were even and lining up the zipper tracks as he carefully pulled it shut, protecting the clothes but without stressing the zipper. Silently, I watched him. He knew he could not fix any of this for me, for us, but he was determined to make it easier where he could, to try to make it right, to do right by me. I was watching him through the arc of the day, through these awful first days, as he was watching me. Looking for what needed to be done, for where some ease might enter in, for where he could siphon off some of the pain. Swooping in for our angsty toddler, redirecting, relieving me from what I could not tend. Running with her, running and running around the camp, chasing her wonder, telling her another story and then another when I couldn't bring myself to lift my head or open my mouth.

Jesse let me be. I could see this now in sharp focus as he finished the task of packing Fritz's clothes away. All his doing let me live. His care for me and for Alice was beautifully functional. We didn't talk in these minutes; all this care was absent narration. He was giving me space to make it through another hour, another day.

He filled his arms with the bags and started out of the room to put them in storage. I leaned back against the wall, my legs stretched out across the empty bed. I looked up at the empty shelf, then back to Catherine, then up again.

I had been holding my breath.

I exhaled. This, at least, was done.

Planning the Plot

Now it was Thursday again. It had been one week, tonight. I loathed Thursday, as if it were the day itself that had robbed me of my son. For months to come, this fourth day of the week would fill me with dread. I reached into the little jar, fishing out the last folded note. The paper was thick, white, textured. A dotted pattern of flocking shifted like drifting snow across the back of the note. I recognized it from the stash of old wallpaper samples in the camp's art cabinets.

I hope your day is filled with smiles & laughter ☺

I could tell this one was written by one of the girls. It was wonderful and absurd, both for reading during labor and for reading during grief. I loved it anyway. Maybe this, too, could be possible.

I strung the notes together, stitching blue embroidery floss in and out along the top edges. Simple as it was, this was my first constructive act since Fritz's death. Ripping off two pieces of tape, I hung the notes on the window, where they swooped in an arc like pennants for a party. It was a strange party in this small home lost in mourning, but still I reveled in them. They hung just above my sightline as I sat in my glider at the dining room table, arms empty, looking out over the gleaming lake. Sun crashed off the water's rough surface, assaulting my eyes with its unrelenting glory. I looked away and found respite from its brilliance in the simple words of these notes, trying to promise that I could do hard things—that I would survive not only this child's birth but his death as well.

My son's funeral would be the fourth I'd ever attended. I'd only been to two actual burials: One was for Jesse's grandmother, on a gorgeous day out in Point Reyes, family gathered casually at the cemetery, and with abundant love. The other, the first, was when I was twenty and serving as an intern at a small church on an island in southwest Florida. The church was mostly filled with retired snowbirds, and I helped, sort of, with a funeral there. At the end of the service, a bagpiper led us out of the church to "Amazing Grace," and on to a columbarium in the church's garden. We placed the box of ashes in a little nook, put the brass plate back in place, and screwed it on. The whole affair was very orderly, cleaned up, cinematic.

Nothing about Fritz's death was orderly. In the two weeks between his dying and his funeral, we had a lot to learn and decide, more than fit in that time.

We were sitting on the fraying couch in Laurie's living room, eating dinner she had made for us once again, when my phone rang. Seeing that it was Phil calling, I threw on my coat, retreated to the back porch, and answered. I was exhausted. Phil was checking in, but he also wanted to help me start thinking about all the plans we needed to make. Choosing the date for the funeral was a good start, but there was so much more. I stared blankly out at the sunset as I listened to Phil urging me to think about where and how we were going to bury Fritz. It surprised me, as my family of origin did none of this.

We didn't make decisions like this, we didn't do burials, we didn't know how. We put it off until it was no longer raw. It had been nearly a year and a half since my mom had died, and we still hadn't decided what to do with her ashes. For all I knew, my grandpa's ashes still sat on a shelf in my grandma's closet.

Phil had other ideas. "Do you want to bury him at camp? Somewhere away from the bustle of life, up in a grove of trees?" he asked. His voice was tender.

I shook my head, before remembering to speak into the phone. "That's so close to the highway, hardly a peaceful spot with all the trucks charging by."

"Close to the water?" he offered, but then cautioned, "But remember that that would be in the midst of it all. . . . Do you want to walk by that spot each day? What about kids playing there—how will that feel?"

There were so many pieces to consider, I didn't know where to begin. "I'll think about it, at least," I said, before telling him goodbye.

The next day and the next, Jesse and I talked, wandering around camp, surveying different spots while Alice ran circles in the dust. We considered putting some of Fritz's ashes nearby at Spooner Lake, where we had hiked almost every day I'd been pregnant with him. Back on the phone again, planning more details, I relayed this idea to Phil. It was up to us, certainly, but he wondered aloud if maybe it would be better to do all the burying at once, with all the people gathered. Maybe, he suggested, this wasn't something we ought to do alone.

There is no perfect place to bury your son, but interring his ashes near the water felt important to us. Finally, we settled on a bluff at the center of camp, an outcropping of land looking over the beach, with enough room for a tree. It wouldn't be quiet, just above the beach where campers swim, and maybe fifty feet from the campfire circle, but we reasoned we'd rather have joyful noises surrounding this place than the sound of semis braking for the tight curves of the highway. This place would be not hidden away, but set in the middle of our lives.

First Run

I couldn't sit still. Fritz had been dead for ten days, and sitting in one place, arms empty, was agonizing, terrifying. The cortisol still pumped; I was ready for whatever crisis might befall us at a given moment. I was wired, but it was a weird high: I was anxious, in overdrive.

Silence made it worse—sitting in quiet, sitting with myself, was unbearable. Not knowing what else to do, I put on shorts and a wicking shirt. I tied on some old sneakers I'd bought the year before for ten bucks at an REI used gear sale, scrawled a note on a piece of scratch paper, and pushed through the door, leaving Jesse and Alice napping. I treaded quickly down our driveway, loose gravel sliding out from beneath my soles.

Very, very slowly, I ran—could I call it that, really?—past the empty dining hall and up the camp's long asphalt driveway to Highway 50. Even just that much was painful. I crossed the frozen highway, breathing hard. I ran. There was no shoulder; cars and RVs and semis flew by, the wind tunnel shaking me in their aftermath. I ran. Sand blew up in my face, stinging as it hit. I ran, pushing up the small swells in the road, lungs on fire with so little oxygen at 6,200 feet above the sea. My body was still wrecked from giving birth: my hips wobbled, loose in their sockets, and I quickly realized that coughing while running would make me pee. I hadn't even stopped bleeding from Fritz's birth—still, I ran.

And for the first time since Fritz had died, running along this shoulderless road with no margin for error, I could bear to be by myself, with myself, alone. My lungs burned more acutely even as my heart ached, but what a relief to give myself over to this entirely physical discomfort for a change. I ran a mile and a quarter out, tracing the edge of the lake, a silver sheet stretching out flat across the water in the gray afternoon. I turned around, a little surprised I hadn't yet been hit by a truck. I ran back, arriving home exhausted and amazed that it had happened, that I was capable of moving my body, that I was capable of doing anything at all.

Sympathy Cards

The shit people sent in cards very nearly drove me over the edge, pouring acid into my broken-open heart. At the same time, the love people sent in cards was saving my life. Neither of these statements is the slightest exaggeration.

The first card had arrived the Monday after Fritz died. He'd been dead for maybe eighty-five hours, and here was a card. A couple more arrived the next day, a few more the day after that. And then we seemed to inhabit a Dr. Seuss book, with cards flying in from all directions, piling on the available surfaces, spilling out, all but coming stuffed under the weather stripping on the window. There was one post office box for the camp, and it held mail for the camp business and for the ten of us who lived on-site. The small rural post office, more of an outpost than a fully equipped operation, was directly across the highway from the camp driveway, just south of the fire station that had sent us the determined but cosmically inadequate EMTs. In the past, Stuart had most often done this chore of retrieving the mail, but because I loved mail so much, I'd largely taken over the job since moving there. Now, though? Now I could not bring myself to go.

The daily mail for our family no longer fit in the post office box, so Sandy, our postal worker, handed it all over the counter, rubber-banded in one massive bundle, cards stacked three inches high. Stuart stopped by our cabin each day to deliver them. I took them from him, thankful, sheepish. Most days, I sat down in my glider, the one I'd been given for nursing, and immediately ripped open the envelopes. It gave me something to do—an event to look forward to—but also something to dread.

I was fast becoming an expert in the sympathy card design market, and I developed a pretty high bar. The truth was that I was glad to hear from anyone, from everyone, and, at the same time, I felt the need to mock some of the crap that showed up. Laughing at these cards numbed a bit of the dull ache, if only momentarily. I was tempted to feel guilty, ungrateful, but I was really too tired to care.

One card featured a particularly creepy baby angel floating and holding a thurible, the swinging brass censer used in Roman Catholic masses and some other liturgical church services. A cloud of incense was rising out of the tiny holes, apparently with the writer's prayers for us. Others used a nature motif: birds, chipmunks, hydrangeas, seashells, flying dandelion tufts, wisteria pressed from foil, birds of every kind, endless butterflies, scenic vistas. The accoutrements made me laugh: golden embossing, velveteen flocking, ghastly explosions of glitter, glued-on sparkles and gemstones. Many people added the flourish of misspelling Jesse's name—he was used to it, it did not bother him, while my anger flashed at the sight. How could you spell someone's name wrong on a sympathy card for their forty-day-old dead baby? I had no patience for such carelessness. I had no patience for anything.

Many of the cards tried to solve the problem of grief in a typeset line or two, rhyming if I was lucky, sometimes tying it up with some scripture to offer a simple reason for my son's death, or sometimes attempting to defend God's honor. One card came from a parishioner of the church where I was serving in Reno. She wrote, "We each have some earthly task to do, and when it is done, we go home. . . . Some ripen young; some take a long time to do it." I was appalled, furious. Fritz did not "ripen"; he had not completed his "earthly task," I thought, seething. How could anyone say that his time was enough? Fuck you, I thought, tempted to rip the card in two. Others sought to jump ahead in time and in confidence. "Know that you will survive and in time your family will thrive," wrote a friend. How lovely, I thought, that *she* knew this—I had no such confidence. It was my hope, but it was not a given, not a foregone conclusion. Not at all.

I had already hated all the "angel" business that gets thrown around when someone dies too young—the trite explanation that "God needed another angel." I do not believe we morph into angels when we die, sprouting wings. Angels are another breed entirely, wild and wonderful beings, holy and mysterious messengers of the divine. We don't *change* into angels, you foolish people, I muttered, clenching my teeth. Where do you even get this? My patience waned further. I wanted to organize a lecture for all the sympathy-card writers of the world. Lesson One: as people, we are of a different substance—human, not angel.

But then some cards taught me. "Saint that he is," a friend wrote of Fritz, and I stopped short. That was what had happened, I thought, eyes wide. My son hadn't magically grown wings and turned into an angel, but he had joined the saints. I didn't know what that meant, really, but it was an idea I could live with, and practice: reaching to connect with this band of saints as I took communion, remembering all the saints on particular holy days, catching bits of wisdom on their place in the cosmic order in a reading on this Sunday or that. I had already lived this practice—it had washed over me for years—but it was only just now dawning on me that Fritz had joined them. It came as some reassurance, this I could at least contemplate.

It astonished me that some people did not expect me to remember them, explaining that they served as an usher at my parish in Reno, that we went to high school together, and so on. Jean reminded me of our connection through school and church back in Indiana, naming her siblings. How could I not remember Jean? She was not confident that I would, though, and yet she was offering what she could. "Call, email, write," she said, "or don't be obligated to reply at all." She expected nothing of me, and I was grateful.

The best cards were the ones that didn't try to make it better, from people who knew they couldn't solve anything but who were willing to join us in the grief. "Words seem so hollow," wrote Tom and Kevin. Seminary friends wrote, "We love you, and we send our love to be with you. . . . In love and brokenheartedness, Reed and Linden." Susanna, my seminary advisor, knew: "There are no words at a time like this. Just the faith that his beautiful, short life was not in vain, and that all he was and might have been is safe with God. And yet . . . we weep." Our college friends Griff and Liz were true, too, in their own faltering: "All I can think of is that our hearts are with yours in the ocean of sadness."

I read, card after card, that it wasn't just my heart that had broken this winter. Fritz's death had broken the hearts of all our people, even those who had never had a chance to meet him. Some of my friends had no choice in the matter, I could tell—his dying simply ripped us apart. But some, I could hear between the lines, some of them actually allowed this death to break their hearts, allowed it to rend them into bewildering grief. They didn't have to be here, yet they were choosing to join me. No amount of gaudy rhinestones and glitter and butterflies could undermine the potency of this sacrificial accompaniment: these people didn't have to suffer, but they were deciding to, choosing to be with us in the exile of this dark place.

One day early on, just in the first week following Fritz's death, a small padded envelope stuck out of the stack of cards that Stuart dropped off. I set aside the pastel envelopes—why are they all pastel? why not a passionate red, or a piercing blue of possibility?—on the dining room table, curled up in my glider, and tore off the top of the yellow-papered bubble wrap, bubbles popping in that tactile and satisfying way as I ripped through the plastic. I reached in to pull out a crisply folded piece of paper, the letter on it typed, and a tin box, no more than two inches across. An intricate pattern had been hammered into its lid and sides, circles and rays radiating out from the center, though the journey had tweaked it a bit, flattening it on one corner. Lifting the lid, I saw some minuscule paper cranes, all different colors, and two rocks, one so white it was almost luminous in my dark living room, the other like hard-pressed coal, a jagged rock to whom life had not been kind. Pulling my knees to my chest—the fetal position was my default these days—I unfolded the letter.

It was from my mom's first cousin. I could never remember if that made him my second cousin or my first cousin once removed, but in practice Carl was more a combination of uncle and brother. He taught me to make dry-ice bombs as a preteen, and had long been schooling me in the fine art of the prank, our time together adventurous and raucous and lighthearted. My eyes raced across the lines of text, delving into another scene entirely.

Carl had been out on a long run in rural Oregon when I called to tell him that Fritz had died. His was one of the phone calls during which it took multiple attempts for me to convey the simple fact that my baby had died. The shock, he said, had doubled him over. At the time, I felt his anguish acutely and, as he was brought to his knees, sought to console him. Now I started to read his account, written just the day after he heard, filling in the picture from the other side of that call.

"I finished that run," he began. One line, solitary, definitive. "But first, I sat by the side of the road and cried for a while, regardless of the cars. I don't think anything has hit me so hard since my dad died."

I tried to conjure the image. Carl had a soft heart but was a tough guy, a volunteer firefighter, one who had for years completed the Firefighter Stairclimb in Seattle, a fund-raiser for the Leukemia and Lymphoma Society that entailed running up sixty-nine flights of stairs wearing full turnouts and oxygen. He was so competitive, a glint quickly flashed across his eyes when any challenge arose. I read on, imagining him crumpled and weeping. I doubled back to that line, though, carefully tracing it with my eyes a second time: "I don't think anything has hit me so hard since my dad died."

Carl was no stranger to grief. His dad died when he was in college. His mom died far too young also—a nasty one-two punch of lung cancer and then a brain tumor when she was not yet seventy. He was close to my mom, too, the two cousins born just seven months apart. That my son's death hit Carl like this was arresting. Even as I'd been paralyzed with grief in these early days, I was hesitant to name how awful this death was. I was afraid to answer, to myself or to the world or to God, that yes, this loss was *that bad*; that this death was the kind of bad that guts you, leaves you empty, festering, gone; that this could be the one you might not make your way back from.

My shock still cocooned me, holding me a few steps removed from the terror of being lost to myself.

The run was one of the most difficult of his life, Carl continued. He'd surprised even himself, that he'd pushed on:

> What usually takes me an hour and a half took almost three hours. I stopped five or six times to cry. At the intersection of two logging roads, something pulled my feet right and uphill. A mile later, I saw why. There was a new clearcut, gaping up the side of the hill, wreathed in a storm cloud, and in dozens of smokes from still smoldering slash piles—perfectly appropriate to the moment. The piles had burned so hot, they had gone underground; there were dry patches of flaky, ashy earth with deep pits of burning embers beneath, steaming and smoking. I took handfuls of ash from one and rubbed it on my face and heart. And that was where the dark stone came from. It used to be clay, and now it's brick from the heat of the slash fire.
>
> I kept running, with no desire to run, but no desire not to run, nor any desire for anything. Nothing seemed worth it. And then, at the steepest point—three quarters of a mile of 20% misery that usually gets me fired up for battle but today left me only with a vague feeling that it wouldn't really matter if I gave up—something miraculous happened. The storm wind came up from the southwest and literally carried me up that slope. I have never felt anything like it.

Neither have I, I thought. Not while racing bikes, or hammering away in rugby, or backpacking well past the point of exhaustion. I had only ever moved on my own power, my own legs, my own self-drawn will and breath.

Just past the summit is a sacred quarry from which you can see
Mt. Hood, Mt. Jefferson and the Sisters on a clear day. It's where
Jeannie and I have gone to grieve the ones dear in our lives.
It's my prayer spot. And that is where the other stone, the little
three-sided quartz purity, comes from.

Carl pivoted beyond the run, my brow furrowed as I tried to track his
leap. He was looking squarely at me, through the page.

If any have ever eaten darkness and shat light, certainly you
are among them. How you could be called to do so again is
beyond me.

Is that what I'm being called to do? I wondered. Eat darkness and shit light?
In my life, I had prayed and wrestled and sought. But truth had not
come from beyond me, luminous, transformative. I trusted in the Holy Beyond, and even as I had made vows to God, life had, until now, been largely
rational, predictable, straightforward. Shit had happened, yes, inexplicably
horrible shit. That seemed to be part of it. But the light? I hadn't been astonished by it. I hadn't born witness to miracles. I'd just pushed forward,
grateful for the love that surrounds.
Carl seemed to see something, though. He seemed to be living something that right now was beyond me. He held the ash and the light together.
He held them both for me, steadying us, until the day when I might be able
to take them in my own hands.
I gripped the paper tightly, flattening its creases, trying to pull these
words into myself. The stark black type on the crisp white page was a welcome change from the glittery butterflies just beginning to accumulate in
the early collection of cards. The letter's austerity matched Carl's words,
his stark willingness to name where we were together, to describe the dark
clouds brewing, the ash that covered us. He was choosing to cover himself
in it, to join me here in darkness.

I folded the letter back in thirds, setting it on the top of the pile, its blank white back covering the sheen of a fancy purple envelope. I turned in my glider to face the window, looking out at the crashing waves, the lake rough in the afternoon wind. The sun's waning light broke out in a hundred directions off each crest and trough. I felt the need to dive in, plunge under the water, eat what darkness lay beneath this dancing light on the water's surface.

Dry Bones

It was the first time that my eyes had ever fooled me. The first time they told me what the truth is by showing me what is beyond. I did not learn how to do this in seminary. We Episcopalians enjoy talking about mystics, admiring them from afar and reflecting on their experiences, maybe, but we don't spend much time being taught to practice in this way. But then, maybe this cannot be learned. Maybe it simply happens to you.

Fritz was not yet in the ground the first time sight came to me. He was dead, out of my hands, but not yet returned to me as a crude box of ashes. It was my third run in as many years, for the third day in a row. I was making my way slowly up the trail, along a bluff over Lake Tahoe. It was thickly carpeted in pine needles at first, but as the grade became steeper, the trail turned harder. Packed dirt, cracked from the drought. Bushes sent their bare, scraggly arms out, trying to jab at me, stab at me, point out my misery and, in my attempt to mitigate it, my hopelessness. *Exercise!* I'd thought that exercise outside might solve this! The branches clawed at me as if laughing.

I passed through a long clearing and moved farther up the hill, lungs on fire, the weak air of high altitude crushing me. Suddenly, I looked up to see the trail ahead of me: the cracked dirt of the trail ceded to thick, loose earth and then—bones. The trail was covered in bones. Thin leg bones, a socket here, the blade of a shoulder there, bones were all my eyes could see. All tiny, splintered, bleached white from the sun. I gasped, horrified. This was my life now, having made death my intimate acquaintance. On the edge of Lake Tahoe, on a pristine winter day, blue sky, blue lake, I had landed with Ezekiel, that age-old prophet who touched down in a valley, expansive, filled only with dry bones as far as the eye could see. Here, too. The ground was littered, bones were all I had to stand on.

I seemed to hear the words the prophet had heard, echoing: "Mortal, can these bones live?" (Ezekiel 37:3, NRSV) God came to him, crashing in, or was it tempting, cajoling? All I could hear now was the cruelty of the question and how I hated it. Punishing my lungs and my legs, I pushed up, gingerly but rapidly making my way around the bones, careful not to step on them, running until I crested the hill and left them behind me, looking back over my shoulder, aghast. "What just happened?" I stammered to no one, to everyone. "Where am I?"

But it's a dead-end trail.

Not even a quarter mile later, I slowed to a stop, propping myself up on the gate, looking into the driveway of an empty luxury lake house. I was panting. I wanted to run downhill, I wanted to go home, but not back through *that*, whatever it was. My body grew chilled standing still, and I gave in and turned back. Coming over the hill again, letting my feet pull me down, the bones had now vanished and the forest floor had returned. I saw only dry white branches, broken bits, twigs.

Death remained, though, all around, before my eyes. And the question lingered, taunting me, ringing in my ears. *Mortal, can these bones live?*

I did not know then. I did not know if life could return after something as terrible as Fritz's death. I simply did not know.

Ashes and Glitter

I can never quite bring myself to say this out loud, but I believe cremation to be horrific. The body I'd worked so hard to create, incinerated? Ground to a fine grit? All done with reverence and care, apparently, yet obliterated.

Burying a corpse was far more complicated, though—ashes did feel right, but in a completely heinous way. I could not bear to think about it for more than a few moments at a time.

We tried to explain it to Alice, in some slightly cleaned-up manner. I was committed to telling her the truth without sugarcoating this mess, but I couldn't bring myself to tell her what was going to happen to the body of her brother, that we would be asking someone else to burn him up for us. It was terrifying. It turned my stomach to imagine the acrid stench of smoldering flesh, the olfactory notion flashing in against my will.

Driving home at dusk from a dinner out, we told Alice that after you die, your body turns into ashes. We left out the teensy fact of how this happens exactly, and for once she didn't ask.

"But what are ashes, Mommy?" she piped up from her car seat in the back, curious.

Even the concept of ashes was new to her, one more in a long string of things she was having to learn altogether too young. The remains of campfires didn't help much, even as often as she saw them.

"Glitter," I jumped to, impulsively. I had no theological backing for this. I consistently roll my eyes at the "We are all stardust" riff, encountering it largely as platitude. I definitely did not have foresight as to where a two-year-old would run with the information that her brother was being transformed into glitter, a word that had fallen out of my mouth.

"He's turning into glitter glue?" her voice cried out from behind us.

"Well, no, not exactly," I said, trying to backpedal, too late.

But Alice was thrilled: A little brother turned into glitter glue—was there anything better?

I sat in the driver's seat, hands clenched on the steering wheel, my knuckles beginning to whiten as my stomach churned again. I was beside myself knowing that my son—essentially my own flesh—would soon be incinerated and that my daughter would celebrate the process as a metamorphosis into a prized craft item.

2

RITUAL

ЯІTUAL

The Placenta and the Aspen

When Fritz was born, Jesse and I had saved his placenta, frozen it at home, and then put it into Camp Galilee's massive walk-in freezer. We'd nested it in multiple bags and marked it very clearly. The outermost brown paper bag spelled it out: PROPERTY OF TICHENORS. DO NOT OPEN AND DO NOT EAT. I had thought it would be lovely to bury the placenta under a new tree, just as we had done with Alice's. Hers was actually under a lilac bush we'd planted in Berkeley—the bush wasn't doing great, the climate too warm and dry for its liking, but it limped along, flowering a tiny bit each spring.

We now called around, wondering if there was a nursery that would even have trees for sale in January, and were surprised when one did. Jesse ratcheted Alice's car seat onto the bench in the camp truck, I threw old towels over the blanket of matted hair from the camp dog, and we headed over the pass and down the hill to Carson City.

There weren't too many options for trees. It needed to be a native, and also one that could thrive without too much care at the camp. We settled on an aspen. I loved the rustling, almost rattling sound their leaves make in the wind, and their white bark is beautiful, even when the leaves are gone. The symbolism was a boon—they are rhizomatic, spreading not by seeds or cones, but by sending out root suckers, which spring up as new shoots a little way out from one individual parent tree. Eventually a whole colony of trees can grow up around one original seedling. And the colonies work together, all connected invisibly underground. If trees are sick at one end of the colony, and a nutrient they need is scattered on the ground at the other end, the trees can actually pass the healing element through their network, bringing what's needed to those that are struggling.

The kind, if slightly perplexed, arborist at the nursery led our scrappy family to the row of aspens near the back of the huge lot. Big buckets of trees stood bare, their twiggy branches blowing and scraping against one another and the high blue sky. The arborist taught us a bit about what they would require for water, now and in the months ahead. It was a different sort of newborn care class—brief and simple. We didn't tell her why we needed to buy an aspen right *now*, in winter. Perhaps my puffy eyes and tight lips made it clear that this was not a spontaneous, happy-go-lucky landscaping project, and she did not pry.

Alice picked her brother's tree, the tallest one in the row, some eighteen, maybe twenty feet tall, the topmost branch arching far above the rest, as if reaching for a heaven whose geography I did not know. The arborist called on a walkie-talkie for the forklift driver, who wove his way through the tight rows of shrubs and trees to carefully wedge the lift under the black plastic box protecting the root ball. Careful, I wanted to urge him. This tree needs to get home safely, needs to make the drive unscathed, I wanted to say, but I bit my lip.

At the insistence of the camp's board of directors, we charged the tree to the camp's account. Back in December, the board hadn't felt entirely comfortable with the plan for me to give birth at home, at the camp—I'd had to sign a waiver, promising that if something went wrong, we wouldn't sue them—but I was quite grateful now for their generosity. We needed this tree, and even at the cheap rate reserved for churches, $250, it was more than we could afford, especially right after the cost of cremation.

Together with two nursery workers, Jesse and I heaved the tree into the bed of the pickup, pulling its base forward against the cab and letting the trunk lean on the tailgate. The workers assured us that it was heavy enough to stay put, even with the steep grade and hairpin turns that lay ahead. We took the curves slowly on the highway home. Back at camp, we guided the truck off the paved drive and all the way down to the bluff overlooking the lake, where the tree would be planted, where we would then bury Fritz's ashes.

The hole required for the tree was enormous. We began digging and watering, digging and watering, as the nursery folks instructed—the hole needed to be big so the young roots would have an easier time working their way into loosened soil. The day was uncharacteristically warm, but so far the weather this entire winter had been bizarre. We were in an extended drought, with little snowfall, and now a warm spell. Alice soon stripped off her clothes and began stomping and splashing in the mud. She claimed responsibility for the hose and joyfully soaked much more than the hole itself, delighted with her good luck in scoring a hose and mud and a dance party outdoors in January. Her glee crashed against the weight of this work, how heavy the dirt was in my shovel, how much I hated this whole project. Yet it was impossible not to laugh at a filthy, naked, dancing two-year-old, the sound of my laughter clashing with the misery that sat leaden within me.

The Bread

Our cramped cabin was too small for us to cook much of anything there; the counter on the one end of our main room was mostly good for making coffee and microwaving leftovers, the stovetop more often serving as storage space than anything else. The morning of my twenty-ninth birthday, Fritz then two weeks dead, I snuck away to the empty camp kitchen just down the hill. Outside of summer camp, the other cabins were generally filled with retreat and conference groups, the kitchen humming with activity from before daybreak until darkness fell again.

The only group this weekend, however, was our friends and family arriving for our son's funeral. The kitchen was still empty, and I left the lights off, choosing to work in the indirect daylight filtering in beneath the tired eaves and through the greasy windows. Cool light glanced up from the long stainless-steel island in the center of the kitchen. I set a matching metal bowl in its center and dragged the fifty-pound barrel of flour down from the shelf. I dumped in five cups, then whisked in the baking powder and salt. Next I needed the wet ingredients.

But first I paused, cradling the chilled sides of the bowl in my open palms. I looked down, and all I could see was ash. I was baking communion bread for the funeral Eucharist. It was a recipe I'd used countless times. But this time it looked like I would be kneading bread out of dry, lifeless ash. I doubled over, trying to find breath, leaning hard against the cold steel of the table. Tears came rolling, quickly, as the sound of my sobs echoed off the cinder-block walls of the empty dining hall. Fat droplets fell, landing deep in the powder, tunneling down. It was all so wrong, and yet so true, making bread from a broken body, bread that tomorrow we would break in the hope of being made whole. It was more than I could take. All I could do was weep.

Finally, I stopped and gathered my strength to finish the recipe. I found the other ingredients, mixing them and then adding warm milk, as if preparing a bottle. I kneaded it until it came together, cohering, compliant: the bread of life.

Alice would not allow me to wallow alone in the darkness for too long in one go, and as I finished wiping up the scattered flour, she burst into the dining hall, eager to plant her brother's tree. I stepped into the walk-in freezer out behind the kitchen, its door marred by a bear's fruitless attempts to break in, and grabbed the triple-bagged placenta. As Jesse and I hustled to keep up, Alice ran to the bluff, zigzagging through the wood chips and down past the stone church, not even pausing at the creaky, splintered jungle gym.

Our people, just beginning to roll into camp, found us there above the lake. We didn't have a clear game plan. The box around the root ball made the aspen particularly unwieldy, and so the work of planting the tree quickly became the kind of team-building activity we might have assigned to our oldest campers in the summer, a puzzle of weight and shifting fulcrums and strangely complicated wing nuts. Confident that her main responsibility was the hose, Alice quickly stripped off her pants and underwear, her naked bottom wiggling below her zipped-up winter coat. It wasn't long until she was totally naked, though, soaking the hole and spinning once more in the delight of fresh mud. When all was soaked, I quietly took the placenta out of its bags and nestled it down into the hole, adding more dirt on top. All this was right, appropriate. Still, I did not want to look at it.

It took all of the hodgepodge gathering of a dozen or so—my brother-in-law and his wife, friends from seminary, co-workers from the camp, a friend from college, a childhood friend—to wrestle the tree into the hole and then to finagle the sides of the box off. Alice, tired of her naked mud dance, pulled me to a big rock just next to the tree, where she climbed into my lap and curled up to nurse. Someone googled "how to plant an aspen" on a phone, reading aloud about layers of dirt and water, correct tamping practices, on and on. Our friends were taking this project seriously, determined to help this tree get a proper start.

Alice was either sated or lured by the fresh promise of loose dirt, and I pulled her too-big pants and dinosaur sweatshirt back on her as she ran to the pile and began hurling fistfuls in around the roots. We took turns shoveling soil and checking the straightness of the tree, watering and tamping with our feet, circling close around the trunk, a practice run for the dirt we would cast into the hole together the next day.

We were just finishing when two more cars pulled up: Alice's godfather and his family, and Phil and his family. The tree carefully and thoroughly planted, I announced that it was time for a swim. It was a ridiculous invitation, on January 24 at Lake Tahoe. But the sun was bright and the water was shining, enough so that we had to shade our eyes from its glare. Everyone except Jesse looked dubious—Jesse was always game.

"Come on, people, it's my birthday!" I yelled. "Swim with me!"

Many consented, in what was clearly an extension of goodwill and maybe a little bit of pity. Suits were quickly procured, and we ran out across the long, drought-stretched beach.

When we hit the shallow edge of the water, shrieks began escaping uncontrolled. We hurtled farther out, a whole gaggle of us, kids and adults and the camp's big yellow Lab, until it was deep enough that we could splash down, immersing ourselves in the clear and frigid winter water. I came up sputtering and hollering, astonished and amused that my friends were willing to do this with me. I sprinted back to shore, quaking with cold, just as a friend I hadn't seen since we were hospital chaplain interns together went running out into the water in his underwear, having only just arrived. We were a spectacle. Heart pumping as I toweled off my numb skin, I realized I was grinning. I was still broken, but coming out of the water, I felt alive. Our friends were here. It was my birthday, damn it. I had at least survived to twenty-nine.

The Ashes, the Cardboard, the Neoprene

Ralph at the funeral home had assured me that Fritz's ashes would be ready in time for the service, but without much time to spare, likely only the day before. It was hard to get ahold of him, though, or to talk to anyone there who knew what was happening. Were the ashes actually ready? Was someone there to let us in? Unclear. But finally, we had shaky confirmation, and with friends already gathering at camp, I pulled together whatever nerve I still had to make the trek. I understood that I couldn't send someone in my place, that this was something I had to do. I would go to retrieve what was left of the body I had grown and brought into the world.

It's an odd honor to confer, asking someone to accompany you to the funeral home to pick up your son's ashes. On your twenty-ninth birthday.

Various friends offered to join me; some even seemed to vie for the spot. Was it a privilege of intimacy they sought? Were they working out their own issues, needing a mission? Some seemed so confident they could help me effectively, which annoyed me. I didn't want to be the object of their mercy. I wanted a companion. A *com-panion*, I thought, remembering its root from some seminary class long past: "with bread," someone to break bread with. But there wasn't bread this afternoon, just one small body. I wanted someone who could come with *com-passion*, someone ready to suffer with me. This was the work of the church, I thought, right here. Empty hands, the desperate time for another to enter into this pain.

At last, I asked Phil to accompany me, trusting he could walk the line with me. We slipped away late in the afternoon, the sun glancing low across the lake and the crest of the Sierras to the west. It was crisp and clear and gorgeous. I drove our Subaru past the casinos and touristy outposts of South Lake Tahoe, retracing the ambulance's tracks, the gray leather of the back seat still holding the impressions from Fritz's car seat.

Phil began to speak. I was trying to watch the road in the waning light, but I turned my head to take in his words. "I'm proud of you, how strong you are, how you seem to be stepping into this grief in such a healthy way."

"There really isn't another option," I said, trying to dismiss the compliment. Then I caught myself. "Well, there are—but the other options all seem really shitty."

We laughed, but it was true. I knew whose daughter I was, whose alcoholic, suicidal genes I had inherited. I was already familiar with the pull, the lure of numbing, the ease of pouring one glass of wine and then another. A couple of glasses let me press pause on a day, stop early, actually fall asleep in the dark. It was a sinister option, but a real one, and I had been flirting with it already.

"This might seem strange to say," Phil continued, "but you are beautiful in this heartbreak."

I squinted back at the road ahead, blinded by the sunset. It didn't make sense to me—I couldn't see any of this from the outside—but his words were a gift. At least one other person I trusted seemed to think I would make it through this, that I might be whole again on the other side.

Through the main part of town and now into the outskirts of South Lake Tahoe, Phil and I passed the funeral home the first time by. I pulled a U-turn just before a curve and then scooted in before the evening traffic plowed through a newly green light. We were the only car in the bare gravel lot. The building was a pseudo log cabin, built in the style of a vacation rental; maybe someone believed this exterior would exude a sense of homey comfort.

I swung my legs to the ground and took a deep breath. Standing, I glanced across the silver roof of my car at Phil. We looked at each other in the way you do when you've run out of time, unable to further delay the hard thing. I sighed. We slammed the car doors, crunched in silence across the lot, heaved open the thick pine doors, and stepped into the polished veneer of the foyer, where vaguely spiritual paintings hung in gilded frames. Vases of plastic and silk flowers, predictable and dusty, stood on the side tables. A stone fireplace filled one wall, mimicking those of the resort lodges encircling Tahoe—all of this working so hard to gussy up death, to somehow render its grittiness more palatable.

Ralph emerged from an office, greeting us with professionally honed warmth, minor chords of pity still leaking into his voice. I introduced Phil awkwardly: "This is my friend—he's also my priest, I guess." It was a funny idea, that you'd need a priest for the ride-along, but here he was—sans collar—in jeans and his gray-checked flannel shirt, somewhat ragged. None of this part of the process would be aided by ritual and pageantry. Not on our end.

Ralph tried to make some small talk, picking up the encouragement right where he'd left off: "More kids will help you make it through this; just focus on having more children. Keep on. Keep trying."

I stared at him, furious, disbelieving. I will not be subject to this conversation again, I thought. Phil lifted his eyebrows but met my eyes, offering silent encouragement: I was under no obligation to withstand this shit.

"Do I need to sign anything?" I asked Ralph through tight lips.

"Let me get the documents," he said, disappearing into his office. He returned with a simple brown cardboard box, the size of a small box of Kleenex. "Of course, we have a wide range of urns, if you'd like to take a look now that you've had more time to think about it?" he angled, the question baited with the suggestion of guilt.

"That will not be necessary," I shot back. "We have no use for an urn."

Ralph had papers in hand, too, on a black plastic clipboard. I was relieved that we were exiting the world of platitudes and euphemisms, even if it meant we had to get real.

"Inside this box is a plastic box, and then within that is a plastic bag containing his ashes," he said plainly. He opened the lid. "Tied onto the bag is a metal tag with the number identifying your son's body through cremation." He showed me the tag, a small brass medallion, like you might have attached to the key for a locker at a pool. "The tag was laid on his chest when he was cremated. Please verify here that the number matches the label on the side of the box"—which he showed me—"and here in the paperwork."

I checked, double-checked. The three digits matched. What a strange way to verify that this is what's left of my son, I thought. Just numbers and ashes now, otherwise anonymous. Ralph closed the box, and I took it from his hands, shocked by how little it weighed, so light you'd have thought it was empty.

I glanced through the paperwork, irritated by how ill-fitting the form was for an infant.

AGE (Yrs): 0
DECEDENT'S PRIMARY OCCUPATION: none
YEARS IN OCCUPATION: 0
KIND OF INDUSTRY: none
EDUCATION: none

MARITAL STATUS: never married

WEIGHT LIMITS. Due to limitations on the cremation cham-
ber, the crematory cannot cremate anyone in excess of 275 lbs.
during the course of normal operation. If the decedent is over 275
lbs. additional charges will apply. Decedent weight: 11.5

Fritz hadn't weighed that much, and they still didn't even have the date
of his death correct. I crossed out *January 10*, pushing the pen hard into the
paper, and wrote with purpose, *January 9*. "Not the tenth, the ninth," I said
under my breath. He lived *forty* days. Not forty-one.

Following the legalese to the bottom of the page, I saw they had mis-
spelled my name as well. I fixed it, confident I knew how to spell the name
of the dead baby's mother, even if I was unsure about every other part of
who I evidently now was.

I flipped to the final page, where the fees for their services were calcu-
lated. Most of the many boxes were unchecked.

"Commemoration of a Lifetime" video tribute: . . . . . beginning
at $475.00

No, absolutely not. No embalming, no viewing, no way in hell I would
want this guy conducting a memorial service. Would he preach about the
big flock of children I should have to fix this little blip? Yeah, no fucking
thank you.

In the merchandise category, two options were checked, the very cheapest ones.

Casket/cremation container: CARDBOARD $95.00
Outer burial container/urn: NEOPRENE URN $20.00

Jesse and I had laughed—actually laughed, finding dark humor—when
we had perused the brochure of casket and urn options. The choices were

all named as if they were hope-filled crayon colors, but with a morbid twist. Why, for just $2,495, we could buy the "Little Angel," the casket specifically made for an infant.

I signed on the various bottom lines, fast, my name barely legible. I passed the paper and slick promotional pen to Phil, who bent over the marble-topped credenza to sign as my witness. I clutched the cardboard box with both hands and uttered a forced thank-you to Ralph after I had already turned to leave. In the dwindling light outside, I dug in my jeans pocket for the car keys, tossing them to Phil as I crossed in front of him to the passenger door.

"I can't drive," I whispered.

He caught the keys, said "I figured as much," and clicked to unlock the doors.

I opened mine and sank down into the bucket seat.

Now it was real. The last two weeks of phone calls and funeral planning had dragged others into our new life, but here I was with my son's ashes resting on my knees. It started quietly: the tears came first, and soon behind them the inability to properly breathe as my whole body shook in spasms of grief. There was nothing to do now but sit in it, reel from it, let it come.

"Oh, Liz," Phil said softly. He wasn't trying to stop me, and he joined with me in his own grief, his own tears rolling freely.

There was nothing to say. Weeping was all there was left to do.

Was it ten minutes of holding on, being held, cradling what remained of my baby, while grief stormed my body? More? Evening traffic continued past the otherwise empty parking lot until finally I was wrung out and dry.

"I'm ready," I said. "Let's go home."

Phil pulled into the stop-and-go traffic, a predictable combination of locals going home from work and vacationers rolling in for the weekend. The gas tank was near empty, so I asked Phil to pull into the Chevron station. I was struggling to keep these basic aspects of life functioning—gas, bills, showers—all still seemed elusive these days.

He hopped out of the car. "Let me get it," he called out, reaching into his pocket.

"Phil, that's ridiculous," I shot back. "You don't have to buy me gas."

"I know I don't have to," he countered, his eyes softening, "but I want to."

"Go ahead, then, knock yourself out," I said, shaking my head. "And thank you." All this was darkly amusing, and it was a relief to feel my face smile.

"Except . . . ," he called back a moment later, sheepish. "Shit. You know what? I don't even have my wallet on me."

We slid into laughter, somehow freed by the absurdity of it all. This kindness—someone buying me a tank of gas—wouldn't change my son's death, but even this comical failed attempt was a balm. I reached back into the car for my credit card, snapped it through the slider, and listened as the pump started clicking away.

"You still have to drive," I told Phil, one eyebrow raised. "Just don't get pulled over."

Back in the car, I fastened my seat belt, grateful for a simple measure of safety and the basic means to keep moving forward, at least mechanically. Neither safety nor movement felt in any way predictable. I took the cardboard box of ashes and set it on the dashboard. Phil pulled away from the gas station, aiming to turn back onto the busy road, but immediately hit a pothole. The box slid off the dash, crashing onto the floor.

"Well, I guess it doesn't really matter anymore, does it?" I asked, reaching to pick it up. Nothing would hurt my son ever again. There were no five-point harnesses to click and tighten just so. The box could sit on the dashboard or not, an uncomfortable mental leap, but I found it hilarious. It was dark, and true. I could drop what was left of my son, klutz that I notoriously am, and it wouldn't make a difference, propriety and reverence be damned.

The sun had already set by the time we made it past all the T-shirt shops and snowboard rental places and seedy casino bars of South Lake, and back into what is largely wilderness, only the shoreline and the edge of the road dotted with cabins.

"You ready for this?" Phil asked. "Ready to dive back in?"

"Not really," I sighed. "I don't know if I can take all those people yet." I pointed to a little pull-out ahead. It was a small parking area, but empty at this hour. We got out, leaving the ashes in the car. If you hopped the split-rail fence and bushwhacked just a bit, you'd find the trail I'd been running, the one that had been covered with bones, then miraculously not. I wanted to go up the other way instead. A paved path led past a sign teaching visitors about the scenic vista and deposited us in front of a giant pile of boulders. I began scrambling up, annoyed with my choice to wear clunky clogs but determined to crest the outcropping. We settled in, leaning back against the highest boulder, standing on another massive round of stone, looking out above all the rest. The sky was losing color now, fast, but the glow of the now pale sky still shone on the lake. Even after living at its edge, I was still not used to this vastness. The sheer reach of its surface, the impossibility of fully grasping its depth and all that it could hold, its needing nothing from me. It was big enough to hold me and my dead son, deep enough to swallow all of us whole, yet still it held the light, lifting it back up to me.

Shivering, Phil and I climbed back down and drove the last mile and a half to camp. It was nearly dark as we wound down the steep and narrow driveway, sheltered beneath the tall Jeffrey pines. The lights were on in the dining hall, which was already filling with people. As we snaked around past it, across the dirt and gravel and up to our cabin, I saw that they were decorating. A mentor of mine stood on a chair, taping up balloons while a beloved priest twisted crepe paper out to the corner of the room. A friend from high school was blowing up more balloons, handing them to the mentor. A seminary classmate stood by, coordinating the effort. Right, I remembered, all of a sudden: it's my birthday. All of these people are here, and it's my birthday. We parked in front of the cabin, set the cheap box of ashes on the kitchenette counter, and walked down the hill to join the party.

Protected Flame

The dining hall was as festive as you can make a rectangular cinder-block room the day before a baby's funeral. When Phil and I walked in, my assortment of friends had finished hanging the spiraled crepe paper, swooping out in all directions from the center of the ceiling, balloons of every color fluttering in the wafts of warm air blowing from the rattling wall heater. By this point, most of my people had arrived: more seminary classmates, friends from high school, college chums. My mom's cousin had just rolled in, Carl, who had taught me how to blow stuff up when I was a young teenager and who had been so rocked by Fritz's death. He was now more verklempt than most, crumpling sweetly into my embrace on arrival. Another contingent burst through the door, this one of people from All Souls, our parish back in Berkeley, where I'd served for my internship in seminary, the church where I'd been ordained a priest, where Phil is the rector.

Our friends, mine and Jesse's, were now coming up in droves to re-create All Souls in exile. I heard the youth minister before I saw her, relieved that she knew it was still appropriate to throw her head back laughing, cutting up, making a scene. Even now, especially now.

The room was full, and good. And overwhelming. I snuck away, into the kitchen. As if Laurie weren't already busy enough getting dinner on the table, I fell into her arms, teetering.

"I don't know if I can do this, Laurie," I whispered, a tremor snaking down through my chest.

She just held on. We stayed there, me clutching, her holding, good at this.

"Yes you can," she said. "You already are. We're doing it together."

I shook, scared, exhausted, while the commotion picked up further through the door—the night was already in motion.

Enough former camp counselors had arrived that the kitchen now worked smoothly, each of them tapping into their muscle memory from summers past. Stacks of plates emerged, then utensils, towers of cups and the big plastic pitchers of water—a dance these friends had done together hundreds of times. Then the feast was brought out: steaming curry, roasted vegetables, fresh naan, great bowls of salad. I pushed others to go first, trying to figure out where one sits on a night like this, or with whom, but they ushered me right into the line to fill my plate. I sat down at one of the long white tables near the middle of the room, and waited.

Tables filled in, some forty, maybe forty-five people settling to eat. The various groups clumped together. I watched as people scanned the room, starting toward me but then faltering and defaulting, always toward the easier, simpler table. They piled onto the long wooden benches with friends from college or high school, or with anyone they knew in the crowd. Some moved into more interesting mixes, connecting with folks from other parts of my life, excited to explore the new relationships. My table remained empty. Jesse had already sat down with some of his extended family, leaving me to be a free agent. Finally, beloved dregs began to fill in around me: the folks who came alone, who didn't know others to join, or who were brave enough to be unfazed by the perplexity of sharing a birthday dinner with the mother mourning her newly dead newborn. This was a spontaneous birthday party of course, derived from the necessity of the funeral tomorrow. *That* was why they were here.

Conversation was awkward, halting. I juggled introducing friends from wildly different parts of my life and reminiscing with each one in turn. Alice ran back and forth between me and all the people she was so delighted to have visiting at once, returning only to ask me why questions and to get spoonfuls of "albo-jam," her special mixture of almond butter and jam, one of the few things besides my milk she reliably agreed to eat.

Time had gone slippery again, and I strained to pull my eyes back into focus. I was not yet convinced I wanted to be at my own birthday party. It seemed philosophically necessary to celebrate—what a remarkable gift that I got to turn another year older—and yet there was a thick wall of glass surrounding me, separating me from all the life and love and goodwill bubbling up from these good people. I could hear them, even touch them, and yet was held back, apart, as if by some invisible force, tethered alone in a desolate place.

This mourning trance was broken by the sound of Sara, the raucous youth minister, hollering at me from across the dining room. We had mostly finished eating by then, and I rose to join her at the back table, grateful for the distraction. Sara was tall, rowdy, and famously loud, and I was now bemused to hear her invite me in close.

"I have a secret," she said, grinning, bouncing excitedly, eyebrow raised for mischievous effect.

I felt some life flood back into my body, as if her enthusiasm were an antidote. "Did you get a new tattoo?" I guessed. It seemed likely enough.

She shook her head. "Better." She cupped her hands to my ear and tried to whisper. "Kristin is leaving All Souls!"

I gasped, pulled back, and looked at her with wide eyes and dropped jaw. "What! For real? When?" My head began spinning with possibility, stirring up out of the muck that had been sucking me ever further down these last two weeks.

Possibility! As if there might be a way being shown to me, out on the horizon. Kristin was the associate rector at All Souls in Berkeley. Her leaving meant the chance of me returning. My dream job would be open.

I stretched out to kick Phil's chair at the table across from us. He turned, surprised.

"Why didn't you tell me about Kristin?" I hissed. "Holy shit!"

He shook his head, smiling at Sara. "I was going to," he explained, "but today didn't seem like the right time."

He was right—the day had been harrowing, and I was grateful to have done the tree and the swimming and the ashes without the distraction of what could be, what might be. I needed to be here, now. Yet there it was: a future.

Here, with Sara's giddiness, her inability to wait until some more appropriate time to share the news, was the introduction of a glimmer. My imagination spun, considering the good life that might be out there for me, down the line. Since Fritz's death, I had not been thinking of what the good life might be—or even that it might exist. And yet here it was, grabbing me by surprise, forcing me to think of it. This was the best gift of the day: the return of hope, of possibility, or at least the possibility of possibility, what

Mary Gordon describes as being the meaning of resurrection. This whisper was a reentry of what Gordon calls the "great perhaps." Maybe, just maybe, there would be more life ahead.

As plates clacked into stacks and silverware jingled into the bins of soapy water, a voice called out for cake, then another. A joyful clamoring began, birthday instinct taking over the crowd's mind for a moment. Cake! Cake! A counselor ran to get a towering stack of small plates; another flipped off the lights. Someone sat me down as Laurie emerged from the kitchen carrying a plate with a dark chocolate brownie. Walking slowly, she processed into the midst of the party with the light, protecting the flame of a solitary candle with one hand. Someone began to sing, and everyone joined in. The singing swelled, filling the room, but at a slower pace than usual. It was all heart, but they sang with the undertones of a dirge. Even as we celebrated, we all still knew why we were here together, marching toward a funeral.

Laurie carefully, almost delicately, set the plate down in front of me. In the darkness, I looked up at all the faces gathered around me, and then down at the single birthday candle. I was twenty-nine. I was still here. I stared at the candle as the silence stretched out, trying to decide what I could wish for on this night. What I most wanted I could not have.

Finally, I inhaled, then blew out the candle. My wish? Only to survive.

Digging the Hole

Jesse and I decided that we should be the ones to dig the hole.

Now eight years into my ministry, having spent much more time working with the funeral industry, this innocent choice of ours strikes me all the more. Typically at the cemetery, you get the full-service treatment: they dig the hole, tidy it up, and complete the burial for you. They mask the dirt with AstroTurf, and often cover the hole with a plank and more AstroTurf, or sometimes dark green velvet—these being part of the *arrangements* everyone's always going on about. The default operation is for the family to gather, have a minister or other hired docent of death say some prayers, and then leave with the coffin or urn still aboveground. The gravediggers and the undertakers will do the dirty work, the *real* work, of burying your loved one.

Maybe Jesse understood why it made sense to do it ourselves, but I did not, not yet. The morning of Fritz's funeral, we went to find our sweet friends Tom and Cheri, to tell them we were ready. A little more than a year earlier, we had asked if they might be our "mentor couple." We didn't entirely know what we meant by the request, but we knew that we wanted to learn from their decades-long head start on a solid marriage. There was much wisdom to glean from them. On this day, still feeling honored, taken aback even, that they had flown out from North Carolina to be with us, we trusted that they would know how to do this unthinkable thing.

Jesse found a shovel up in the rusting Quonset hut that served as the camp's toolshed, and the four of us gathered down on the bluff. It was chilly, the sun not yet high enough over the eastern ridge to shine on us. We stood at the chosen spot, looking for a long time at the aspen we'd planted the day before. Tom and Cheri wrapped their arms around us, warming us, helping us to stay upright. We talked, we laughed, surprised that we could.

As good as it was to talk with just the two of them—it was a sacred space, a rare one, with just the four of us gathered—I knew we had come here with a clear job to do. After a long spell staring at the unbroken ground, I slowly trudged over to pick up the shovel leaning against the trunk of a tall pine. Carefully placing the shovel's edge a few paces in front of the thin new aspen, I held the handle and jumped onto the shovel, forcing the blade down into the ground. The sandy soil gave way easily. Again and again I hurled myself onto it, taken aback by my body's eager strength for this chilling task. The quiet ground parted to form a shallow divot, and then a hole, and then a darker, deeper place. I traded with Jesse, watching as he pushed farther below, the pile to the side growing taller as sand and dirt sailed onto it. After some time, the three of us watching, he stood back.

"Is this deep enough?"

We didn't know, no one having taught us how to dig a hole for a baby's ashes. Were we doing this properly? What did *proper* even mean?

Tom and Cheri had stood witness to more death than we. Early in their marriage, they had moved home to Maine, to share an old farmhouse with Cheri's ailing grandparents and care for them as they died. That they weren't strangers to the process was part of why they'd shown up for us.

"That is a good hole," they assured us. "It's plenty deep."

With Fritz there was so little to bury.

We set the shovel aside and stood together again, the four of us now staring into the hole.

Cheri turned to confer quietly with Tom, trading a few questions back and forth.

"Should I now?" she asked.

"Do you imagine a better time?" he returned.

Understanding their exchange required background that we didn't have, but together they decided that yes, this was the time.

"Let's. Now's good."

Cheri worked her fingers into the front pocket of her jeans and tugged out a fabric envelope, small enough to fit in her palm. She opened it, then gingerly handed me its contents: a thin gold ring, six prongs holding a blue sapphire.

"We want you to have this, Liz," Cheri began. "It's the color of Fritz's eyes."

I didn't know what to say. No one had ever given me something like this—for engagement presents, Jesse and I had exchanged bicycle helmets. The ring was little; it would fit on my pinky but not over the big knuckle of my ring finger.

I, too, held it gingerly. "Where did it come from?"

"It's been in our family for a long time," Cheri explained. "I won't tell you the details—it's for your story now. But its story has been about a mother and her son, and the great love that was between them."

Normally my curiosity would have demanded more, but this was enough for me today. I turned the ring over in my fingers, slipping it on, clutching it. I was grateful for something to hold on to, to see. The two of them held us together, lingering above the open hole. But it was time to get ready. Soon everyone would gather.

The Box

Hunched over our dining room table, I began cutting thick white paper I had scrounged from the camp's art cabinets, creating two large squares. Satisfied by their right angles, I started to fold them. I made one box, and it kind of worked but seemed flimsy. Would tape help? I began in on the second. It wasn't cooperating, I was becoming flustered, and time was running out.

A quiet knock sounded on the cabin's warped aluminum door, then the squeak of the hinges. Phil let himself in and sat down by my side. He studied my project, clearly surprised that I was folding paper boxes half an hour before the funeral.

"Liz? What are you making?"

I was frustrated, on the brink of tears. "I'm trying to make a box for Fritz's ashes. All we have is that awful neoprene thing, and I can't stand it."

He could see that my plan was unworkable. Scant as they were at just a cup and a half, if that, the ashes would be too heavy for the paper box—this would end disastrously.

Phil rose with a deliberate calm. "Let's see what else we can come up with." He glided slowly around our cramped living room, scanning the floor-to-ceiling pine shelves. His eyes landed on a small box, some four by six inches, dark brown in a flat wicker weave. "Could we use this?"

It had been my mom's, for makeup, I thought. Hardly a reverential container for my dead son. But it was lovely, as I saw it again, and it was the right size. It had been hers, was now mine, and here it stood, ready.

Phil pulled it down from the shelf and emptied it of our collection of lake rocks, then sat to help me with the ashes. I slid the neoprene box out of the cardboard box, and pried off the lid. Drawing in a sharp breath, I lifted out the clear plastic bag. The bag itself was enormous, the ashes filling only one small corner, reminding me of how you might squeeze frosting into the corner of a bag to pipe florets on a cake. I felt the ashes through the plastic. Rough, granular. Ground bone, some larger chips. As I traced the mix with my fingers, my eyes fell on a softly rounded piece, maybe an inch and a half across. Was it part of his pelvis? A shoulder blade? A shard of skull? I stared, unable to move. Phil sat with me as together we bore witness. We lingered in silence for a minute, then another.

"Here," he said, finally, helping me move forward. "Let's cut the bag, so it fits in the box."

I held the bulb of ashes while he fastened a twist tie around the gathered plastic above them. He reached for scissors and cut off all the unnecessary plastic.

"There," he said, "that works."

We nestled the bag into the woven box and fastened the lid's string around the box's wooden toggle.

"It's time to do this, Liz. Get changed, and I'll come back up to meet you here in ten minutes. We'll walk to the church together."

Phil was still in his gray flannel, I in camp clothes. Having run out of ways to delay, I retreated to the bedroom. Black slacks, yes, but a bright blue cardigan. I dressed Alice, too. She would wear a party dress: she had no black funeral clothes in her 2T wardrobe.

The Rite

Soon we were walking down the gravel driveway, Jesse carrying Alice, I carrying the ashes, Phil at our side, now looking more official in his white robe and stole. Cars were shoehorned into every corner of the parking lot, and more cars lined the driveway up to the highway, filling in on the dirt between pines and boulders. We stepped into the little stone church at the center of camp to see that it, too, was filled. Laurie stood waiting in the entryway, holding the paschal candle that had been brought up from All Souls for the day—a massive candle, some three feet tall. Each year they make a new one out of the stubs of the beeswax candles from the previous year—it's then lit at the Easter Vigil, still in the dark of night: one flickering light piercing the darkness, promising that the darkness will not overcome us, that death will not win.

An artist at All Souls painted a different design on the new candle each year, always some symbol of the Resurrection. When we had been planning the service, Phil asked if he should bring it. I had checked in the church at camp and was disappointed to see they had an old paschal candle, covered with a gaudy plastic decal.

"Yes," I said. "Yes, we need a really good candle!"

The previous Easter, then pregnant with Fritz, I had followed this same candle into the darkened church. Now it would lead us forward as we went together to bury him.

Laurie gripped the candle intently. Just above her callused chef's hands, I saw the familiar image of a pomegranate bending around the pillar in careful acrylic paint, its bright seeds bursting forth in all directions. Its message: life, and the possibility of life, could not be contained, would not be held back.

Jeff, the priest from Carson City who was leading the service, locked eyes with me, nodded, and walked up the bright blue carpet to the front of the church. Standing beside the first pew, he raised his voice to welcome everyone.

This man was perhaps the most unhinged priest I'd ever met: hilarious, flippant, uncensored, jarringly direct, generally well past irreverent. Now, though, he was already choking back tears as he greeted the congregation.

He wiped his eyes. "We're going to need a lot of these this morning," he hollered, waving a box of Kleenex above his head. "Why don't we just pass them around?"

Jeff had decided folks needed some instruction before the liturgy.

"You're at camp, so things are going to happen a little—well?—differently here," he said. "You're going to need to participate throughout the service. Here at camp, we don't believe that blessing is just the function of the guys and gals running around in collars. Yeah, I know it might be a little surprising for you real Episcopalians here, but you're gonna need to help. When we get to the table, I'm going to invite you to extend a hand, to join in blessing the bread and wine. We think of it as a form of divine reciprocity: as we bless the bread and wine, the hope is that God blesses us to become the Body of Christ in the world; it goes both ways. And then, we're going to lay hands. Jesse and Liz and Phil and I will lay hands on Fritz's ashes, and bless them."

Here Jeff's voice cracked, stopped, then slipped into a jerking, warbling, ripping cry. He rubbed fiercely at his eyes. I straightened my back, surprised. Jeff had suggested this ritual in one of our planning phone calls. But I'd never seen something like it, nor had Phil.

"We don't bless the dead," Phil had said. "They're fine, they don't need it. We bless the living."

And so we'd agreed not to bless the ashes, as this didn't make theological sense to us.

Apparently, however, Jeff had decided we were going to do it anyway. He'd just spoken the act into being—explaining how this makeshift congregation would help bless and bury this child's ashes, and how they would, in turn, bless us. And now, still wiping his eyes, Jeff walked to the back of the church to join us.

A seminary classmate arose, unannounced, to point out where the various hidden exits of the church were—the place was so packed it was apparently making him nervous. He was vigilant, seeming to sense we were stepping into liminal territory, somewhere uncertain and maybe dangerous.

Then Christopher, the dear, bald music director from All Souls, bent over the electric keyboard he'd brought up with him from Berkeley, worried that the old organ wouldn't be enough, insistent that this service needed to sound just right. He began playing softly. The tune was lodged deep in my bones from years of returning to it. We sang the chant in Advent, when we were deep in the waiting, the getting ready for life to happen, for God to come. It was a song I sang when I had been waiting, hoping to become pregnant for the first time, wondering month after month after month if it would ever happen. I returned to the song when I came up to my due date with Fritz, and then past it, and then a week past it, and then two, and then all but three weeks late, waiting, hoping. "Open my heart." Just three words, longing, pleading, deciding, inviting. Three lines of melody intertwined, re-peating the three words again and again. Many of the people gathered knew it well, and their voices split into the layers of harmony without instruction or hesitation.

I choked on the words, the song gargling out through the tears stream-ing down my throat. I could not do this. I had to do this. It was already happening. "Open my heart," we sang. "Open my heart, open my heart." Laurie turned to face the church, and began walking slowly, deliberately, forward, leading us with Easter's light. I followed. Jesse walked at my side, carrying Alice, her legs flopping and playfully kicking, her thin blond pig-tails bouncing with each stride. I clutched the woven box of Fritz's ashes, trying to sing while clenching my teeth.

As I trudged forward, all but ground into the floor by the weight of this seemingly empty box, my eyes widened to see who was present, standing with us, trying to sing with us. There, in the back, just to the right of the aisle, was the doctor, the one we saw at urgent care, the one who'd told me Fritz was fine. He looked terrible, I thought. I wondered if he was on the verge of becoming sick, shoulders hunched forward, his lips only faintly moving in song. Next to him was a clump of teenage counselors from the summer before who seemed out of their depth yet determined to be there. Looking up as I continued in, I saw the back of my father's head, his wavy brown hair more gray than I remembered, but still a head taller than anyone around him. I was stunned. My father? I thought. Even my father came? I had seen him only five times in the last eight or nine years, our relationship having faltered so mightily after his divorce from my mother, back when I was still in middle school. And yet here he was, he, too, *present*.

We continued walking numbly forward and arrived at the front, stopping before a small wooden table covered with a baby blanket a parishioner of mine had knit, a framed photo of Fritz looking straight into the camera lens, and a pair of newborn pajamas covered in red, yellow, blue and gray lions, all things I'd carefully arranged earlier that morning. I placed the wicker box of his ashes in the center, completing the grim tableau below the paschal candle, now in its tall brass stand.

We had added a row of chairs in front of the pews to stretch the church's capacity. Jesse's parents were already there, standing near the granite wall and the small stained-glass windows depicting different glorified mountain scenes, angels trumpeting above the snowy peaks and blue waters. We slid in beside them, no shelter now between us and the work of the service, nothing to hide behind. Alice ran to her grandparents, delighted, twirling as we sang. I clung to Jesse, then pulled Laurie to my other side, needing her support as well.

The service began for me as a haze of moving shadows. Phil and Jeff recited the ancient Resurrection Anthems back and forth, their voices frayed, watery. Friends rose to offer the scripture readings, stopping suddenly to fight back tears, or racing to finish as emotion overtook them.

I sat between Jesse and Laurie, clutching their hands in my lap, heaving. It wasn't that I needed the closeness, but that I was certain I would physically fall out of my chair if they didn't hold me up, that I was just moments from wailing, writhing in a heap on the blue carpet. I squeezed harder, turning their knuckles white.

The service was a big medley of all the truths we were clinging to, hoping to be true, trying to trust. Songs and readings that I had been singing and hearing and studying for years cascaded over us. One friend rose to read, then wept out the desperate truth that nothing, not even death, can separate us from the love of God, a line I had first been taught around a fire as a kid at summer camp. We prayed an old hymn in four-part harmony: "Abide with me; fast falls the eventide; / The darkness deepens; Lord, with me abide." We had sung this hymn endlessly with our college friends years ago, unwittingly practicing for this day. My friend Tripp plucked solitary, lilting notes from his banjo, leading us in singing lamentations as we went on. The Twenty-Third Psalm had it right, worn as it was: here we were, all of us settled squarely in the valley of the shadow of death.

My eyes were mostly open, but I was having trouble tracking through my waves of tears. Phil stepped into the pulpit, a little fortress traditional in its carved wood and octagonal walls, far more substantial than the lectern we had to brace ourselves on at All Souls. I watched him take a deep breath as the congregation settled, then let it out slowly. He took another. I felt sorry for him. This kind of assignment was a preacher's absolute worst nightmare.

"I believe two things to be true this day," Phil began, his voice strong, insistent. "One is that this is not how it is supposed to be. And, I believe that nothing, not one thing, no one, is lost to God." He paused, breathing. "Friends, this is not the way it is supposed to be," he said again, his eyes wet. "Sweet baby boys are not supposed to die—forty days is simply not enough."

Even as I was locked on his words, my mind wandered, unable to grasp this seemingly alternate reality: my mentor, the one who had taught me how to preach, was now preaching my infant son's funeral.

"I cannot comprehend what Jesse and Liz have been living these past two weeks. Hell, I don't even know all of what I have been feeling. For standing at the edge of this chasm takes one's breath away," he continued, his voice teetering, sounding young, almost adolescent. "And when we come to times like these, words fail us." His voice broke, faltering, the words refusing to come out except jaggedly, ruined.

Phil spoke of how completely alone we can feel. "We come face-to-face with the utter darkness of loss," he said, naming my new home. He voiced my constant fear, that "the shadows of the places of danger will overcome us." He seemed to understand that I did not know if I would survive this. I was not simply grieving; I feared the worst. But Phil did not try to solve the problem of Fritz's death or offer reasons for why it happened. He just gave witness to the gut-wrenching pain of it, the terror of what we were living through, and the way we had to carry on together. "*This*, friends," he said, "*this* is why we are here." We were here to bear witness, together, and to bear one another up.

He stepped out of the pulpit then, and brought forward a box, a huge one, and set it on a table in front of the altar. Phil began to tell the story of the Good Shepherd, telling it the way we tell these stories to our youngest children, so simple and beautiful as to contain all truth. He pulled massive story pieces from the box, unfolded the green felt pasture on the table, spread out the cool, fresh water, showed us the silhouettes of the sheep. He paused, seeming to summon the courage to continue, to tell us of the shadows, the places of danger, these places where the sheep could get lost. But even there—I watched him carry the Good Shepherd, searching—even there, he showed us, anywhere, even in these places of danger, the Good Shepherd seeks out the lost, carrying them home. I watched, motionless, holding my breath, the story permeating me.

The service proceeded in a blur. The familiar words of the Eucharistic prayer rolled past me, happening around me, not penetrating. I suddenly realized I was bone tired, nearly too exhausted to stand. Alice danced through the gaps in the altar rail, circling one wooden post again and again, her own personal merry-go-round. She discovered that another post was loose, and it made a satisfying squeak as she spun it in circles.

Jeff invited us to raise our hands in blessing. The bread was broken, chalices filled. "The gifts of God for the People of God," he said, raising them up, offering this meal that we somehow trusted would be enough, as if even bread baked of tears could somehow still strengthen us.

Suddenly, the sound of music pulled my body into the hinge of Easter, the moment when all-consuming darkness just starts to give way to the faintest flicker of new light. "Within our darkest night," we began to sing, the Easter chant that named so precisely where we stood on this day, in broad daylight. The late-morning sun ricocheted off the surface of Lake Tahoe, bright enough that I needed to shade my eyes from the front wall of the church, where the one window of entirely clear glass looked out over the lake. And still, the darkness enveloped me. "Within our darkest night," we sang, "you kindle the fire that never dies away, that never dies away." It is the chant that we begin in total darkness at the Easter Vigil, late on Saturday night, gathered outside in the cold dark. "You kindle the fire," we chant, striking a match to light the new fire, to mark our remembering of the Resurrection, and our trust that it is still happening now. "You kindle the fire that never dies away, that never dies away," we sing on and on to God that holy night, willing it to be true again, waiting for Easter, the harmonies swelling into the night sky as the sparks catch hold of the wood, smoldering, jumping, finally glowing hot. "Within our darkest night, you kindle the fire that never dies away, that never dies away. Within our darkest night, you kindle the fire that never dies away, that never dies away."

We sang it now, on this day far from Easter, breaking bread, being fed, taking the cup, shoulder to shoulder. Alice turned to see Celeste come forward for communion. She was the midwife's apprentice, the one who had coaxed this absurdly late baby from my body. Alice was absolutely taken by her, planned to become her, and now threw her slight body at this woman, who was still somehow ready to catch life. Still not fully comprehending what we were doing, Alice could revel in the joy of having all her favorite people now gathered in the same place.

Once fed, we stood to sing the kontakion, an ancient funeral chant, ending with its perfect exhortation to life: "All of us go down to the dust, yet even at the grave we make our song: Alleluia, alleluia, alleluia." This, this I wanted inscribed on my heart. Still, even here and now, I willed myself to sing, to give thanks. I would not be robbed of that.

Into the Ground

Jeff led Jesse and me from our seats to the small table where Fritz's ashes lay. Jeff stood behind us, as did Phil, each putting a hand on our shoulders. "And now we bless these ashes," Jeff began, asking us to lay a hand on the box. I did, but was unsure, shaking. Jesse rested his hand next to mine, our fingers overlapping. I still didn't know what it would mean to bless these ashes. Fritz was gone, I knew, but the prospect of parting with him further was rending my whole being in two. Jeff spoke words, and I felt goodness and love flowing out through me, into the nothing, into what had been, and what could no longer be, a blessing given to ash. Jeff uttered the commendation, the words through which we ritually gave whatever was left of Fritz over to God. I picked up the box, holding it tight, and we turned to leave the church.

People cascaded out of the pews and flooded into the aisle to form a somber parade behind us. I plodded forward, pushing through the towering wooden doors, squinting in the striking light flashing off the lake. I listened to the bodies following, quietly kicking down through the wood chips, past the rusting jungle gym, filtering in around the scraggly sage bushes, finally gathering at a safe distance from the hole we had dug. Jeff implored everyone to come forward, to join us, to huddle in close.

I stepped to the edge of the hole, Jesse close behind me. Slowly, I knelt on the sandy dirt, alone. I unwound the string and opened the lid of the box. I lifted out the small plastic bag that we'd cut down to size and set the box down on the dirt. I had brought this babe into the world kneeling, birthing him into warm water, using all my might to do so. Loosening that thin twist tie on that bag was harder, the force required was impossibly more demanding than giving birth. I turned it once, twice, then a third time, and the tie fell into my hand. Bracing myself on the ground with one hand, I felt it was warm from the sun. Grasping the little bag, I reached my other hand deep into the hole, into its cold, beyond the reach of light. I paused, faltering, and then slowly, gently, carefully poured out his ashes. I saw them there, a small, light pile, some bone shards still visible, in striking contrast to the dark, wet dirt. And then I sobbed. My head bowed heavy, too much to hold upright, I sank to the ground and there I remained, on the dirt, crumpled, my hand dangling in the hole, unable to move. I was undeterred by all the people looking on, oblivious to any pressure I might have felt to pull myself together under their gaze. There was nothing but ashes and cold dirt, and me, inextricably bound to them, yet unable to be buried myself.

Jeff gently lifted me up, led me to the pile of dirt. "We have to do this part. We do this part together," he reminded me, quietly.

I took a fistful of dirt and returned to the hole, dropping it in, then another and another. Jesse joined me, and Alice. Our daughter was an eager and prolific burier, as it turned out, elated that this somber gathering had somehow now turned into a dirt-throwing event. Finally, Jeff pulled us back; it was time to let others help us. He took dirt and let it fall out of his cupped hands, into the hole. Phil did the same. Then others began to come forward, slowly, one by one, picking up fistfuls and casting them in. I held on to Jesse and raised my head to Phil, motioning for him to join us—I needed someone on either side to hold me up. I clung to them, clung as if my legs were broken, watching in horror and gratitude as our people helped to bury our son. Alice danced in and out between them, taking all the turns she wanted to with the dirt. It was hilarious, watching her great joy in this most wrenching task. I giggled, unable to stop myself. "Even at the grave," I remembered, "we make our song: alleluia, alleluia, alleluia." I wasn't sure I could voice it, but I let it soften me, my deep gratitude for this girl who would somehow keep me going.

It took longer than I expected to bury him, fistful by fistful. Nearly everyone came forward. I watched as one after another, people were caught off guard, grabbed and shaken by the palpable grief contained in a fistful of dirt. This was not sanitized or gussied up; there were no rose petals, no bright AstroTurf. Just us, our hands, this dirt, the hole. When everyone who was willing had come forward, Jesse took the shovel, filling it the rest of the way in, pushing it down, the ground now made whole again, level at the foot of the aspen. I looked down to see that my hands were shimmering, golden. The dry, sandy dirt had a mix of fine-grit mica, some sort of fool's gold spread throughout. Glittering, it now coated my hands, still shaking from this awful act. The shimmering dirt seemed to bless them, save them, cover them in salve.

Then it was over. We sang an old Irish blessing, the familiar words wafting out across the water. Phil and Jeff anointed me and Jesse, and we prayed, but it was already over. There were still hordes of people to greet, hugs to receive, food to eat. But it was over. We had put our son in the ground. My task was now to walk away and leave him there.

None of It Is Glamorous

Most of the funeral guests had drifted away—we'd eaten lunch, I'd visited as much as I was able. As the crowd had thinned, my dad and I had found our way to each other, hugging. I found myself searching for words, though I knew I didn't have more than my awkward, surprised gratitude that he had come. I had then seen off other well-wishers, starting to feel brittle in my repetitive responses, realizing I could take no more. Many people had already begun the drive home; others had gone up to their cabins to sleep, exhale, regroup before dinner, drink. Out of the corner of my eye, I saw Phil laughing with Kirk, another priest serving near Reno, over in the parking lot. They were whispering, then really laughing, laughing hard. My mouth watered at the sound, now run dry from tears. I was so, *so* ready for respite.

I made a beeline over and shouldered my way in between them. "What's so funny, guys?"

They grinned, impishly, shooting each other curiously hesitant looks as they tried to decide how to respond.

"You have to tell me," I cajoled. "Come on!"

"Fine," they acquiesced.

Kirk was wearing a leather jacket, zipped all the way up to his chin. It struck me as an odd choice as the sun beat down—I was warm wearing a

ing on a little stool on top of the counter, and then still up on her tiptoes to try to reach the top of the kitchen wall, holding the very end of the paintbrush handle.

My mom had flown out from Indiana to visit, to help us prepare for this baby, her first grandchild. Trying to cover the years and years of accumulated grime throughout the apartment, long neglected by an order of elderly monks who owned it before my parish bought it back, she was repainting the kitchen white. Jesse and I were moving in, trying to get settled before our daughter was born, knowing it could be any day. Biologically speaking, I was prepared to be a mother, having completed the supposedly requisite training period of one entire gestation.

As I watched my mom reaching up, teetering, helping me with this nesting, I called out, "It never really ends, does it? This mothering thing?"

She laughed, shooting a grin at me, gleeful. Well into adulthood, I still needed her to show up as my mom. And here she was.

"No, it keeps on going," she replied. "You sign up for the long haul."

It was natural that she would be here: turning a dilapidated old place into a home was who she was, it was what she had been doing for as long as I could remember. She made art out of nothing when I was young and we had no money, because she could, for the sheer joy of it. A couple of scrap two-by-fours, cast-off nails, and kitchen string became a loom for weaving rugs out of strips of cloth cut from worn-out clothing. Otherwise discarded scraps of felt and ribbon were trimmed, cut, sewn together, and stuffed with bits of rag to be Christmas ornaments: a festive drum, a heart—we still had them. It seemed she could make anything out of almost nothing.

This was the woman who brought our old house in Iowa back to life. It had been built in 1870, and it was not an easy house. It needed work— the electric-blue shag carpet, the layers of hideous wallpaper, the finicky wiring—but there was such potential. My mom could see it, even hidden under more than a century of neglect. She uncovered ancient floorboards in the attic, pried loose the old square nails, and ripped them up. She carried the massive planks of pine, some as many as eighteen inches wide, down the narrow stairs one by one; she stripped and sanded them till they glowed. She ripped up the carpet in the kitchen and dining room ("Who puts carpet in the kitchen, anyway?" she said, laughing) and replaced it with this gorgeous if totally irregular pine floor, painting on coat after coat of polyurethane to protect it from our spastic dog's toenails. That was the kind of project she could envision, and still make happen, by herself.

In those early days, she mostly finished projects, too. A jungle gym, built from scratch for me and my brother, while a roving gaggle of neighborhood kids attempted to "help." A new deck, a fresh coat of paint on the old house, flower beds, vegetable gardens.

My mom could work this spark. She rode the light of creating beauty with us and for us, and just for the delight of it.

The Call

Fifty-one weeks later, toward the end of August 2012, I stepped out of the old brick building that sits on the crest of the hill of my seminary campus. A collection of seminaries from a range of denominations and traditions stood clumped together on the north side of the UC Berkeley campus, mostly an easy walk from one to the next. The schools wove in and among the old apartment buildings and small craftsman bungalows, the cedars and sycamore trees reaching above most buildings in the bright sun, radiant in a form that seemed apt for this place nicknamed Holy Hill. It was late in the morning, but the neighborhood seemed to be still slowly waking up, set as it was in the midst of student housing. Classes were still not quite in session, the sidewalks empty. I had just met with my spiritual director, and as I wound my way through the maze of stairs and turns on the campus, I pulled out my small red flip phone. A missed call from my older brother—exceedingly rare. I listened to the voicemail.

"Liz, it's John, please call me when you get this. I love you. K, bye."

Even in his steady calm, clearly the voice of a well-trained military man,

I could hear the urgency. I tried him back but landed in his voicemail. I knew it was bad. I tried my mom's landline and then her cell, leaving cheerful but deeply anxious messages on both.

"Hi! Just calling to say hi! Hope you're well. . . . Call me, okay? I love you!"

I sensed the futility of these messages. I walked the five blocks down the hill, curving past floods of blooming jasmine, taking the long-cut to loop past the best garden in the North Berkeley neighborhood, with its daisies and horsetails and black-eyed Susans spilling out in every direction. I made it back to our apartment, stepping over the toys and dirty clothes of my eleven-month-old daughter and into the bedroom whose lavender walls my mother had helped me repaint almost exactly a year before. My phone rang again. My brother. I sat down on the edge of the bed, bracing myself as I inhaled sharply. This was it: *that* call, the one I'd always dreaded.

"Liz, I'm really sorry to have to tell you that mom passed away this morning."

"What! What happened? Did she wreck?" I could believe that. I'd been worrying about that for fifteen years.

But not this: "She took her own life."

"Holy shit" was all I could utter. "Holy. Shit," I said again, slowly, deliberately, stunned.

This was one thing I had not worried about, even after all those years of pouring out the hidden booze, of stealing her keys, of trying desperately to rally her for rehab, of urging her to work the steps or get a sponsor, anything that might help.

"Oh my God. What happened?" I begged. I felt like I might be sick later, but I was still surprisingly steady, following my brother's lead.

Jesse came and sat next to me on the bed, quietly leaning into me.

John continued. "We're still piecing it together. But what we know is that she had an awful lot to drink yesterday and then went out driving, presumably to get more. Someone saw her passed out at the wheel at a red light, there on the corner of Hillside and Henderson, right by Templeton

Elementary. They called the cops, and by the time they caught up with her, she'd kinda wrecked the car into the hill of someone's front yard in that subdivision. But she didn't hurt anyone. They took her in."

Jesus Christ, I thought. Why could she not stop? Why was it so impossible?

John went on. "She spent the night in jail, downtown. They let her out first thing this morning, like at seven. She walked out. She walked across the street to that parking garage; she went up to the top and jumped."

Our mom had jumped off a parking garage to her death! Of all the ways I feared—expected, even—her alcoholism to take her, this was not it. Not *jumping*. Nothing so intentional, deliberate, final.

"She died immediately. She didn't suffer," he said. "Now we need to focus on the positive—remembering her well."

He offered this in one string—the suicide, and the not suffering, and the focusing on the positive. John had always big-brothered me so intently, trying to take care of me, showing me the way forward. I knew that his words were rooted in love, but I was flabbergasted as to how our mother could have not suffered. What! I thought. She didn't suffer? She committed *suicide*!

We agreed to talk soon to start making plans. I numbly told him that I loved him, said thank you, and snapped my phone shut.

I folded pitifully into Jesse's arms. It was finally over, this debilitating, crippling, terminal disease of my mother's—still, I had no way to hold this sort of ending.

Relief and Wailing

We headed up into the Berkeley Hills for a family walk that first evening, as we usually did. Alice would turn one the next month, and she was strapped to my front in a green hand-me-down baby carrier. Even as the shock of losing my mother began to settle in more deeply, I recognized that relief was right there, too. It was the relief that was surprising.

"I have been bracing for this for *so fucking long*," I let fly to Jesse.

If he answered, I didn't hear, lost in my railing monologue.

"Since I was thirteen, maybe, and old enough to understand what she was doing, driving drunk. I always assumed her drinking would kill her, a car crash. I just never thought it would be suicide." Maybe it was partly the shock taking over, allowing me to keep functioning. But the relief was palpable, *so real*, too. "Finally, now I don't have to worry if she's going to die this time, or—worse—if she's going to take anyone with her."

I knew this now that it had finally happened. With the bizarre weight lifted, I felt almost euphoric, sickening as this was to realize. My life sentence, conscripted service to the duty of worrying, was commuted. I was *so relieved* she had not killed anyone else. I knew, viscerally, that that would be worse. Suicide was ghastly, but my mother killing innocent people on her way out? I was uncomfortably grateful for the simplicity of this otherwise complex, grotesque kind of death and grief.

"At least it wasn't that," I said over and over to Jesse. "At least she didn't kill anybody else."

He nodded, sympathetic, patient.

Three days later we were flying east. The seminary classmate's wife who drove Jesse, Alice, and me to the Oakland airport seemed perplexed, maybe even concerned, that I was making jokes, carrying on, already trading in dark humor. The high of cortisol pumping through my veins sheltered me, supplying me with its artificial armor of shock throughout my being. And shock or no, there were jokes to be made! I needed the humor if I was going to keep my head above water, if I was going to keep on going.

When we landed in Indianapolis, it was Mike, my stepdad—or, since he and Mom had divorced, my former stepdad? ex-stepdad?—who picked us up at the airport. I felt a surge of comfort in seeing this person who had spent years raising me. Sturdy, muscled, thoroughly tanned from all his time spent outdoors, Mike remained my most involved parent—he started dating my mom when I was in middle school, not long after she'd divorced my dad. While I'd had my share of adolescent brooding and resentment at the beginning, the reality was that he was all in, fully committed to being my parent. He had vowed to stick with me, with me and my mom both, even through the ugliness of her drinking, to see me to adulthood. We didn't always see eye to eye, but he was there.

As he hugged me tight at baggage claim, my mind lagged in recalling the messiness of his recent split with my mother, just months earlier, and suddenly I wasn't sure what to say. The layers of complicated relationships, braided and unbraided, were only compounded by my mother's suicide.

"But hey, what's a little more awkward dysfunction?" I asked Jesse out of the corner of my mouth, as we trailed behind Mike with our suitcases.

He smiled knowingly; by now we were used to it.

The four of us arrived in the dark at the farmhouse, where together with my mom and Mike, I had lived for my last few years of high school. My stepsister was there already. She had driven up from Tennessee and was trying to help her dad bring the house back from being a man cave toward being a home. The last time I'd visited, just seven months earlier, my mom had still been living there. It existed then as now in a state of perpetually unfinished renovations, and while she was already on her way out then, their divorce rapidly proceeding, it still felt fully lived in. Now everything *home* was gone: plants, art, books, edible food. The fridge contained Velveeta, mustard, Miracle Whip, bananas, bread. The sight of it all made my stomach ache.

Jesse, Alice, and I slept in my old room that night. The walls remained the blue, teal, green, and purple that I had painted them at sixteen, but now they felt tight, the room threatening to collapse in on me. We pulled a mattress onto the floor, and I clutched my daughter through the night, but even surrounded by the familiar sounds of crickets and the particular creaks of that house, along with the warm smell of growing hay wafting in through the open window, I was unable to sleep. Some of my senses delivered an automated response that I was home. But looking around, my eyes still open in the dark, I knew this was not my home. I was suddenly unsure if it ever had been.

Waking the next morning after only a little sleep, I knew I couldn't stay there. Too exhausted and weary to worry about offending Mike, hoping that he would just get it, I asked him for the key to my mother's house. We crammed our things back into the suitcases and piled into my mom's Rav4. Had my brother brought it out to the farm? I didn't know, but I was grateful for the freedom it afforded us. We moved Alice's car seat over from Mike's truck, then drove the twenty minutes to town. Never having been to her new house, I had scrawled out Mike's directions on a piece of scrap paper. We passed the middle school where I attended seventh grade, then the dentist, and turned into a subdivision of seemingly identical houses all in several shades of beige arranged in cul-de-sacs, a bland jungle where you might be lost for days. We pulled into my mom's particular cul-de-sac and rolled up her driveway, stopping before her garage door. Sunflowers bloomed to our right. Raised beds that she had built stretched along the side of the garage—sugar snap peas, Roma tomatoes, basil. Blooms cascaded out from planters on the front stoop. Yes, *this* was Susan, *this* was my mother's place.

I pulled open the storm door, turning the solitary silver key in the doorknob, without even a key ring to grip. Already I was grasping for something to hold on to. Pushing into her home of five months, I stepped over her flip-flops: cheap black ones from Old Navy, flimsy, bearing the steady impression of her feet, kicked off as she had stepped inside.

My mother's death was suddenly real.

She had only moved into this house that spring; she was still painting, settling in. A philodendron spilled down from the top of a bookshelf, a small dresser from my childhood doubled as an end table in the entryway, holding mail, her keys, a small collection of beautiful little vases, shells, unusual rocks. Even with her unfamiliar splurges on new furniture throughout, I felt immediately that she belonged here, but she was gone. I started sobbing.

I wept now as I had not yet done, moving from room to room, as if I were looking for her, as if I were a small child lost in a sea of other women's knees in a busy department store, trying to find my mother. Alice toddled behind me, still new to walking, fascinated to see her mother unhinged. My own mother was not in her kitchen or her dining room. My sobs became more frantic; I was at once gasping for air and letting out wrenching noises, foreign even to me. I kept searching, knowing it was in vain but unable to stop myself. She was not in her bedroom or her den. She was not past the sliding door on her patio. I backtracked through the den, into her bathroom. Her house was full of her things, full of signs of her, full of everything except herself. As one last futile attempt, I stumbled into her walk-in closet. It was packed, yet empty. I fell to the carpet, wailing, undone. It was real. My mother was dead, and she had chosen it.

The Post-it

I lay ragged in my mom's closet for a long time—was it half an hour? longer? I couldn't say—sobbing until my body gave out. Then I just lay, curled on my side, motionless, unable to rise or speak or do anything but abide in this awful new world. Just existing in it, continuing to live within it, was unbearable. It was four days now that my mother had been dead. I lay, still, listening to my breath in the stagnant closet.

Then I heard the soft creak of young feet. I listened as Alice grasped the doorframe to steady herself, then set forward again, tottering, until she reached me. She put her hand on my head, not asking anything of me, not batting at me as a demand for play. Seeing my still body, moving only from my deep and weary breathing, she brought her head down close to mine, bending herself the way only a toddler can. I felt her warm, milky breath on my face, and only then willed my swollen eyes to open. She stared back at me, just two inches from my face, blinking. Holding her close, I smiled weakly. We would continue, I thought, even in this freakish world. I would be able to do it with her, because of her.

I slowly pushed myself to sitting in my dead mother's closet. Pulling Alice into my lap and wrapping my arms around her, I began to look around me, to see where we were. All I had seen thus far was my mom's searing absence, and the signs that she was not here: her flip-flops empty, her bed neatly made, her driveway vacant. I looked up a bit to see the piles of shoes. We had this in common, but she was a much more accomplished collector than I. A hodgepodge of shoe racks sported countless pairs, many all but indistinguishable to the untrained eye. Pumps and slides and cheap slip-ons, some—with tags still on—clearly acquired as impulse buys. Shelves and rods packed with clothes lined three walls of the closet, organized roughly by type. Suits, blazers, dresses, sweaters. Cardigan upon cardigan. Accessory belts, scarves. All things that were Susan-like: fun, but also an attempt to be taken seriously as a small blond woman in the world of sharp businessmen. In my mind, I could see her flexing her muscles and her intellect, reaching for respect.

I wondered what else I might find, how I might get to know my mom more in her death. I wondered if I could find answers here. I rose, slowly, picking Alice up and holding her close to my chest. Stepping into the dining room, I stood and scanned. Jesse came next to me, placing a hand on my shoulder, squeezing it, silently acknowledging the tension of my grief. Papers and file folders lay stacked on her new dining room table—an impressive choice, that table, one she had excitedly told me about picking out. Big enough to entertain, and for the first time in her life, it was neither a hand-me-down nor a Formica slab. Eight leather chairs arched their black backs around the table, deserted but ready. I looked into the kitchen, saw the sink still full of her dishes. A wide red saucepan, a Le Creuset knockoff, sat full of water with red chili oil beaded on the surface. Glasses littered the counter.

Something closer caught my eye. There, on the island separating the kitchen from the dining room. A pale yellow Post-it note. I walked around the leather chairs to pick it up, turning it right-side up with my one available hand as I held Alice on my hip. It was my mom's last to-do list, just three things written on it:

 —*Pick up dry-cleaning*
 —*Write will*
 —*Get stamps*

I handed it to Jesse.

He smiled, shaking his head. "So close!" he exclaimed.

"Yes," I agreed.

"She tried," Jesse said, his eyes curling farther into a smile. "She wanted to make it easier for you." Jesse, as ever, was kind and generous. Even now he respected her.

This was just so her, full of good intentions but struggling with the follow-through. To have intended to write a will, but to have wound up killing herself before she could quite pull it off.

"Yeah, at least she meant well," I said, chuckling. "Classic."

The Preemptive Note

My mom's therapist had reached out to me after she heard the news of her death, saying my mom had been keeping a journal, that there might be clues there. After finding the Post-it note, I wandered through the house, picking up trinkets to inspect, scanning. I saw it on her bedside table: a composition notebook—the classic kind, with a black spine adhered to a mottled black-and-white cover, a small space to write a name or title on the front. "Susan," she'd written a few times over with a dull pencil. I sat down on her new green couch with its clean lines and a gorgeous soft weave. She picked it well, I thought as I settled in, classy but comfortable and just a little funky.

Inside the front cover of her journal lay a once-crumpled, then-smoothed sheet of paper from a notepad advertising the antibiotic Zithromax, its pale purple border offering an unnervingly calm boundary. Her handwriting detailed the homework assignment from her recovery group: *Story in 1st person—awakened in jail/hospital + find out you killed family of 4.*

Behind this note was a plastic heart made of two sheets of contact paper, sealed together. It had yellowed with age. Inside were pressed flower petals individually plucked from violets, also now yellowed with the many years since I made it. At its center, a dried-out four-leaf clover.

I set it aside, turning to the next sheet of loose notebook paper.

My mother, doing her homework, had imagined an almost-real scenario, her handwriting clear, in unwavering black ink:

> *This is the end. The worst has happened and I have now entered a permanent hell. I have killed 4 people, and caused immeasurable sadness in the lives of many others. There is no atoning, no amends, possible. I will most certainly be looking at a long stint locked up—I may not see mom again, and likely will see my children and granddaughter rarely if ever. I have lost my job, my house, everything. And for what? I was doing so well—what minor annoyance could have prompted me to go down this horrifying, and ultimately inevitable, path? I would so much rather it had been me so that I don't have to wake up each and every day to a fresh realization of the horror.*

I was stunned. I read it again.

Hell. No atoning. Everything lost. She used the word *inevitable*. She wrote: *I would so much rather it had been me.*

"This may be the closest we get to a suicide note," I told Jesse, pushing the journal across the couch to him, trading him for Alice.

I disagreed with her, vehemently, that she would be alone, that we wouldn't visit her, that her drinking and driving were inevitable. And yet, for her, it seemed it was. She could see no other way to prevent this immeasurable sadness.

In July, just seven weeks earlier, she had been hospitalized on a seventy-two-hour hold for life-threatening intoxication. My brother had put her in after she'd been admitted to the emergency room. But after seventy-two hours, they could not hold her any longer against her will, and she—once sober—was so charming, articulate, convincing. She had a plan. Outpatient programs: twelve-step meetings, recovery groups, individual therapy. She insisted that she had already learned everything there was to learn in an in-patient program, or even in an intensive outpatient program, for that matter.

Taking the journal back from Jesse, I looked for more explanation. There was one page detailing her recovery plan, both in the coming weeks and further out: meetings, their frequency, whom to call, church. I turned more pages: some cursory journal entries; a few lines per meeting, mostly describing the interesting people she encountered there; a few points of inspiration. I turned the page again. One more entry: just four meetings recorded. I flipped through the remaining crisp pages, all blank.

One loose sheet fell out: a letter to me and my brother. It was the other half of the assignment she had asked me about several weeks earlier. She had invited us to write letters to her about her drinking, to be read aloud in her recovery group, and she would do the same. I had spent hours working away at my letter, naming the full truth, loving her, forgiving her, hoping with her. I held her letter up. A half page, and a small page at that. Some quipped apologies, regrets, rosy turns on how her drinking had made us more independent, promises of love and declarations that now she'd always be there.

I threw them to the floor, hard, the paper and the book. The book smacked down, sliding across the polished wood. "What bullshit!" I exclaimed. "She wasn't trying to get sober at all. No wonder she thought it was inevitable that she would drunkenly kill people—she wasn't even trying. *Four meetings!*" I was ranting now. "*Four fucking meetings* she journaled about! And this letter to me and John? What a fucking joke. No wonder she didn't send it to us. It's pathetic."

Alice's eyes grew wide, tracking my flailing arms.

"It didn't have to be this way, and she couldn't even try hard enough to see that." I was disgusted, furious.

And even as I raged, kicking a pillow across the room, I recalled that I was also grateful. Rage at the seeming futility of it all shook me, even as relief washed over me again. Thank God she hadn't actually killed that family of four.

Home Parish

By our own design, my brother and I had only a few days to plan our mother's funeral. Jesse and I had flown to Indiana on Monday, three days after her death. The funeral would be three days later, Thursday. I'd had no clear expectation of what we would be able to do, what we could agree to, my brother and I. My brother? I didn't really know what he believed. He had long ribbed me for my religious practice, but then he'd recently converted to Roman Catholicism. When I somewhat cautiously raised the question, though, he had deferred to me. "You know this stuff, Liz, you can plan the service." Did he want input on readings? Music? Was he okay with an Episcopal service? No, no, and yes. We found a date and time that worked for us all—soon enough that Jesse and Alice and I wouldn't have to return to California and then fly back again, but still with enough time for some other family to get there from out of state. Beyond that practical measure, though, John handed the responsibility to me. Now in my last year of seminary, I felt as if I'd just been assigned another project for a liturgics class, only we wouldn't be playacting our way through the service. It was my mother's death; all this centered around her ashes.

The service would be held at Trinity Episcopal Church, in the heart of Bloomington's downtown. It's a lovely limestone church from 1909, its building sturdy and steadfast without edging toward ostentation. It had been the first church I'd ever attended, the first experience I'd had of Christianity beyond the glancing cultural exposure I'd gotten from living in Iowa during elementary school.

We had moved to Indiana before the start of my sixth-grade year, my brother rounding out middle school in eighth. We were settling into a split-level ranch house full of sea-foam-green walls and sea-foam-green carpets and sea-foam-green laminate countertops, flecked with gold. This bustling suburban world was foreign to me after very-small-town living in an ancient house on the Iowa plain—all except the Jesus part, which people in this new place were just as worked up about as people in the old place had been. So

I asked my parents at dinner one night, earnestly and with great curiosity, if we could go to church. They must have been taken aback, but they did not laugh me down. Back in New Hampshire, before we lived in Iowa, my mother and brother had been baptized in an Episcopal church on the same day—she just twenty-two, he an infant. I followed two years later, also baptized as a baby. That bit of sprinkling had been the extent of our involvement with the church.

When I asked that night if we could go to church, my father, Irish Roman Catholic by origin but long since lapsed, chuckled, dimples showing. He and my mother, who had been raised nothing, then lobbed fragmented lines back and forth across the dinner table, attempting to piece together the whole of the Lord's Prayer, but struggling. That fall we ended up at Trinity. The Episcopal Church seemed like a logical median between "Roman Catholic" and "nothing," a place that might have room for us.

We had jumped headlong into that church—my brother and I into Sunday School, my mother into the alto section of their remarkable choir, bolstered by Indiana University's School of Music nine-tenths of a mile away. Soon my brother and I were vesting in white robes and serving as acolytes. Eventually, our endlessly charismatic and helpful father was elected to the church's vestry. It was everything my twelve-year-old self somehow knew to want: structure, ritual, and big questions, yet a complete lack of Bible-thumping. But more than that, the church offered steady adults, ready to catch us when it all began to fall apart. Maybe I knew we were already slipping, already precariously close to the edge.

We'd been in Bloomington and there at Trinity not even a year and a half when my parents announced they were divorcing, a surprise in the timing of the proclamation but hardly in its content. Even as a naïve early teen, I could tell they weren't happy, that they hadn't been for ages. Soon we kids were splitting time between two houses, soon my mother was drinking more and more; then, not long after, my father was moving to California with his new wife. Shell-shocked and reeling, my mother now scraping to hold it all together as a single parent, we fell away from church. It wasn't until I earned my driver's license that I could get myself to and from Trinity, driving alone through the quiet Sunday streets. It was a haven for me: reliable, standing in as kin, offering something real for me to lean on. As my mother spiraled deeper into alcoholism, the church became all the more critical for me, buoying me up until I could leave for college.

How fitting then, I thought, that we would hold her funeral here. It was somehow appropriate that this congregation would be carrying me through again. I had gone alone to meet with the rector, Charlie, new there since I'd left home. It was pretty straightforward, really—I'd come with a list of hymns and readings I liked, I had no interest in hosting a reception, I was ready to be clear that I did not want to sugarcoat anything or pretend that my mother's death was anything other than what it was. After all, the news had made the front page of Bloomington's *Herald-Times*, so her death being a suicide was no secret.

But being such a novice to funerals—despite having studied the rite in seminary—I had not really considered the possibility that Charlie would ask if I planned to speak. I'd swallowed hard when he offered the idea, not sure what I would say or even whether I could say anything. I shook my head, feeling guilty in my reticence.

"I don't think I want to," I had said, "I just can't do it."

My brother didn't want to speak, either, so we decided to leave it to the dean of Indiana University's business school, where our mother had taught, and to Charlie, the preacher. I would try to listen, thinking even that might prove too much.

Jesse and Alice and I arrived at the church not long before the service was to start, slowed as ever by trying to dress and feed Alice while simultaneously readying ourselves. Not yet eleven o'clock, it was already getting hot; August 30 was sweltering and especially humid. We gathered first in an anteroom, off the side of the church—I did not want to face the throngs of people already filling the sanctuary. Right at eleven, we filed in. The front pew of the church had been reserved for us: my brother and his girlfriend first, then Mike's daughter, then me and Alice and Jesse. I had only ever sat farther back in the church, never in the front, where the wooden half-wall boxed in the pew, worn from a century of palms resting on it, the rack still holding the hymnal and the Book of Common Prayer. I could feel the thrum of the swelling congregation behind me, but could only glance back peripherally, I could not bear to take in all these people here to mourn my mother.

I clung to Alice as she wriggled, as we sang, as these readings I had chosen wafted over me without penetrating. The dean rose and read a patchwork of students' tributes to my mother's teaching, gathered from years of class evaluations: her use of a circular saw in one class to illustrate an accounting concept, her singular ability to create intimacy in a lecture hall with 250 seats, her unwavering commitment to her students. She *loved* them, I knew, even when the insidious disease from which she suffered sometimes kept her from showing up. I knew this—I knew it because it was how she had been with John and me.

I stared at the urn, placed on a small table at the transept of the church, just before the stairs rose to her old choir stall. I had picked it up before the service—or tried to. Massive, carved of white marble, of my brother's choosing, it was almost too heavy for me to lift. Now my arms were filled with my impatiently squirming eleven-month-old, who was hemmed in by the green-and-white dress my mother had bought her four months earlier, appliqué daisies ringing the skirt. Alice tugged at my shirt, hungry, oblivious to my heaving chest, feeling only curiosity toward my watery cheeks. As I gave in and let her nurse, she began playing with the necklace of my mother's that I now wore. It was the same one she had once fiddled with endlessly, tugging and twisting it against my mother's collarbone, when my mom had visited us in California, and then again when we'd met in New Hampshire for my ordination as a deacon just months earlier.

Switching to my other breast, Alice stretched to brush her foot against my face, wetting her bare toes with my tears. I turned my head to avoid the full brunt of her kick, and saw again my stepdad, Mike, sitting behind me, next to my aunt, uncle, and grandmother. Mike didn't have to be here, I thought. It had been so tough for them, so painful for him and my mother both at the end.

I didn't know if he wanted to be here or not, for himself, but I could feel the care he shared with me, his brown eyes wide and warm. I faced forward again, realizing I hadn't heard much of what the preacher was saying, but instead heard my brother let out a just-audible sob. I turned my head to see him—this U.S. Army Ranger—shaking, then burying his face low in his hands, his back rhythmically rising and falling. This was how bad all this was.

The service sped past me, around me, over my head; nothing stuck. Now we were rising to say prayers, now we were passing the peace, now suddenly I was at the altar rail receiving the bread and wine, now I was straining my arms and fingers to lift my mother's urn and leave the church, tunneling out through the hundreds of people, so many of whom I did not know—her scores of students, her colleagues, but then my high school friends, too, my teachers, summer camp friends, parishioners who were still here from a decade earlier. Stepping out into the noonday sun, I squinted and walked self-consciously around the corner, inelegantly lugging the unwieldy, hulking weight that was once my petite, beautiful mother. I followed the clergy back to the church's anteroom, having been told that I could not, in fact, just leave, that I had to stay to greet people, at least for a little while.

I stood, feet rooted, while person after person hugged me, gave their most sincere condolences, shared what a light Susan had been. I knew that, I thought—she was, she was a delightful, inspiring, lovely ball of light, except that she was apparently miserable, too, and a drunk who had killed herself. She chose for us to be here, had made it happen, and I could not hold these truths together, not for the finest liturgy in the world, not for all the kindness these strangers and old friends could offer me. I only wanted to leave, to go eat lunch, to sit alone in the quiet of her house.

Emptying

When there is no will written, the sorting game of who gets what after a person dies can play out many different ways. My brother and I split our mother's modest retirement savings fifty-fifty. Her life insurance still came through, amazingly, even though her death was so obviously a suicide. As a gesture of goodwill, John suggested we split that policy four ways with our now former stepsiblings. We knew she'd taken them off as beneficiaries in the last months—it had been a rocky time, with sides taken, lines drawn— but I agreed. In the long run, it seemed right to reach for peace.

Then came her things.

"What do you want, John?" I pressed.

He shook his head, pursing his lips and wrinkling his nose slightly. "Nothing, really," he answered, his voice neutral.

I couldn't tell if he had matured beyond needing or wanting material things, or if the thought of having our mother's things was too much for him.

"We should leave some of the new furniture to stage the house, though," he added, always practical.

"I'd like the piano. And can I take the mattress and the sofa bed? We could really use those. . . ." I trailed off. I was sentimental and would take all the mementos of her I could fit in our home and garage. And I also had fresh in my mind our ramshackle collection of furniture sitting awkwardly back in our Berkeley apartment, many of the shelves and chairs and housewares found on the side of the road in the week of college students moving out. Her new pieces would be a definite upgrade.

"Sure," he said. "If you can use them, go for it. But let's leave the dining room set and the other sofa. And the art on the walls. It's going to be hard enough to sell this place as it is."

"Great." I exhaled. "Thank you." This divvying up was far easier than anything we had been forced to share as kids. Still, I worried about him. "Don't you want anything else?"

"Eh, no," he started. "I don't need anything."

"Really?" It made no sense to me, though I knew I had always been the more sentimental one.

"I'll take the stuffed duck," he said, his voice calm, "if that's cool with you?"

"Seriously?" I almost laughed, then saw that he was, in fact, serious. "Yes, definitely, it's all yours."

The stuffed duck in question was easily seventy years old. When our maternal grandfather was young, he had shot it and—as the story goes— stuffed it. It was mangy at this point and, as far as I could see, had nothing to do with our mother; I wondered if there was more to the story.

That evening, we went back to Mike's to have dinner and to go through my mom's jewelry box. My stepsister had snagged it from the house before we got there, to protect it in the event there was a break-in, and she had done a thorough inventory by the time I sat down with the box. John called me back that evening, with a second request: In addition to the stuffed duck, could he have the sapphire bracelet? I immediately knew the one he was talking about: a stunning white gold bangle, sleek with alternating diamonds and sapphires. He wanted to give it to his girlfriend.

I felt a twinge of jealousy rising but held it back. "Yes, of course, it's all yours."

He would take the duck and the bracelet; I had free rein over everything else but the props for staging.

For living in a small house, and for having moved there only five months earlier, my mom still had enough belongings to present an adventure. The house was a window into what she was thinking, what she was hoping for, as she worked to set up a new life after her second divorce, on her own again at age fifty. This had been the first time she'd ever lived alone.

The den was filled with new toys and books, ready for Alice, for other hypothetical grandkids, alongside the best things she'd saved from when John and I were growing up. Centered on one wall stood the sofa bed, a fancy one that automatically inflated so that you couldn't feel the bar in the middle of your back. All this was *so nice*, she'd clearly hoped it would make her little one-bedroom house work for me and Jesse and Alice to visit her.

There were so very many shoes. Shoes upon shoes, shoes hiding behind more shoes. I cursed the fact that my feet were two sizes larger than hers.

Extensive glassware, of all kinds, lined three cupboards. Sets of martini glasses; margarita glasses; stems for red wine, white wine, champagne. Highball and double old-fashioned and pilsner beer glasses. Alcohol was everywhere, in plain sight and hidden deep in the crevices of the kitchen, the cleaning closet, moving boxes, the garage, booze as pervasive as air. Why had she gotten into the car that night, I found myself wondering, when there was more than enough alcohol right here to last her?

There were good things to eat, and we did eat them, still reeling from the Velveeta desert at the farmhouse. Fresh carrots and heirloom tomatoes and bunches of thick, hearty spinach with leaves as big as my palm. Gingersnaps she'd baked a few days before filled a tin. The recipe box sat beside it, painted in dots and curls of every color, so stuffed with tattered, stained, greasy index cards it couldn't close.

A worn cardboard box on the living room floor was stacked full of empty picture frames and a jumble of photos ready to be matched and assembled and hung on the freshly painted walls, along with the art my mom had splurged on: a lithograph print of a rook in a tree, a print of people on horseback, matted, then framed.

Cleaning out her house became a community affair. Andy, who was first my college boyfriend, then later a friend in seminary, drove down from Indianapolis. Carl, my mom's soulful cousin, and his yogi wife, Jeannie, were there, helping to sort and heave boxes and weep. Friends from summer camp arrived. Katy came. She was the mom of the boy who picked me up for high school for a couple years, who took me places when my mom couldn't drive; she was especially tearful. A high school teacher who'd befriended me, together with her wife and young daughter, also came. My best friend from high school and her little sister were steady and prepared, bringing extra food and tape and scissors. We ordered pizza and sat knee-high amid the boxes, sorting. We hauled armload after armload of suits to a nonprofit for women trying to get jobs, packed carload after carload of housewares and kitchen goods to outfit the new residential community at the Episcopal Campus Ministry: glasses, flatware, spatulas, pots, Swiffer sheets, a vacuum—everyone seemed grateful, happy to take it all.

All the while, I had another pile going. It grew big enough after a few hours of digging and sorting that it started sliding and falling over. I tracked down a Rubbermaid tub, maybe three feet tall, slapped some masking tape on it, and labeled it PRESENTS FROM SUSAN.

I didn't know if it would work or, if it did, how exactly. But it struck me that I could likely find enough neat gadgets and books and toys and generally lovely or intriguing things to let my daughter have gifts from her grandmother; there might even be enough if I had another child, too. The project began to snowball. I scoured my mother's house for things appropriate for any age. The toys she'd prepared for Alice were easy. Then her oil pastels, a sequined box. Binoculars, a book titled *Drawing on the Right Side of the Brain*, our old Erector building set, Legos. Dollhouse furnishings. Costume jewelry. A mini quick-dry towel for backpacking. A booklet of "Sun, Moon, and Stars Armband Tattoos." A stack of Calvin & Hobbes books. An embroidered purse she had brought back from China and used for years when I was young. A child's T-shirt that we silkscreened with palm trees and stars, one of many we ran off as Christmas presents one year when money was especially tight. A small woven box, an antique noisemaker, paintbrushes, fresh canvases. A paper fan. A blank journal, a book of card games from the 1950s, wooden blocks, a guide to reptiles and amphibians. It would not be enough to give my children their grandmother, but the box was full.

Filling that box was the treat of packing up my mother's house. Bittersweet, but a way to yoke myself to some semblance of hope. But there was still the fact that we had to haul the furniture and these remnants west. Jesse rented a truck to drive across the country while I flew home with Alice. He backed it into the small driveway, and my cousin Carl and several camp friends dragged and begged and shoved the upright piano—in our family for four generations, or five counting Alice—up the rickety aluminum ramp, its wheels stubborn enough to add more drama to the task. A web of rope soon held dresser and mattress and lamps and bike and tools and stacks of boxes more or less in place, leaving room for the sofa bed to still pull out in the back so that Jesse could just sleep there on the drive home.

We dripped with sweat, Indiana's August humidity lying oppressively atop the weight of all that furniture and mourning.

That's Gonna Fuck You Up

Back in Berkeley, it was the first Community Night of the year at seminary—an evening Eucharist, students and families and staff and faculty praying together, followed by dinner. We were stepping back into this weekly downbeat of the school year, and I had just returned from Indiana. People were kind, though some seemed skittish around me—seminarians were usually eager to practice pastoral care on one another; we just weren't very good at it yet. And *suicide*? Generally people just don't know what to say to the survivors. Suicide is grotesque, disturbing, also fascinating.

The room was festive, dozens of banners hanging down from the skylights overhead, each bearing the seal of a different diocese. Some looked professionally done; others were artistically handcrafted; still others involved rickrack and glitter and glue. Bougainvillea spread outside, encroaching on the wall of windows.

As plates were beginning to be cleared after dinner, Tripp sat down next to me. We'd been friends since he'd arrived this time last year, but we didn't yet know each other well. He was fifteen years my senior, a seasoned Baptist pastor now going for a PhD in liturgics.

"So how'd she do it?" he asked matter-of-factly.

"It was suicide," I said. I hadn't yet grasped his question.

"I know, Liz," he said, softening. "What'd she do?"

Ah. Most people were intrigued but too afraid to actually ask. Tripp was asking, sincerely, but it seemed the question was more for me than for his own morbid curiosity. I figured now was a time I could cast off pleasantries and euphemisms.

"She jumped off the fourth floor of a parking garage," I said flatly, but with my eyebrow raised just slightly.

"Damn," Tripp said, smiling with his eyes, tugging a bit on his white beard. "That's gonna fuck you up."

It was the most honest thing anyone had said to me since she died, and I loved him for it. In those five words, there was permission—suddenly, magically granted permission—for this to be a veritable disaster. I didn't have to hold it together for my daughter. I didn't have to be stable for my ministry. I didn't have to make progress on this degree. I could just let this fuck me up, as it was bound to do. This was the natural course of things. What's more, Tripp was not afraid of any of this, and he was not afraid of me.

4

RETURNING

RETURNING

The End of Leave

After Fritz died, after the funeral had come and gone and life had receded back into quiet emptiness, I waffled between thinking I should just jump back into work and wanting to hide out, to never return. Practically speaking, though, it was complicated. Both the camp on Lake Tahoe and the parish in Reno had worked with the same church insurance company to administer my maternity leave benefits. After I gave birth, we had been going back and forth by email—trying to sort out which organization needed to pay whom how much, which forms were still outstanding—and hadn't yet solved it all. And then Fritz died. A few days later, I realized this was yet another piece that needed working out: What happens to a mother's maternity leave when her baby dies?

Up until that point, I had been annoyed that maternity leave was covered under the umbrella of short-term disability. How is being a mom a disability? I wondered. A woman's ability to grow and birth a child is fantastic! But now the bureaucratic judgment call was working in my favor. If I was recovering from the disabling event of giving birth, my recovery did not actually depend on the state of the child, in that the insurers had given me time not to bond, but to heal. The insurance rep had to check with the legal advisers, but in the end I was still entitled to twelve weeks away.

Ultimately, I split the difference, returning to work two and a half weeks after the funeral—just over a month after Fritz's death, but still almost two weeks before my maternity leave ran out. The interim rector, my boss, was a fumbling old man, entirely well-meaning but out of touch. To his credit in that moment, though, he told me I could take as much time off as I needed. I was grateful for that generosity, because I dreaded going back.

It took an hour to drive from our home at the lake up and over the pass, down the long, winding highway into Carson City; up over another ridge; through the Washoe Valley; and then over a final pass before descending into Reno. Some of the drive was gorgeous; some stark and desolate.

It was now my first day driving back. I fiddled my Bluetooth earpiece into place and called Mike, my stepdad, once I reached Carson, as the cell signal was usually reliable for most of the drive thereafter.

"I'm driving to Reno," I started. "Today's my first day back at work."

"Oh, fun!" he exclaimed, his voice resonant with excitement.

I winced, shaking my head at the mountains rising up before me. "I'm not convinced it'll be fun, actually. . . ." I paused. "But I'm doing it, at least."

"Oh, it'll be great," he cajoled. "It's good to get back in the saddle."

Part of me knew this was true, but I also longed for space for it to feel hard and awful and just plain wrong. How could I face the other staff, or my parishioners? What would I do with all their questions? I ended the call quickly, driving the last twenty minutes in silence—at least the quiet expanse surrounding my Subaru would not tell me what to feel, how I might proceed.

Parking in the lot facing the church's offices, I hung my head. I couldn't quite identify the reason, but I sensed that this church was not going to be a place of healing, but rather an environment to be endured. I waited a few more minutes, sitting in the car, futzing about, gathering my things into my bag until only one minute remained before the staff meeting was to begin. Downtime would be my enemy here. That would be when people would say all the things I did not want—could not bear—to hear. I wasn't ready, but I shuffled inside.

As I sat through our droning, fluorescent-lit meeting in a room untouched by daylight, I was numb, clenching my teeth. I will get through this, I decided, but nothing says I have to be entirely present.

Those gaps of time, though, those openings that people fill with all manner of crap? Unavoidable.

In the copy room after our staff meeting, a parishioner who had stopped in to help with an office project cornered me. "I'm so sorry about your son," she began.

I nodded, quiet.

"I've just been thanking God you're so young."

I furrowed my brow, not making the connection. I would hear the same words many times, but this was the first time someone was saying them.

"I mean," she went on, "thank God you still have so much time; you can have lots more. I'll be praying that God gives you another baby real soon."

I stared at her, unable to form words. "Yes," I stammered, "it is good that I am young." I pushed sideways past her, almost running to my office. Then I remembered that I had to share that space, too, and pivoted again to make a beeline for the bathroom at the end of the hall. I locked myself in the big stall and stood against the wall, leaning my head back. Is this what it's going to be like? I wondered. Is this how people are? How will I handle the coming Sunday?

After hiding in the bathroom as long as I could, I retreated dejectedly to my shared office, grateful to find it empty. I lifted the phone to my ear each time I heard someone coming down the hallway, just in case. I didn't know whose number I would dial, but I needed to appear occupied. I needed to be ready to avoid the next sympathy attack. My armor, by now, was seriously riddled.

On Sunday I was forced to dive in again. I started the morning in the sacristy, the little vesting room off the side of the massive sanctuary, where the priests and lay leaders dress for the services, where all the sacred objects are stored. It was quaint, with a few closets to hold our robes. Older church ladies bustled in and out with the silver chalices and linens, preparing the altar. Tall windows filled two walls of the room, each separated into countless diamonds by thick lead lines. I reached into a closet, grateful that my muscle memory was beginning to take over after ten weeks away. I had to think twice, though, reminding myself to pick up my cincture, the white rope that ties the waist of the robes. The last time I had been here, my pregnant belly was far too large to accommodate it, but now it slid around my midsection easily.

And there, before I even stepped in among the people of the congregation, it began.

Todd, also a priest, turned to me, leaning down on the high counter. "You know, I've been thinking a lot about Fritz's funeral," he coughed out awkwardly.

I suspected he'd been working up the courage to say this; his words had the shape of rehearsed lines.

"Yeah?" I asked, wondering where this was going ten minutes before we were to begin the service.

"When everyone came forward to throw dirt in the hole, I didn't. I just couldn't. I know it was beautiful and good and all, but it was awful. It was just too real for me. I couldn't do it. Throwing dirt in the hole would have just made it too real."

The longer Todd went on talking, the wider my eyes grew. He seemed to be making a confession to me. Was he asking for my absolution? Was this an apology? Why was he even telling me this? I never would have known otherwise; there were far too many people at the funeral for me to keep track. And what did it matter? It occurred to me that this had been weighing on him, but he kept talking, going on and on about how it was a beautiful gathering, but just *too hard, too real*, and so on.

Fuck this shit, I seethed, silently. If you cannot ask for an absolution, I'm sure as hell not giving it to you, I thought.

"Yes," I finally cut in, finding my voice. "Yes, it did feel *real* to throw dirt in the hole—*it was real.*" I was furious, but more than that, I was so sad. This is a priest standing in front of me, I thought. If he can't do this with me, who can?

I reached for Phil's words in my mind. When we were talking through the logistics of Fritz's funeral, I had asked if it was too much for him to come with me to pick up the ashes from the funeral home. "Of course not, Liz," he had responded immediately. "It is the priest's job to accompany the body. This is *our job*, Liz. You will not do that alone."

There in the sacristy with Todd, I slowly shook my head. What kind of priest refuses to help bury ashes? How dare he now try to garner my understanding and absolution for his cowardice? My mind spun, but I could not stay there fuming. It was time to start the service.

That hour of worship was fine. Nearly all of the spoken interactions with other people were prescribed, already written down in the liturgy. As I processed into the sanctuary during the opening hymn, the grandeur surprised me. These last two months had passed in small places, dark rooms, and beside the starkly unadorned lake. I squinted in reaction to the ornate architecture, the sculpture and painting and gilt. I could feel the gaze of parishioners as I glided by. I tunneled my eyes into my hymnal, but I could sense people searching me out, trying to gauge how I was, really. Arriving at my chair, up five steps and squarely in front of the congregation, I pulled back my shoulders, trying to convince us all that I was steady. Avoiding anyone's eyes, I began voicing the printed words of the Good News, but they felt misshapen in my mouth.

I did not hear the sermon that morning. My mind was fearfully locked on the determination to survive this, my first Sunday back. Nothing else stuck. Halfway through, I made the unthinking decision of leaving the relative safety of the chancel—the area cordoned off behind the altar rail, reserved for the clergy and choir—during the passing of the peace. Mingling briefly with folks in the pews, I heard them start in, even around the well-worn script of "Peace be with you."

Dave, a tall man in cowboy boots who I only sort of knew, clasped my hand in both of his. "You doing okay? You okay, really?" he asked. His tone was earnest, concerned, scared. There was only one correct answer to this question, he was telling me with his eyes.

"Yes," I said. "Peace."

"Good," he answered. "You're okay. You're okay." He shook my hand again, twice, firmly, as if we were entering into a contract.

He wanted my promise, my assurance. Maybe I would be okay, but there were no assurances yet. Again, I retreated. I was beginning to see the pattern already—opening myself up to people's reactions, then running for cover. I sat down hard on my chair, grateful for the altar rail I generally would have preferred to dispose of—for the time being, it separated me from these well-meaning people. Relief settled briefly: there was still at least half an hour before I would have to talk to any of them again.

There was no escaping all the words, though, not in the end. Following the service, I had no choice but to greet the people, to actually talk with them. Many were fine, maybe even most. They just gave me hugs, told me they loved me, even though they didn't really know me, as I'd only worked in this place for three months before Fritz was born. I appreciated this simple love. But then there were those who felt the need to say more.

Gloria came in quickly. She was in her late eighties, and always showed up with both class and great humor. I'd fallen in love with her almost immediately when I'd begun working here. She grabbed both my shoulders and held on tight, looking up into my face. Resigned, not knowing what she'd say, I let my arms dangle at my sides.

"I am so sorry you lost your baby boy," Gloria said, tears in her eyes already. "But my word, he sure was a smart little baby to go back to God so very quickly! Such a smart boy."

I blinked. I rejected this sort of theology in every way. And yet what could I say? She and I were separated by more than fifty years and a sea of cultural differences. I nodded, feeling like I was losing some part of myself in assenting to her proclamation.

People sifted past me, on one side and the other, the crowd winding and swirling before my dizzy eyes, some coming in close, others taking a longer route through the pews and side aisle in order to avoid me, me wondering how much of this awkward dance was actually happening and how much existed only in my head. I looked up to the great arcs of the vaulted ceilings, trying to ground myself to something steady. I made my way through more bumbling apologies and shoulder pats from the line of people slowly leaving the church.

The pews and aisles mostly empty, I walked across the center aisle to greet Sally. She was of indeterminate age, but probably eighty, at least. This being Reno, she had her fingernails done professionally, a different color and dramatic design each week, often with rhinestones affixed. Her clothes were usually lavishly adorned—sequins, glitz, animal prints, often all at once. Today was no exception. She was shaky on her feet and hard of hearing, so I knelt down close to say hello.

She took my hand. "How's that baby of yours?" she asked excitedly. "He must be getting big by now."

"Oh, shit," I said under my breath. "Oh, Sally, I'm sorry you didn't hear the news. My son died suddenly about a month ago."

She looked down at the kneeler. "I am sorry," she said, stretching out the words. Then, bracing on the pew in front of her, she popped up, sitting straight, and swiveled sideways to look me in the eyes. She grinned. "Well, just keep trying! Have more soon!" she exclaimed cheerily.

I stood up, turned, and walked away. I could not do this. I was done.

For this day, this first day back, I decided that not punching anyone defined the metric of success. A low bar, sure, but I *had* managed to reach it. I knew they cared, I knew they meant well, but in that moment I was too tired to feel ashamed of how much I resented their god-awful responses. I drove home in silence, grateful for the vast emptiness of all that western land.

Plumbing the Depths

Leaving that first Sunday back at work behind me, driving higher and higher up into the Sierras, I felt everything acutely. I was exhausted from the people, especially the ones who seemed to want me to take care of them, or who wanted to make it all seem all right, palatable, survivable, understandable, done. This transaction cost me, took place at my expense. I resented their clamoring inability to walk with me where I was. I didn't know what I needed from them, really, but I knew it wasn't this chorus of platitudes and cheap, false encouragement.

I rolled to a stop in front of the cabin, sitting, staring at my home from the silent car. There was nothing planned for the rest of the day, an agonizing openness that yawned before me. I slowly swung out of the car onto the half-frozen gravel and plodded into the cabin. I was hoping to find distraction inside, anything that would get me moving again, something to occupy the void. Empty silence still physically terrified me.

The front door creaked as I pushed it open, the metal panels so tweaked out of shape that they no longer fit the doorframe. It creaked again as I pushed it shut, using my hip to force the latch, but that metal click was all I heard. The cabin was silent. Straight ahead of me, the door to my bedroom—and Fritz's—stood slightly open. I hadn't made the bed when I got up in the dark that morning. The covers lay knotted from my thrashing, but the room was motionless, vacant.

I dragged my feet forward, noticing how tired and awkward they felt stuck back in dress shoes for the first time in months. I peeked around the corner and saw the other bedroom door closed, and realized I could hear the faint sound of the white noise machine making a steady rainfall in that end of the cabin—Jesse and Alice were in there napping together. Turning the other way, I took the two short steps into our one main room. My work bag fell from my shoulder and I let it land there, in the middle of the floor. My body, too, succumbed to the physical weight of grief, and I slumped down into a chair, then flopped forward onto the table. I had regressed, losing the ability to hold my head up without support.

My head lay sideways, my cheek on the pine table. I stared blankly forward, the empty wall in front of me mirroring my emptiness. Grief was fucking exhausting. But even this position was untenable. Within a couple minutes of sitting, of doing nothing aside from existing in loss in this one place, I began to twitch. It began in my neck and shoulders, this shuddering twitch, creeping tendrils rising up into my head and then winding down my spine. Sitting still, unmoving, felt like both all I could do and imminently disastrous. The sitting, the remembering, the thinking without anything else to restrain or occupy my brain quickly became unbearable. Refusing to even move my head to the side, out of the far corner of my eye I saw clean laundry piled on our couch. From within the mass, I noticed a bit of my running tights. I knew this was my way forward today, my way out, and slowly I rose. Creeping around the squeaky parts of the cabin floor, I attempted to change out of my clergy collar and into my running gear quietly enough to prolong Alice's nap. I didn't actually have the energy to run, but sitting still by myself in a grief this profound was too much to bear.

Ten minutes later, I parked at a trailhead just down the highway and clambered over the split-rail fence. It was an official scenic vista, and that day, as on most days, tourists were walking out to the high rise of boulders for a sweeping view of the lake, the same spot where I'd caught my breath with Phil on my birthday when we'd left the ashes left sitting on the dashboard. It was mainly locals who knew about the trail down below, and in winter it was generally deserted. There wasn't much of an established path, so I followed the weaving sets of faint footprints in February's old, thin snow until the hill dropped me onto the wide trail tracing the curves of the lakeshore.

Since that first run ten days after Fritz died, I'd been slowly edging back into this movement as a practice. Each time out, my lungs burned a little less and my muscles remembered a little more of how all this worked, even in the cold. Crashing down through the loose underbrush, I landed at the center of the trail, an out-and-back in either direction, both ways remarkably uphill. Leaning into the pattern I was slowly building, day by day, I turned, heading to the right. I went first to Ezekiel's place of dry bones.

The thing about running, I was realizing, was that I could think in motion in a way that I could not bear to when sitting still. In stillness, thinking threatened to overpower me, sink me, destroy me. There on the trail the thinking rolled with me, the hill itself forcing me to breathe. I didn't know what I would pray for, if I were to pray—anything resembling formal, direct prayer had eluded me since seeing my breathless son—but my feet struck the hard-packed dirt in just such a rhythm that they seemed to speak that wordless prayer, the one I wished I knew how to find, that I might offer it up. When I was moving, I could actually bear remembering. Much of the time, my eyes settled on my fingers. My left ring finger now bore the simple sapphire ring that Cheri and Tom could see held the color of Fritz's eyes, the thin gold band now stretched to fit over my fat knuckle. It traded glimmers back and forth with the lake as I ran up the ridge above the water. It was hard to see where one blue ended and the other began.

In front of the water's backdrop, I moved each of my fingers independently, mimicking the motion Fritz's hands had made. From the beginning, he was wild with his fingers, plucking instruments we could not see, exploring the air currents swirling about him. Only here could I do the same, while I was running. It was the only place where I could tolerate being with it all, and to do it I had to be moving.

Reaching the gate at the end of the trail, I turned around to run back down this hill and up the other side, tracing the edge of the lake. I made it slowly to the other end, then stumbled back to the center of the trail, near where I started. This short mile and a half was an accomplishment, faster than my last run and so much better than nothing. I stopped to catch my breath at the edge of the rocky bluff. Wind whipped across my face as I lost myself in the churn of the frigid waves crashing onto the perfectly smooth boulders thirty feet below.

I was mesmerized by the water's power, and by the strength of the rocks. What would it be like to throw myself down? Would I die quickly, or would the process be slow and painful? Fractures? Hypothermia? Would I float out into the massive blue and drown? These questions both disgusted and fascinated me. I didn't want to die, really, though that would be so much easier, I thought, than living. More truthfully, I wanted *to want* to die, almost. I sometimes wished for the careless bravado of my mother in her relentless pursuit of oblivion.

But I didn't want that. I wanted to survive, and right now, surviving was a slow and tenuous slog. There was room for that grind here, the lake ancient and in no hurry; it knew that it was more than enough. My mind jumped back to the drive home from Reno, the one I'd done countless times now, and that I had particularly hated this Sunday. That last valley in Carson City is low down, utterly desolate. The earth is dry, cracked open, exposed beneath the scattering of scrubby pine trees, sparse sage, ugly plants with thorns.

And now I remembered that this lake is *deeper* than that valley is low. All that winding, climbing, up and up and up to cross over the pass—and still the bottom of Lake Tahoe is two hundred feet farther into the earth than the barren Carson Valley. There is all kinds of lore surrounding the lake, and each summer the teenage camp counselors were fascinated by it. One piece they often repeated was the hypothesis that there exists a particular depth of water with a certain temperature and level of pressure such that dead bodies neither sink deeper nor float higher. They just stay there, preserved, much like they are in the snow on Everest. The lake is so deep and so cold that it's hard to know what's really known; it defies thorough research.

As I stood there, wanting to want oblivion, looking as far into these thousands-feet-deep waters as I could, it occurred to me that the maw of this lake might be big enough to hold my pain. This was part of the lake's appeal for me, part of its beauty. Supposedly God could take this pain, hold it with me, for me. I trusted that. But I couldn't see it yet. Right now, I could only see this vast lake. Maybe there was a depth in the waters where, even as dead as I felt, I couldn't sink deeper. I kept returning to the lake, I thought, because it was silent and it could handle me.

I kept returning to the water, too, because of what I'd seen that one dark night, trailing behind the ambulance, behind the paramedics pumping in futility on the body of my son. As I watched them work, my mind had begun to wander. Was this awful? I had wondered. How could I be thinking of anything else while following the ambulance that held my dying son? Nothing had been pronounced at that point, nothing was yet final, save in his body—still I knew.

As we had silently continued behind those flashing lights and along this unfathomably deep lake, I had seen my son. Not Fritz, but another son, not yet come. He came before my eyes as a vision, with his name clear. *Sam.* How could I be thinking of my next baby before this one was even cold? I was horrified by my traitorous brain. I questioned my loyalty, my sanity. Fritz could not, would not, be replaced. There are not substitutes for people, I thought, the worry ricocheting in my mind. And yet here was Sam, presenting himself from out across the night lake, a life on the horizon, a companion making himself known to me already, even in complete darkness. Constrained by shame and confusion, I would not admit this unlikely introduction to anyone for a long time to come. I had felt such loathing toward suggestions that having more babies would help me that I found myself asking how the glimpse I'd had was different, even as I knew that it was. I did not know what to make of what I'd seen, and yet even as I had pushed it away, I held the vision close, tucked it somewhere safe, to hold on to, to ponder later.

I now picked up the vision of this new son again, the bright lake crashing before me, down below me. It was still all mystery, but with it there was possibility. This lake held it all.

I took one more long, wistful look at the cold rocks and the pounding waves, and I turned. I still had to climb the hill back to the car. It was slow going after pushing on this run. Alice was probably awake by now, though, the child who existed already, who was still here, and it was time to go home and go back in.

Coaxed

After just a few of my runs, Jesse realized how necessary they were, noticing how I came back from the snowy trail a little more myself, a little more alive. He could tell they generated a certain kind of margin, where afterward I could be nominally more patient and present to him and Alice. He pushed me to go out. I simultaneously longed for it and resisted; at any given moment, it seemed much more desirable to stay asleep, hibernating under my quilt in our dark bedroom. It could be any afternoon, it happened so often. I nursed Alice to sleep, grateful to be relieved temporarily of my unrelenting milk. I fell asleep, too, snuggling with her, cocooned. An hour passed. Then another half hour. The door creaked open, and Jesse slipped sideways through the crack. He moved quickly, turning to close the door and keep the light from rousing our sleeping girl. I watched with weary eyes, my lids only just slit open. He leaned over the tall bed and stroked my shoulder, very gently trying to wake me. I looked up at him in the darkened room, and he shifted to working his thumbs into a persistent knot lodged in my shoulder.

He bent down close to me. "How about a run?" he whispered, kissing my forehead.

I grunted in reply. I knew he was right, but it sounded miserable. Just the thought of running for healing was terrible, even though it worked. I resented that I had to do it. I looked back up at him, whining softly. No, I didn't want to leave this bed. I wanted everything else to go away.

"C'mon," he tried again, "let me help you out just for a little one, while Alice is still asleep. It'll be easier to leave before she wakes, so you don't have to listen to her asking you to stay."

He was right, her pleas against even temporary abandonment were awful to hear these days—I caved to them immediately.

"Here, take my hand."

Jesse was warmly ignoring all my protests, helping me swing and pull to standing as he had done so recently when my belly was huge. He shouldered my slumping weight out the door, grabbing my running clothes off the shelf as we snuck by.

How could he do this? I wondered. How could Jesse see clearly right now, and reach out to me beyond himself? That reaching escaped me. For now, even receiving his reaching out was a stretch. Grudgingly, I changed in the living room, then hugged Jesse, beginning to lose any momentum I had. He felt my gravity sinking and took my shoulders, pulling me up tall again.

"You should go now; she'll be up soon."

He was clear—not controlling, not pushy, but grounded in what he knew to be both true and necessary. He smiled, his eyes showing always this intense combination of sympathy and solidarity. This was hard for him, too, and still I thought I was a mystery to him, no telling what might really work to bring me back. He was pretty sure running would help, though, and ushered me out the door.

We rehearsed this dance again and again as spring came. I was always glad to have gone, grateful for the time and space when I could actually think and even pray pounding the trail with my body, but actively choosing this healing usually still eluded me. It was Jesse who helped choose for me, day after day, coaxing me back into myself, leading me outside and beyond myself again. He knew I would choose it for myself, if I could, and that eventually I would, but for now, he had to do the choosing for me.

Wrestling Trauma

I had known from the time I was young that I should be in therapy, but when I was a teenager, I was scared to broach the subject with my mother. "Mom, since your drinking is fucking me up, can I please see a therapist?"—this was the kind of question that would likely backfire, that would leave her feeling guilty, and then she'd most likely just drink more.

In college, I went to the student health center once and did the intake interview about mental health. They agreed that therapy would be a good thing for me, and I could even get it for free without my parents knowing it! Relief. Then came the news: so many students needed therapy that it would be months before they'd have anyone available to see me.

Thanks, I said, and never went back.

Therapy became the kind of thing I put off until I couldn't. When my mom killed herself, it was clearly time, an obvious breaking point. I started with a decent intern accruing her clinical hours, for a wonderful eight bucks a session, and I was able to make my way through those early turns of grief. Nine months after my mother died, I was four months pregnant with Fritz, Alice was not quite two, and we moved to Tahoe. It was overwhelming to start over, to try to find another therapist, let alone somebody good. I figured I'd be fine for a while. Then Fritz died, and the deep lake lay there beckoning, and I knew I could not go it alone.

I wondered if there might exist a therapist who had experience working with grieving parents, and who was also comfortable with clergy. Only barely back to work, I knew my being a priest was going to add an odd twist to my grieving. Much of it was going to be conducted publicly as I stood and spoke and moved forward in front of my congregation. It seemed like a tall order for a therapist, especially in Nevada, and most of my googling attempts produced people who had experience supporting those who had been abused by clergy rather than working with the priest herself. Eventually I stumbled onto one woman who seemed promising. Rosey had worked with clergy and had a background in trauma; plus, her language didn't seem vague or too New Agey for me. I called her, and quite to my surprise, after only ten minutes, I was baring my soul and crying over the phone. This seemed like a good sign.

I began meeting weekly with Rosey, grateful for a space where I wouldn't have to take care of anyone else, where I could just tell stories and weep and try to see the way ahead. I was still telling the story of Fritz's death to Alice many times daily, but I now needed to tell this story to someone else, tell it for my sake.

One afternoon, I confessed to Rosey that it felt like part of my body was physically gone. It had taken almost two months to fully realize this, to identify what the physical ache was. It wasn't just that I was sad or fearful or weary, but that it also felt, concretely, like a chunk of my heart was absent from my chest.

"Say more," Rosey said, with her typical catchphrase of probing.

I explained how, when Fritz died, we were still essentially connected, only partway through what's called the "fourth trimester," his nursing constantly, the only thing he ever consumed coming from me. He slept on me, day and night. We were rarely apart; I could count on one hand the number of times we'd ever been in different buildings. In a way that was at the very core of my being, part of this being—part of me—was gone.

I stopped talking, and Rosey sat quietly, seeming to mull over my words. Finally, she opened her mouth. "No, Liz. Fritz was Fritz and you are you."

I caught her eye briefly before turning my attention to the shelves full of small plastic toys, animals, and action figures that presumably helped people work out their issues. "What do you mean?" I didn't understand how what I felt could be wrong.

"I mean that you are your own person, and he was his own person. You are feeling something else."

"Yes," I retorted, surprised to be arguing in therapy. "Of course we were different people. And we had only just begun separating. I don't know what it means, or why it is, but still it feels in my body like a part of me is gone."

Rosey pushed back again.

Growing more flustered, I then tried again to explain this physical, aching absence. "Maybe it's like the phantom limb," I suggested, "only worse. If that could happen with a leg, why couldn't it happen with a newborn?"

She circled back, more forcefully, deliberately, trying to convince me that what I was feeling was inaccurate.

I gave up, dejected, suddenly hating her, wondering what it was that I was feeling, then, still positive that even if an ultrasound could not detect it, a chunk of my body was missing. I quietly turned inward, holding that void closer, protecting it. I tried to hallow the hole, trusting that even the absence of this life was beautiful, even as the loss terrorized me.

The terror was real, too, and I brought it to therapy, still cautiously hopeful that Rosey could help me. The sordid dreams that came, awake and asleep: moving through Fritz's death again and again, retelling the progression of my mom's jump on loop in my head. The dreams reached out, weaving Alice in, too. One night she would drown; I would see her reaching for me through the deep, cold water just barely too late to save her. Another night it would be our home, engulfed in flames, the rampant fire separating me from her as she wailed for me. Car wrecks, kidnappings, killer Tahoe bears—my brain was loaded with countless ways Alice was likely to die, right now, imminently. I rehearsed the possibilities asleep, and these strikingly vivid dreams would stick with me. The dreams lingered, haunting me during the day, as if I could see the screen of this alternate reality—was this memory? dreadful foreshadowing?—overlaid on the present world. I struggled to decipher what was real, constantly reliving these chilling, spectral dreams.

"How does trauma play out?" I asked Rosey one week. "What can I do to step out of this awful loop?"

"Oh, these deaths weren't traumas," she responded matter-of-factly, her voice surprisingly kind, considering the words it carried.

"How were they not traumatic?" I asked, cocking my head, confused.

She stood and walked back to the stained whiteboard that hung above a Nevadan variation on a Zen sand garden tray: rustic, a twinge of frontier-style kitsch, but still holding the miniature meditative rake and a few small rocks. She began scribbling notes, triangles, models for how, as she learned in her doctoral studies, trauma functioned. It had to be violent, she said. It must involve perpetrators, malice, aggression. My deaths were sad ones, but simple ones. They were straightforward in their tragedy. They just happened, absolutely unfortunately, but without malice. My experience did not meet her qualifications for being judged traumatic, and we would not be exploring ways to survive trauma. "It would be inaccurate," she said, "misleading."

I was flummoxed.

I was sad, but I knew that I was not *just* sad. My body shook as I watched Alice play, hovering while trying desperately not to become a helicopter parent, but terrified that she also would suddenly die. Jesse's daring sense of adventure left me unhinged. I was sure he would die, falling from the towering Jeffrey pines he climbed, or off the top of the granite crag as he was placing the lead ropes for young rock climbers. "Be careful!" I'd holler at him. It quickly became a worn refrain, no doubt obnoxious, though all but involuntary. Jesse always smiled, nodding, promising that, yes, he was keen to do his best to avoid falling to his certain death. At times my own breathing oppressed me, sometimes too rapid and other times almost stalling. I forgot that I needed air until I became dizzy. I was not just sad about these deaths, but undone. No matter what Rosey said, I was, indeed, *traumatized*.

I was beginning to see that therapists were just people. The discovery didn't come all at once, but to my surprise, it grew on me session by session. Of course I knew this, but on some level I had hoped that this woman would be able to fix me, teach me, tell me how to survive my nightmare.

Of course, she *was* teaching me. But I was realizing that I actually had to do more than just show up. I had to choose what to take, what to keep and work with, and what to let slide right past me. Much of my surviving was going to be up to me.

Carried

Jesse was insistent, persuasive, relentlessly encouraging—I kept running. Daily now, nearly always the same trail just down the shoreline at Logan Shoals, my secret haven. I was getting faster, day by day, and running farther. I tried to do both, each time. Faster, farther, every day. I was pounding, unyielding, trying to force my body to be strong, going for a personal record—a PR—each time. This was my goal, unsustainable of course, but for now the PR kept me going, riding the thrill of a steep bodily learning curve as I kept burning off residual adrenaline from our baby's death.

Early on, I started tracking my mileage and my times, sharing the log, a Google Doc, with Laurie. She had taken it upon herself to add an extra column where she recorded encouraging comments after each run. "Is it snowing? What is this, winter? Speedy speedy speedy! You must have had your greens today," she typed one day, when I made it out even through the falling snow. Another day, celebrating a faster time with me, she simply added, "Hot damn!" The next week, "Hey, girl, heeeeyyy!" I could tell she was working to jostle my spirit alive, to get it moving alongside my body. Her words didn't make me laugh yet, but they sometimes squinted my eyes into a little smile, a start.

I still couldn't pray, not with my own words. I couldn't sit still; I couldn't sit alone with the flood of memories and questions. But I could run it all, and I felt somewhat less leaden now as I did so. Shuffling quickly downhill, through the loose forest floor to the Logan Shoals trail, I now instinctively turned right and pushed up the hill. The lake glittering to my left, I wove from one edge of the dry creek bed to the other, jumping from rock to rock before settling into the longer stretch of hard, sandy trail. I ran through the dry bones, having grown used to them now. I still hated them, but they were familiar. The bones were becoming part of my home, a scattered cairn on the map of this steady pilgrimage along the lake.

Slapping my hand on the dead end's gate as I turned around, I began picking up speed, cresting the hill and then pushing harder, faster, downward. The lake was steady at my side, all but hugging my right hip as I watched the ground shifting before me, dodging twisting roots and suddenly tumbling rocks as I picked up speed. And then the forest, the ground, the lake—it all began to melt past me, and I was now flying down the trail. Something had come behind me, hemming me in. It was lifting my legs, each in turn, quickly. It raised my right foot, gently hurtling it forward, placing it ever so briefly on the trail, ready to spring forth, while in the same instant picking up my left. It was a wind, a force, pushing them forward, landing each without my careful eye, then raising the other to race me forward. This wind was fast and powerful, and yet I could feel, too, that it was protective, that it kept me from dashing my foot on these stones, carrying me over and past the roots that threatened to trip me. I had never run like this before, sailing. I realized that I was not running. Something, someone, was carrying me, flying me along that trail above the lake. Something was driving me out ahead into what was beyond. This movement was a prayer, asked and answered as I moved, being prayed from outside my living body.

The force slowed as I did, and we both came to rest at the center of the trail, the path stretching out of sight to our left and to our right. I stood tall, breathing but not so hard, not like I panted after an all-out sprint.

"That wasn't me," I said aloud, slowly, quietly, decidedly. Something carried me there, carried me down the hill, back to this starting place. The waves crashed, but today they did not entice me. All I could see was the light flashing on the water's surface, all across the lake.

Respite and Terror

Part of me had been trying to believe that I could summon enough tenacity to survive the entire ordeal of Fritz's death alone, through the power of gritted teeth. Settling back in at work was seriously challenging that belief.

I'd been a priest for not quite a year and a half at this point, and I loved this work, felt born to do it. And I was beginning to realize how much it all depended on the team of people I worked with, the colleagues who surrounded me, the people available for collaboration.

Back in the fall, when I had only just begun at the parish in Reno, I had already been scratching my head at some of their practices. The interim rector was reusing sermons he'd written God knows how many years ago, and it showed: they were stale with age. The church siphoned off families with kids into a separate service on Sundays, a practice that I suspected was put in place partly to preserve the quiet of the "real service." I could work with practices like these, and yet . . . ?

More than anything, it had come clear in my short time back from maternity-turned-bereavement leave that not many folks there were willing to join me in my grief. There were exceptions, of course, but they were hard to find. After the empty platitudes and bizarre theological assertions that first Sunday back, interactions had fallen into a fairly predictable routine. It seemed most folks either wanted me to reassure them by saying that, yes, I was okay, or simply wanted to hear no more about it. I was not convinced that either one of those options made sense—I now longed to be with people who could accept my grief for what it was.

Yet my long commute did offer time for me to find solace on the phone. One afternoon, Tom and Cheri's voices crackled through my Bluetooth headset, the sweet sound surrounding me in the desert, assuring me that they got it. I edged deeper, wondering if I would find a limit. They had helped us dig the hole for Fritz's ashes—what could they take now?

"Sometimes it's hard to look at Alice when she's sleeping," I tested. "She'll lie there with her eyes the tiniest bit open, revealing a sliver of her big pupils, and all I can see is death. In that moment her eyes look just like Fritz's at the end: mostly closed, but just a little bit of his eyes showing through, vacant."

I was coming upon this realization: the night lake dwelled in everything.

"Mmmm," I heard from across the country. "Oh, yes, I hear that," said Tom.

"Of course you see death right now, Liz," Cheri added in. "It's got to be everywhere."

Their voices were warm, unflinching. I turned off the highway into Carson City and drove past a trucking company, a beauty school, a neon sign advertising dancing nudes in the middle of the afternoon.

"Even when she's awake, even when I'm by myself," I said, "still sometimes all I can see are his dead eyes, not fixed on me or on anything."

Tom and Cheri assured me that this was normal, that I did not sound insane to them.

I wasn't actually too afraid of being crazy, though. I might or might not be. What felt dicier was finding people who were strong enough to listen to me say these things. These two, anyway, could.

I realized I wanted to go to visit them. I wanted to get out of Nevada, a state I now resented. I didn't think Nevada had caused Fritz's death, but it did contain it. Even if no one was to blame, I hated this place because my son had died here.

Back at home after the call with Tom and Cheri, I pitched the idea to Jesse. He had just brought up plates of dinner from the dining hall. We didn't want to cook, but I didn't want to eat down there among retreat guests, who might ask me how many children I had. Or, worse, among the ones who were here last summer or fall, the ones who had seen my growing belly. They would ask me how old the baby was now; they'd exclaim how big he must be getting. I hid from them. We shared another dinner around our little table in the one main room of our cabin.

"Jesse," I started, "when Tom and Cheri invited us to Asheville, do you think they really meant it?"

"Why wouldn't they?" he asked, sliding a forkful of noodles into Alice's mouth. "It was their idea; we weren't hinting for it." He had a point.

Back in January, Tom and Cheri had offered that we could come stay with them when we needed some sabbath time away.

"I mean, we'll bring you out here," Tom had clarified. "We have plenty of miles from all my traveling for work, and we have lots of room for you to stay with us."

"Oh," I had said. "Oh, wow." There was no way Jesse and I could pay to fly there ourselves, not now. But having the time with our friends, especially in their own home, was tempting. "Thank you," I said, along with Jesse. "We'll see."

It was the sort of grand generosity that is hard to accept. Three round-trip plane tickets across the country? That was enormous for us. I didn't doubt they meant it, but still. Jesse and I talked about it a bit back then, but we were reluctant to take them up on the offer.

"You're right," I now remembered aloud to Jesse. "They did offer, out of the blue. Maybe we could really do this?" It had only taken being back at work a little while for me to reach for a braver place in asking for help. "Let's see when we can go."

We pulled out our laptops, juggling calendars and our plates and Alice's, comparing the church calendar and the camp calendar, and found two weeks in the spring that would work. I quickly wrote to Tom and Cheri before I lost my nerve, Jesse still feeding Alice bites as I typed. I swallowed hard, pressing send. It was horrible, asking for something this huge.

But they were Tom and Cheri, and of course they had meant it. Soon itineraries landed in our inbox and I began counting the days.

The Joy of Ash Wednesday

When Ash Wednesday arrived, falling early in March that year, I was oddly overjoyed. Finally, my parishioners and I could all be in the same morbidly introspective place: almost sullen, quieted by the looming presence of our mortality, our finite being, our total dependence and utter lack of control. I had been living in a web of loss for nearly two months, and I had been lonely there as others moved more steadily through the bright desert winter.

Work was beginning to feel somewhat more routine now. I could predict which conversations to avoid, where to deftly change the subject before someone said something that left me feeling hurt or infuriated. I had even less patience for platitudes now than when I'd first returned to work. But Ash Wednesday? This year it felt made for me.

Three services, morning, noon, and night. It meant a long day, leaving in the icy car at daybreak, returning home after Alice was asleep.

The services were quiet, almost no children present to interrupt our focus on the surrounding darkness that tempts us, pulls us astray. The music was pointedly somber, directing us through the gate into Lent, guiding us toward penitence and self-reflection.

I trembled with excitement as we neared the middle of the service, when each person would come forward. It wasn't the sort of excitement I would feel for seeing an old friend or receiving a wonderful gift. It was more of a quivering awe, a deep shivering respect for the thing we would do together. Rising, I took the small pyx, a round silver container with a hinged lid, which was ordinarily used to carry consecrated bread to someone at the hospital or at home but which held ashes this one day of the year. I cradled it carefully in my left palm. Made from palms kept from the previous year's Palm Sunday and burned the day before, these ashes were a much darker gray than Fritz's had been. Here was nothing but fine, soft ash, no coarsely ground bones.

I walked slowly, carefully down the white marble steps, my back to the imposing altar, and stopped in front of the first person standing at the altar rail: an older woman, her hands clasped meekly in front of her. I pressed my right thumb deep into the pile of ashes and lifted it to her forehead, brushing her hair out of her face with my other fingers. "Remember that you are dust," I said, tracing a lopsided cross on her forehead. "And to dust you shall return." I paused a moment, then pulled my hand away. A small clump of ash drifted down onto her nose. I shuffled to my right, to her husband, and repeated the words, tracing this symbol of execution and of life returning over the deep wrinkles of his forehead.

Again, and again, I plunged my thumb into the ashes and traced them onto foreheads. I laid my fingers on thick slicked-back hair, crooked wigs; I wove my way through curly bangs. Some people came forward and pulled their hair back tight on the top of their heads: earnest, shoulders squared, ready. Others knelt gingerly, leaning their weight on the smooth wood of the altar rail, as if they needed to borrow its sturdiness to withstand the ritual. I looked into people's eyes, the ones who were willing to look up, and told them whence they came and where they were headed. Reminding people that they're going to die is an odd way to tell them that you love them, a priest friend told me once. It is true—true that it is odd, and true that it is an expression of love.

It's one of the most honest days of the church year, when we come together and name that we've gone astray, name that we will die, name that now is the time to turn about together, to turn back to our God. This year, my life fit the rhythm of the community, at least for a day. Lent would be a comfort.

I sank deep into each exchange. The more people I crossed with ashes, the less aware I was of anything else around me—who was on one side of me or the other. It was just this person in front of me, their skin, this pile of ashes, my thumb. Our breath, intermingling in the two feet between us, for this time, while the moment lasted. Finally, nearly everyone had come forward; there was no longer a line reaching up the center aisle. Even the ushers, who had been helping people forward, had received their ashes. I stepped right, aware only that these were the last people. Standing in front of them, I had to adjust my sight downward.

A small woman stood before me, holding her baby. I gasped, then turned it into a cough, trying to mask my horror—or was it terror? Maybe she wouldn't really want ashes on her baby's forehead, I thought. Maybe she was just coming for herself and of course had to bring her baby along.

I raised my hand to her forehead, gently blessing her with the sure prediction of her death. I paused, steeling myself, opening myself. I believed in this, I told myself. For everyone. I nodded to her baby, who was gazing at me with wide eyes.

"Did you want . . . ?" I asked softly, my voice trailing off.

"Yes," the woman answered firmly, nodding, with a soft smile.

I didn't recognize her; I doubted she knew who I was, much less my story.

"Yes," she said again in a raised whisper, looking me in the eye.

Her eyes explained her insistence, they told me: "It's the truth."

My throat was already tightening, my eyes hot. I blinked furiously as I looked down into the shining pyx of ashes. The pile was smaller now than when I had started, but only barely. We never ran out, ever. There was always plenty of ash to foretell our shared mortality. I laid my thumb in the hole of ashes, coating the pad with an even dusting, soft and black. I lifted my hand to the baby's head. Hair still wispy and short, none to push back. My fingers wrapped around the whole side of his head. He looked into my eyes. Calm. Trusting.

"Remember that you are dust," I uttered, tears beginning to pool in my eyes. I carefully carried my thumb down the center of his forehead. "And to dust you shall return." Then left to right, making the cross bar.

The baby wriggled in his mama's arms. I stood, shaken, knowing that this woman was right, that her eyes saw clearly. It was the truth. I smiled weakly at her, grateful for her courage.

Slowly, I spun on the balls of my feet, my robes swishing against my slacks as I climbed the steps back into the chancel. Tears rolled down my face as I ripped open the wrapper of an individual hand wipe. My back was to the congregation, but I didn't bother trying to hide my face from the choir, who sat right in front of me. I scrubbed the black from my thumb, but the dark stain stuck in the cracks of my skin. I sat down, hard, on my wooden chair, relieved that another priest would lead the rest of the service.

Whatever joy I had felt stepping into this day, into this dark season, was still present. But now, having enacted it, actually living out this ashen exchange with other human beings, my joy was a heavy one and it weighed me down. I was grateful to have been honest together. And it was all real, piercingly raw. This was my life, now, this my new home.

Back in the Pulpit

I sat at our dining room table, the back of my chair nearly grazing the door of the fridge right behind me. The cabin was silent, and I stared at the blank Word document open on my computer screen, its cursor quietly blinking as if taunting me.

Though I had only been out on leave for ten weeks, I hadn't preached since the end of October, more than a month before Fritz was born. He was so late, and my boss didn't want to schedule me to preach and then have me out giving birth, so we left ample leeway. And then when I returned, I think my boss was afraid to put me back into the preaching rotation. What would I say? Could I handle it? Would I be—you know—all *emotional?* More than five months had passed, and I was rusty.

Tell me again: How does the Good News work? I couldn't really remember what any of this was, or how I might go about finding out. The idea of proclaiming the Gospel, of actually forming my own words to express God's hope for the goodness of our lives—all this was eluding me entirely. I had been ordained to guide people in the Good News, to help lead them toward resurrection. I stared harder at the blank screen: nothing. I was clearly not up for this, not the one for this job, I thought. I didn't have even the most mediocre news to share.

An old joke goes that we preachers preach first to ourselves. We preach what we need to hear, what we're wrestling with, what we're trying to believe. It's funny, and it's always felt more or less true to me. I wasn't even sure, though, what sermon I needed to hear.

I tabbed from the blank Word document back to the lectionary website containing that Sunday's scripture readings. At least I wouldn't have to choose those, too, I thought. Some denominations leave it up to the preacher to choose the lessons from scripture, but the Episcopal Church joins Roman Catholics, Lutherans, and others in using a set rotation of readings, helping us to get through a wide range of scripture Sunday by Sunday through the liturgical year. Sometimes it cramped my style, but at least today I was being offered a starting place.

I began with the Gospel. Jesus makes mud with his spit and restores the sight of a blind man, but the blind man's community still rejects him, even after he's healed. *What?* I had nothing to say there. I flipped to the Old Testament reading and made it through the first line: "The Lord said to Samuel, 'How long will you grieve over Saul?'" (1 Samuel 16:1, NRSV) I clicked the box to close the window. Saul wasn't even dead, just rejected. I still had no patience for the Lord's supposed quashing of grief, no matter what followed. I turned to the New Testament reading, grateful to at least be able to choose from among several different lessons. "For once you were darkness, but now in the Lord you are light," Paul wrote to the Ephesians. Really? Am I? Maybe the Ephesians were, but everything was still looking pretty dark here to me. Paul went on to encourage them to live well in various ways, ending:

> Sleeper, awake!
> Rise from the dead,
> and Christ will shine on you. (Ephesians 5:8, 14, NRSV)

It seemed so simple. You just decide to awaken? Oh yeah? To rise from the dead? And Christ's light will beam down? Is it that straightforward? I wondered. Is this some sort of up-by-your-bootstraps theology for recovering in the wake of death? I didn't understand this, and I couldn't preach it either. Not yet.

Last possibility: the Psalm. I almost never preached the Psalm, tending to find more meaning cracking open the stories instead. But here I was, having already discarded them. I clicked through to the Psalm and let out a strange sound, half laugh, but balking, exasperated. The universe, I thought, is truly fucking with me. This Sunday, the fourth Sunday in Lent, we were being dealt the quintessential funeral Psalm, the one people know even when they knew absolutely nothing else of scripture: Psalm 23.

"Fine," I said aloud to the empty room, to the pines swaying outside my window. "I'll do it." Now six weeks back at work, I knew that most people were reluctant to hear about Fritz's death, my grief, how much work it was just trying to survive. I wouldn't touch it much in preaching, I thought. Only a very few times had I heard preachers really own up to the darkness of their own lives in a sermon. The despair that afflicted other people, sure. Speaking to their own darkness, though? Rarely. And yet I wasn't sure I could pretend the darkness hanging over my head was absent, either.

The valley of the shadow of death—this was still my home. I would have to preach from within this shadow, too. *Though I walk through the valley of the shadow of death, I shall fear no evil.* (Psalm 23:4, BCP) My church held on to this older, more lyrical translation, at least for this particular psalm. More modern translators tended to render it as "the darkest valley." For once, I disagreed, appreciating the haunting flourish of the lines that Myles Coverdale first translated into English back in 1535. It seemed to wind its trembling tendrils into my soul, approximating the depths I wandered, void of most all light. I read it again. *I walk through the valley of the shadow of death.* The words were worn from use, yet they were true. The darkness of death still hovered overhead, blotting out the direct light of the sun, causing me to wither, day by aching day.

The second bit, though. *I shall fear no evil.* I choked on the words, awkwardly spitting them out. I feared everything right now. I was fearful of conversations with friends and family and parishioners and even the dental hygienist—she, too, had last seen me pregnant. I feared I wouldn't make it through this, that the death of my son would push me over the edge. I was fearful that a third shoe would drop, following my mom and Fritz. Deaths came in threes, did they not? I saw it at church: you had to watch out for the third funeral in a row, you braced for it. I feared for Alice's life, even without any particular dangers or threats, and for Jesse's. My eyes drifted across the room to the counter, where I saw my bottles of wine standing in a row, waiting for me. It felt like they helped with the fear, some, even as they added to it also, reminding me of my mother, hinting at what could be. I wrestled with the thought of just one glass, but it was a little early, so I turned back to my writing. This fear—I was afraid of everything, every piece of life.

It struck me that this tiny verse, potent far beyond its brevity, was not descriptive, but aspirational. Reading it aloud again—*I shall fear no evil*—I understood that it was not a statement narrating my current life. I was tethering myself to a trust that existed beyond me, seeking to lean hard on grace even from within the darkness, deciding to step out, freed from the binding fear. I could say these words; I could try to choose not-fear as a way to see promise even within the darkness, even when no way forward was yet evident.

I sat, wondering how that would become a sermon. "If you must, preach from the scars, not the open wounds"—that is what we'd been taught in seminary. "Don't use the congregation as your therapist, especially not in the pulpit." I wondered how I could be honest, when nothing was yet healed over.

The more I mulled, the more it seemed that this was not the time to wallop my congregation with a grand overture of vulnerability, forcing them to acknowledge the dark undersides of life, while crucifying myself in the process. I would dangle my toes in the water maybe, test it, but not go all out in baring my soul.

Just stepping up into that pulpit, now on the other side of Fritz's death, terrified me. I imagined walking up the couple of steps, leaning on the sturdy old wood, looking out and down on the massive nave, its rows and rows of pews. I knew I would feel naked. If I had to be seen there, if I had to speak, I would have to find a more clever way to speak truth than being unflinchingly direct. If nothing else, I simply did not trust my parishioners enough for that. I didn't know if they could really handle my whole truth, or what they would do with it if I placed it in their hands.

I had to find my way in with a story, and so I told one.

When I was fifteen years old, just out of my freshman year of high school, I flew to Japan. I had joined the Solar Bike Team at school. It was an oddity, this sport: some students had designed and built bicycles that used solar panels to fuel small motors, offering an assist to the cyclist. We had won the national race in Topeka, Kansas, and then raised enough money to continue on to the world race in Ogata-Mura, Japan. We packed up the heavy, clunky bikes and shipped them in cargo crates to Japan, catching up with them a few weeks later. The race was its own excitement, but what I most remember from that time is the adventuring that followed. We took bullet trains around the country, eventually arriving at the base of Mount Fuji.

By coincidence, it was some sort of national "Climb Mount Fuji Day," and the trails were packed with enthusiastic pilgrims. There were huts every five hundred vertical feet or so where you could get something to eat and, toward the top, spend the night. When our crew of fourteen American teenagers and two coaches staggered into the penultimate hut, one of the few students who had studied Japanese back in our Hoosier high school translated the host's warning that all the huts at the top of the volcano were full. We would need to either claim futons here or head back down to a lower hut. We were determined to complete the pilgrimage and watch the sunrise from the very top the next morning, so we threw down our packs on the last four futons.

We slept briefly, exhausted but restless, squeezed onto the thin futons so tightly that we had to coordinate flipping to the other side, even the coaches too tired to bother with trying to segregate us by gender. Someone's watch began beeping at 2:00 a.m., then another. We jostled one another to sitting, groggy, disoriented. Dim lights shone in the hut as hikers pulled on still-damp socks and laced up ash-covered boots. We strayed from what we guessed were best practices for a pilgrimage and gulped down PowerBars for breakfast, then set out. The air was chilly but calm. A few lights shone right at the entrance to the hut, but once past it, we plunged into darkness upon darkness. The rising mountain loomed before us. We stumbled over loose rocks and ash as our feet tried to find the trail, our headlamps helping less than we had imagined.

The clear sky far above us was littered with countless stars, gleaming but too distant to guide our way. We crashed into one another, stepped on one another's feet. Someone bashed their shin on a boulder in the middle of the trail; someone else headed into the scrub before we heard their misguided footsteps and called them to come toward our voices. We huddled closer while trying to progress forward and up, coursing back and forth around the switchbacks, each turn presenting another chance to lose ourselves to the mountainside.

Finally, suddenly, my eyes adjusted to the dark. From within the slate of black above me and below, a twinkling began to emerge. It moved, slowly, both leading us and following. It wasn't much more than the stars, but it was warmer, and near. Pricks of light flashed, then shifted, then went dark for a moment, emerging again in a new place. I took off my headlamp, letting my hand fall to my side, my pupils dilating farther with its close glare gone. I widened my gaze, up and down and then up again, as the lights kept slowly dancing, moving.

Oh! They were people! I realized, astonished. Each carrying a small light, walking the trail ahead of us and behind us. Because others had begun the darkened journey before us, they were showing us the path ahead. Others glittered on the trail behind us, showing us how far we had already come. A parade of mostly silent pilgrims, climbing up and up through the dark, all managing not to get lost or hurt, even in the depth of this night. From the light of our own headlamps, we could only see a foot or two in front of us, just enough to keep from falling as we clambered over boulders and slid through ash. Together with the other pilgrims, however, we made the winding path visible, the way forward opening.

Just as dawn was breaking, we came safely to the top. We were cold and tired and hungry, but whole. We turned out from the volcano's caldera, gasping at the view: range after fading range of mountains, all the way out to the sea, swept up in fiery clouds, glowing with the rising sun.

Back in Reno, this is what I preached. "Friends," I said, late in the sermon, grounded in this story I hoped was true beyond that high school adventure, "the months since my son Fritz's death have been filled with darkness for me. There is no getting around it. I know the valley of the shadow of death, and I know that you do also." My voice trembled, threatening to crack as I held tight to the top of the pulpit. Just saying his name out loud, acknowledging him here, in this holy place, acknowledging that the worst had happened—this shook me. I hadn't been sure what would happen if I showed up fully, but I looked out and saw that the walls were not crumbling. There would be no controlling people's reactions, but I'd said his name in the pulpit, and that was a start.

I quickly retreated into safer territory, imploring my listeners to look for the light, to place our trust in the promise—not that there would not be darkness, but that even there, even in the valley of the shadow of death, even there God would bring light. I knew I had believed this once. I longed to trust it again. Living in constant fear was exhausting, excruciating, killing not just the present but any and all future, too. I wanted to choose this verse—*I shall fear no evil*—as my way forward. I didn't know yet if it was possible. I preached this light instead, hoping that maybe I could speak it into being for myself, that if I said it convincingly enough, I might be able to trust it again as well. The light shines in the darkness, and the darkness will not overcome it. "It will not!" I proclaimed. We will walk through the darkness, but we need not fear it, "for we do not walk alone." I desperately hoped this was true.

This is the preacher's way. We preach to ourselves. From within this darkness, I tried to call present the light. I tried to tether myself to that light, to Light itself, even from within my trembling, terrible fear.

Landing

On the last day of March, Jesse, Alice, and I landed in a small North Carolina airport where the gates were filled with lovely rocking chairs. It was quiet, nearly deserted, a long way away from the pent-up madness of the ever-blinking casinos we'd left behind in Reno.

Tom and Cheri's house in Asheville was at the end of a cul-de-sac on which each home carried its own distinct character, deeply lived in, rooted, settled in to over time. Towering deciduous trees were beginning to leaf out, forsythia and hostas were bursting from the recent rains, grass—real grass!—was growing in their backyard.

The next morning, I sat on a bench on our friends' front porch and drank coffee from a thick ceramic mug that some artisan had made by hand. I looked out into woods, the light filtering down through young April leaves, the ground mostly bare save for dried leaves and scattered branches. Alice popped out the front door, barefoot, and began collecting sticks. She wandered, free, meandering in and out around the tree trunks. Penny, Tom and Cheri's elderly German shepherd, slowly tagged along behind her, seemingly grateful to have a new charge to protect. I sat, watching, taking another sip of coffee.

"This is okay," I said to the openness, feeling my eyes soften and relax in a way I hadn't for a long time. "Life is all right here. I might be all right here, at least in this one place."

I sat, still watching, my hands wrapping the mug. This was a home where I could be safe in my anguish, and that simple fact disarmed the terror. I was lost in my thoughts, unafraid of what might come.

Mostly, the days of our vacation were a quiet, playful respite. We hiked. We read to Alice, both Jesse and I together. We ate different versions of comfort food: orzo with basil and cheese and tomatoes—that was Cheri's favorite. Homemade pie—that was mine—then grilled chicken, and finally huge salads, these always Jesse's doing.

Later in the week, Tom and Jesse and I decided we were ready to try something a little more adventurous. We set out to hike a mountain, packing lunch and strapping Alice into her car seat in the back. We were nearly to the trailhead when we were sidelined by the discovery that the Blue Ridge Parkway was closed. Blocked off, completely shut down. Tom thought he knew another way, and tinkering through maps on his phone, he found a series of back roads that should get us there. They did, mostly. An hour later, a half hour since we'd seen another car, we rounded a corner on the dirt road and stopped just short of a locked metal gate.

"Well, damn," I said. "That was a valiant effort, anyway."

We'd been bested by the roads twice; I figured that was that. With a two-and-a-half-year-old in tow, you only get so many attempts before you have to concede defeat. But Tom was already out of the car, examining the lock and chain. "Yeah, it's definitely locked," he said, but with a glint in his eye. Unfortunately, it needed a key to open—Jesse and I had watched a friend crack a combination lock before, but picking one that required a key was beyond our skill set. Tom rattled the chain on one post, then jimmied the joint connecting the gate and post on the other side of the road, quietly talking to himself. We climbed out of the SUV to watch. He cheerily sauntered back to the first post.

"All right," he said. "Jesse, why don't you set yourself under the main crossbeam, down by that far post. Liz, come join me at the chain."

"What?" I said, taken aback.

"I think between the three of us, we can slip the chain off and keep going. Come give me a hand! And Alice," he added, "could you please go stand on the far side there, just up the road? We'll need you to cheer for us, okay?"

Alice ducked low as she scampered under the gate and took her position. The three of us braced ourselves, following Tom's instruction to lift and push with our legs, not our backs—if we were going to trespass, we should at least be safe about it. And then we heaved, lifting this impossibly heavy iron gate. Jesse pulled the joint to its highest capacity on one end, Tom on our end, while I tugged at the chain, trying to slip it over the post. We got surprisingly close, just two inches away, when the gravel began giving way under our feet and the iron slammed back down. Sweating, we leaned hard on the gate we were trying to free. I quietly noticed that while my breath was intensely labored, in this moment it was from exertion, not from terror or anguish. I was just working hard, for fun. My body was responding. I grinned.

"Okay," Tom called, rising again. "Alice, you ready? We're going to need even more help from you to do this. Can you cheer extra loud this time?"

"Yes!" she shrieked. "I am ready to help, because I can be so loud!"

We braced again, and on the count of three, we heaved. Alice clapped and jumped up and down and hollered that we could do it. Our feet slipped, one by one, but we were able to pull them back into place.

"So close!" I yelled. "Just a little bit farther!"

I pulled and jammed and pried each link of the chain in turn, inching each one just the smallest bit higher, until all of a sudden it slipped over the top of the post and we all stumbled backward. The gate swung open ever so slowly, creaking its bid of welcome. We stared at it, not entirely believing our success. Alice was less surprised, though, running to hang on the gate and swing it the rest of the way open.

"Well, there you have it," said Tom contentedly, not wasting any time. "Let's continue on up!"

He rolled the SUV through the open gate. I pulled the gate closed behind us, artfully arranging the chain on top of the post without actually locking us on the wrong side. The road ahead was yet more treacherous: huge washouts that required careful stacking of gathered stones as makeshift bridges, shale that crumbled under the slipping wheels, leaving us spinning out, downed trees to dodge or haul out of the way. Finally, though, we made it to the top, just before this old, closed road emptied onto the shutdown Blue Ridge Parkway.

We walked across the completely empty highway, into the completely empty trailhead parking lot, and started up the trail.

"This is usually packed," Tom told us. "It's one of the most popular peaks to climb around here."

On this strange day, it was here just for us. No one else had found a way through, and we were left alone to explore the thick mud from recent rains, and the twisting, knotted, age-old trees, and the sweeping tresses of grass braiding across the mountain's peak in a little patch of prairie.

When we had summited, Tom dropped his pack in the clearing and pulled out two woven straw mats, unrolling them on the ground and spreading his arms in an invitation for us to stretch out.

"You seriously carried these all the way up here?" I asked, perplexed.

"Oh, yes!" he exclaimed with relish, the suggestion of mischievous delight creeping into his eyes. "It's important to rest well at the top."

I shook my head, smiling at this funny guru, our guide sent to bring us farther up the path. I pulled off my muddy shoes, peeled off my socks, and timidly stepped onto the mat closest to me. It was cool and smooth on my tired feet, made up of hundreds of thin reeds held together by the weave of fine but sturdy thread.

I sat down, first stretching my stiff legs out in front of me and then letting the unexpected comfort of the mat get the best of me. I lay back on it, the early-afternoon sun quickly coaxing my eyes shut. I exhaled, noticing that now I was breathing slowly, with enough ease to examine the wafting smells of plants, nearly all new to me, circling in the breeze. Maybe I don't have to constantly pound, I thought. For the last two and half months, I'd been running always faster and farther, needing to do *more* to feel like I might be surviving. And yet here I lay, stretched out in the quiet sun on a straw mat someone else had carried all the way up here for me, atop an astonishingly private mountain, abandoned for this day only. I breathed it in, deep, and exhaled again. I needed this, too. I thought of the paralyzed man in the Gospel of Luke, whose friends carry him to Jesus on a mat, hoping for him to be healed. They are thwarted by thick crowds, kept away from the healer, and so instead carry him up to the roof and lower him down through a hole, down to Jesus, who healed him there on his mat.

There had to be more ways to move through grief. I was still frozen in it, and even as I pushed my body forward, much of my soul remained paralyzed, petrified, bound. This friend's mat, spread for me on the highest point in sight, was a good place to start. Maybe this could be a way toward healing, too—simply *resting*, enjoying ease.

On our last night in Asheville, we made a bonfire. We'd been talking about it all week, and as a child of the drought-ridden West, Alice was gobsmacked by the idea. A fire? Outside? Incredible. Tom was a self-proclaimed "fire man"—he started fires in their fireplace with a blowtorch—and he reveled in the engineering and tending of fires, loving to tinker with wood and flames. After dinner that evening, he built a robust pile of dry branches and logs he'd been saving from all around the property, carefully stacking it higher and wider, until it stood a good five feet wide and three feet tall. This wasn't one of the massive bonfires of my youth, but it was the biggest I'd seen in a long time. He lit it, again using his blowtorch, poking and prodding his way around the circle to get it really going. I stood back several feet with Alice, who mostly refrained from blinking.

Cheri, who is a painter, had brought a spare canvas and box of pastels into the backyard, and she invited me and Alice to join her in an art project there on the grass. Alice eventually knelt by the canvas, shifting her attention back and forth, back and forth, between the emerging art and the ever-changing fire. I sat down next to them, just watching. Watching Alice, as she created, unperturbed. Watching Tom, gleeful in his project of burning brush. Jesse had retrieved his guitar and joined us in the grass, beginning to sing in hopes that someone would join him. I sat and watched, still. The mat had worked for a little piece of time, but its salvation had worn off and I now found myself paralyzed once again.

"Whatcha thinking?" Cheri quietly asked.

I paused. I looked down at Alice, working intently with the pastels. I glanced across at the fire, shuddering. I tried to look for some bit of courage but found none. "Oh, nothing much, just watching."

I was watching, and finding myself lost, trapped, in that watching. Fires—once my fascination and love, a sport of choice for me, like Tom—now made my insides quake. I fixated on the licking flames and could almost see them engulfing my baby's body. It was what I had wanted: I liked the idea of returning to dust, of that dust being carried away into the soil, into roots, into the water. And yet the thought of incinerating the body I'd grown and fed and clung to—this simply stopped me. I had mostly tried to avoid it, ignore it, gloss over it. But sitting in front of this raging fire, flames whipping around the logs, the smoke thick as the wind shifted toward us, that cremation was all I could see.

Terrified by the image, I finally turned to Alice and Cheri, picking up a turquoise pastel. I lay down on my stomach, propping myself up on my elbows in the grass, and found an opening on one corner of the canvas. I added a curve, a twist, stripes to the wild abstract art they had begun. While everything burned behind me, I had to create something new, anything. If I had any chance of surviving this terror, even just tonight, we would have to make something new together.

Never Again

"How did you know you were ready for another baby? Ready to try?"

A mom asked me that recently, years later, now that Jesse and I have two kids running around, now that we can pass as a normal family. Her daughter had died at birth, six weeks earlier.

"How did you know?" she asked.

Her voice—heavy with longing—sounded almost pleading. It seemed unfathomable to her now, deciding to try again, as she was still lodged in the raw immediacy of grief.

I was terrified to broach the subject with Jesse in the days and weeks and months after Fritz's death, but already it hung in the air between us. We had always been clear that we wanted to have two kids. One seemed lonely. More than two seemed too expensive, too exhausting. Also still hanging in the air was the decree I'd made just minutes after Fritz's birth. Coming just shy of three weeks late, he was born at home on the last day before even the lax regulations of the state of Nevada would have forced me to be induced in the hospital. The day before, as a last-ditch attempt, I'd chugged three rounds of a castor-oil-and-orange-juice concoction. It was wretched. I was terribly sick for a time, then lay, massive, exhausted, watching movies through the afternoon. I'd slept more deeply than was reasonable to hope for that night and woke at five the next morning to a hammering contraction. The contractions kept coming, rolling, building. Even the early ones threatened to shatter my midsection.

The midwives arrived. The teal birthing tub was set up in our one main room, the giant Visqueen liner arranged inside, folding over the edges of the tub. Jesse stretched the hose, snaking from our bathroom faucet through the cabin to the tub, and imperceptibly slowly, it filled. The tub covered all the empty floor space except for a small walkway around it, forcing Jesse to scoot sideways past the raw pine bookshelves to help me, the midwives sitting on the couch, knees bumping the tub. I groaned and yelled obscenities and slid down in the water between contractions, resting my head on a cold washcloth.

I thought I would actually, literally, explode. I thought it was the hardest thing I would ever have to do.

Fritz was born and, in so doing, blew apart my body. He was massive. I pulled him up out of the water and rested him on my legs, still half in the water, as I leaned back against the wall of the birthing tub. We all marveled at how huge he was: a chunky baby, thick arms, full cheeks, big bear-paw hands. He squinted in the midmorning light, flailing his arms, already beginning to gurgle out a squawk—half complaint, half bemused utterance of curiosity—or so I surmised. Fritz was not delicate, nothing like Alice, who came out all tiny and birdlike, her skin sagging off her arms. Twenty minutes later, cradled in the cloth swing of the midwife's scale, he weighed in at nine pounds, seven ounces.

Eventually I passed him off to Jesse, who wrapped him in a towel, holding him close to his face as Fritz bleated about this strange new world. I slowly climbed out of the tub, and as I walked to the shower, I turned back.

"Jesse," I hollered, "I'm never fucking doing that ever again!"

Everyone laughed.

He smiled at me. "All right," he said, "I think we're good."

I wanted to be clear, though: "If you ever want another baby, you're going to have to buy it, or make someone else grow it, because *I am done.*" I was carrying on, of course, and somewhat delirious. I knew it was crass, and I had great respect for adoption. But about giving birth again? This had been an agony, and I was absolutely serious.

I had not fathomed a situation in which I would ever want to do it again. For all the stuff they teach you about sudden infant death syndrome (SIDS) and proper car seat installation and avoiding even the most minute taste of honey for the first year, the possibility that our baby might die seemed too remote to consider. I had read statistics about infant and maternal mortality in the United States, how we were pretty lousy compared to almost all other developed countries, but they were just that—statistics. I had chosen home births to avoid all the unnecessary interventions that had become common in American hospitals. I exercised. I didn't smoke. Jesse and I were young, our bodies healthy. It never crossed my mind that our son could become a number, a freak accident, a biological anomaly that sometimes just happens. It was easy to say never again, and I meant it. I was done.

Until I wasn't. I remembered my words—*I'm never fucking doing that ever again!*—but sometime in April I began contemplating the possibility. I felt guilty for it, ashamed that I wanted another already. Would people think we were trying to replace Fritz? I had no interest in using a child like this.

But the longing remained, the desire to raise siblings. I had wanted to have them close in age, close enough that they could really play together. I didn't want one to have to babysit the other, both resenting the other for the power and annoyance each wielded in turn. But that ship was quickly sailing. Alice would be well past three years older than her sibling, even if we conceived right away.

Still, I didn't feel ready. I didn't even know how to talk about it. What would it mean to have another child but not have Fritz there with us?

Almost every day while I was pregnant with him, we had walked the two and a half miles around Spooner Lake, a small lake at the very top of the pass between Tahoe and Carson Valley, me slowly waddling forward while Jesse carried Alice, or I bribed her forward with a raisin or a chocolate chip each time we made it to a bridge. After Fritz was born, we had gone out for a snowy walk around the lake, the four of us, just once. Fritz was snug against my chest in a Moby Wrap, zipped inside my oversize down jacket. Unless you looked close enough to see the top of his hat sticking out, you'd have thought I was still pregnant.

As we came out of the woods and back along one of the outcroppings above the frozen lake, Jesse quietly remarked, "We're finally all here. This is so good: this is us. We're here."

I smiled, tired but satisfied. "Yes," I agreed. "This is our family."

We had arrived. No more waiting. We were complete.

With or without another baby, now we would never be *all here* again. There was something about the idea of looking complete, in that quintessential nuclear-family way, that scared me. Two parents, two kids. We would blend right in, our loss no longer readily visible. I didn't want to stick out, but I didn't want Fritz to be erased, either. As a baby whom so few people had met, he hadn't left much of a physical trace, at least not one that other people could easily see.

Even before Jesse and I talked about it out loud, the ideas circled in my head. I did the math each month. I wondered when my period would come back, when getting pregnant might even be an option again. It had taken ages for it to return after Alice, but I had also breastfed her almost exclusively for a good eighteen months. She would try other food, for the novelty of it, then demand milk as her actual meal. I was still nursing her now, for her comfort and for mine, and still pumping for our friend Abbie's baby, Ruthie, but I was beginning to dial that back. I was tired of the hoses and funnels and mechanical sucking.

One night in bed, now more than three months after Fritz's death, I hesitantly broached the subject with Jesse. We lay close under the low, sloping ceiling, our legs tangled together for warmth. Cool, dim light came through the one window, but it was too dark to see anything more than the outline of Jesse's face.

"What do you think?" I began, tiptoeing in with the question. "Do you think you'd want another?" I didn't need to say another *what*.

He was quiet for a long time. This was Jesse, his way, always. Absolutely thoughtful with his words, careful to the point that I often didn't know whether he hadn't heard my question or was just pondering his exquisitely chosen response. But here, as we held each other, I could tell from his stayed breath that he was thinking.

"I know that being pregnant is really hard on you," he started.

It was true. I'd had horrible morning sickness with both kids—only it hadn't just been in the morning. I threw up daily, the whole way through each pregnancy, and nothing helped. I'd also had wild aversions to smells and foods, and complete exhaustion.

"But . . ." He paused, searching for words. "But . . . yeah, I still do want to raise siblings. I want Alice to grow up with a brother or sister."

It had been hard those forty days of Fritz's life, teaching Alice how to love another tiny person. How to share. How to make do with less of our attention, survive without being the automatic center of all things, yet we could already see how it was good for her; she was rising to the occasion. Stretching, reaching to be kind and responsible, even as young as she was. We wanted that for her, and for ourselves.

"Me too," I answered, softly. "But how will we know when we're ready?"

I could feel Jesse gently shaking his head. "I don't know."

"I don't know either," I said, tears beginning to roll down my cheeks, pooling in my ears. "I don't know how I could do it again. I can handle the vomit, but I know I'd be petrified from beginning to end."

"Do you think that will ever go away?" Jesse asked. "I mean, do you think there would be a time when it would be less scary?"

Something clicked. "I think it's going to be terrible no matter when we do it," I answered, jarred by this clarity. "Terrible, and so good. But if we wait to try until I feel ready, until I feel healed enough to dive back in, I'm not sure we'll ever have another. Or, at the very least, the baby will be way, way younger than Alice."

"So . . . ," Jesse started again, then faltered. He delicately traced the length of my arm with his fingers. A long pause. "So maybe we should just go for it? If it's going to be hard no matter when we do it, our kids may as well be closer in age?"

"I think so," I answered, surprising myself. Maybe I would be more healed, more ready, by the time a baby was born. Nine months was a long time. And maybe I wouldn't, maybe I wouldn't ever be. But maybe that shouldn't stop us. "I think we should, yes."

"All right," Jesse answered, simply, definitively. He wrapped his arms around me, tight, as I burrowed my face into his neck, tucked under his beard. I could hide here from the dark and the fear and all the rest. And maybe it actually was simple. Maybe we could just choose this. Maybe we just had. We lay there, quiet, considering what we had just done together.

I thought again of the vision I had seen on the way to the hospital the night Fritz died. I looked back at it often. I still could not yet speak it aloud, though. Guilt welled up, closing my throat. Guilt that the vision had come to me in the first place, as if I'd abandoned Fritz before he was even fully gone. But I couldn't help it. My mind turned to the baby I'd seen on that awful, dark night. *Sam,* I had heard, clearly, spoken out of the darkness. That was his name. I'd already seen him.

I fell asleep with Jesse holding me, relieved that maybe our lives would not be so totally bound by death.

Racing and Waiting

The digital thermometer came out again. This time it would live on the windowsill next to my bed. I found a promo code for Fertility Friend, the ridiculously named but legitimately helpful fertility-tracking website I'd used before getting pregnant with Alice and Fritz, and I signed up once more. I easily fell back into the routine of recording my temperature right when I woke up each day; supposedly, this made it easier to predict when I was going to ovulate. I'd done it for months and months before conceiving Alice. She had taken ten cycles to show up. Fritz came on the first real month of trying. I had no idea what to expect now. I didn't know what to hope for, either. But waiting was its own slow torture. I was glad to have a project, even just the simple routine of tracking my temperature, something forward-looking.

It wasn't just my heart that had been torn apart by Fritz's death; my body was still reeling, recovering, healing from his birth.

But a few weeks after Jesse and I decided we would try for another, my period returned. It was as if my body were listening, trying to help me along. I kept running, kept moving toward weaning Alice and the pump. I wanted more of my body for myself right now, especially if I was about to lease it out again.

I tracked, we tried, we waited. Nothing, that first month. I was relieved, but at the same time more disappointed than I could have anticipated.

Another month to push harder, I told myself. Another month for myself. I had been steadily working up to running a half marathon and had chosen one the week before Mother's Day. I chose it because both Laurie and I could make it, but quietly, maybe more importantly, I needed to see how strong I was before launching headlong into that fraught holiday. I expected it to be a sandwich day, pressing in on me from both sides as children celebrated their mothers and mothers gave thanks for their kids.

I had long hated Mother's Day. I tried to ignore the scourge of greeting cards and floral arrangements and skincare gift packs that dominated what seemed like every store. The cards in particular dredged up memories and fueled my resentment, aimed at everything and nothing. My mother and I had always taken joy in making cards as little works of art. No matter the occasion, she and I would find interesting paper, something to make a collage with, swirling smears of pastels, or ribbon cut into a little fringe. The mass-produced cards in the stores were ugly, I thought, and I wanted no part of what felt like a hollow holiday. I ran.

I was no longer running alone, though, at least not in the same way. And I was no longer allowed to go as far as I could and as fast as I could on every single run. Six weeks earlier, I had begun working with a running coach. It seemed like a nutty choice to me: extravagant, bougie. Jesse and I were not the kind of people who used personal trainers. But I wanted to be fast, and strong, and still sort of safe. I didn't want to destroy my body.

Laurie had told me about her sister-in-law, Ruth, who was a trainer. Ruth competed in Ironman races, lived in New York City, and was, as far as I could tell, exceedingly and inexhaustibly optimistic. Even as much as her positive attitude clashed with my innards, I trusted her, maybe because she was so clearly authentic. There was no question she believed all the enthusiastic encouragement she offered. But she was in New York. It was an odd setup, but a hiring a remote coach who came with a friends-and-family discount made more sense than going out to find a stranger. Ruth and I talked through Skype and tracked workouts on a shared Google Doc, and she sent me questions and cheers by text.

I learned that "recovery runs" were a thing I ought to do from time to time. That is, intentionally going for a short, easy, slow run. Weekly, even, or more. I learned that I should be taking days off from running, that running every single day would soon have diminishing returns, and that ultimately I would almost certainly injure myself. I also learned that I should stretch. I balked at these suggestions but tried to be obedient. "Ruth races Ironmans!" I repeated under my breath. Surely she knew what she was talking about.

The easing up frustrated me, though, left me reeling. It was far easier to let the runs be punishing, all out, to work myself ragged. If my body hurt, maybe I wouldn't have to think about how much my heart hurt. If my aching body could heal, maybe my soul could piggyback along. Letting myself rest? I hated it. Going slowly, "just for fun," as Ruth put it, was not fun; it was terrifying. Going slowly drummed up angst: if I did not go fast and hard, I would not get stronger, would not survive. I was afraid of what would come into my mind if I slowed from the pounding, what would flash before my eyes, dry bones haunting me in the broad daylight without the option of running beyond them.

But I slowed down, some of the time. It felt like a perverse act of trust, a raw experiment that I would discard as soon as it proved to be as bogus as I presumed.

I kept getting faster.

Jesse, Alice, Laurie, and I drove down to the Bay Area, and Jesse's mom met us there for added support. There next to the murkier water of the Bay, Laurie and I joined what turned out to be a scrappy little race, just a couple hundred entrants, most of them there for the 5K or 10K options. A mix of single-track dirt paths and then wider gravel and some pavement wove around in loops through a shoreline park in Richmond, a largely industrial city just north of Berkeley. Richmond seemed appropriate: like me, it was rough around the edges. We fit together. It was an objectively perfect day: calm, sunny, warm but nowhere near hot. The gun went off and I sailed. It hadn't occurred to me what a difference it would make training at more than 6,000 feet elevation. I swam in air, I breathed more luxuriously than I knew was possible. I flew past the Bay and through the giant, swaying eucalyptus groves, blasting far through the pace I'd hoped I could pull off. The race's underlying purpose was for me to prove to myself how strong I could be. I didn't anticipate that it might also be fun! That was more surprising: not that I was strong, but that I could enjoy myself, that I could ease from grimacing at the grind of my race pace and instead grin freely at the volunteers, thanking them as I downed their Gatorade.

Nearing the end, I did the math from the numbers on my GPS watch and couldn't make the laps add up to 13.1. I added them together a second time, and still came up short. Frustrated, I asked someone at an aid station how the course was measured, if it was a full half marathon. He wasn't sure.

Dammit, I thought. I'm doing this. I'm doing it all, even if they're wrong. The distance of 13.1 miles was completely arbitrary, but I had set my sights on it, planned my goal time around it, and was determined to finish it. Picking up speed as the finish line came into sight, I pushed harder, relishing the cheers from the small crowd.

"Where are you going?" Jesse called out as I kept running off the course. "You finished!"

I shook my head, plowing forward through the warm, rich air. I checked my watch: 12.9. Panting hard, I raced forward, past the thinning crowd and resting finishers: 13. A little farther, across the bridge to the parking lot. All out, I pushed, until at last I saw the numbers change: 13.1. I did it. I finished it all.

I bent over, desperate for more air, stopping my watch: 2:05:30, more than seventeen minutes shaved off my only other half marathon, when I was twenty-two. Not bad. Very slowly, I walked the quarter mile back to the finish area. Swigging more Gatorade, I explained to Alice and Jesse and his mom what I'd done, triumphant to have run a *real* half marathon.

Laurie cut in, laughing. "The GPS on my watch was off, too," she said. "It said I'd done 13.6 by the end. I think we're just in kind of a dead zone for satellites."

I looked at her, disbelieving, my mouth now filled with Oreos but hanging open. I blinked. "Really?" I mumbled.

"Really," she answered, grinning through her own sweat. "I asked one of the race officials. They measured it with one of those rolling wheels and everything."

"Well, damn. I guess my run past the finish was unnecessary." I sighed, exhausted. "But there was no way in hell I was coming all the way here and not running a full half marathon."

My body could do more than I thought it could, I was learning. I was stronger than I knew. And I could become even stronger, a little bit at a time, if I gave myself to the work and to the rest each day. I hoped that the strength in my muscles could translate into getting strength back into my soul, too. I was still so scared to be trying for another baby.

The month of May came and went without a positive test. No baby, not this time. Again the relief, again the disappointment. And a different kind of fear, just a little bit, began creeping in around the edges: What if we had to wait a long time for this one, as we had with Alice? What if I had to fear both not getting pregnant and getting pregnant? It seemed like an awful trap. I tried to ignore the fear, set it aside, bury it. I ran and ran.

I would do another half marathon, I decided. Just over a month after the first one. It was brash, generally inadvisable to stack two races on top of each other like that, but I didn't care. Coach Ruth raised her eyebrows, curious, trying to hide some of her reticence when I told her my plan. I agreed to more recovery time and slower runs than I wanted. My blisters quickly healed from the first race, and the toe that had lost its nail wasn't bothering me. Running in early summer came with its own challenge—the old snow was now gone from the trails, replaced with the unpredictability of warm days followed by sudden flurries. I never knew what a particular day would bring.

Race day came at the end of the staff training week for summer camp, the first week in June. I had convinced enough of the crew to come, either to run the 5K or 10K or just to enjoy the day in Truckee, that we had to take the camp's fifteen-passenger van. It was another small race, just a couple hundred runners. The description on the website had been vague, without even listing the elevation gain, only warning potential entrants that it was challenging. When we arrived in Truckee that Saturday morning, well before the race began, the ground was already radiating heat. I pinned on my race bib and stretched in the grass, sucking down water.

The gun went off and the gaggle of runners quickly thinned, spreading out into the wilderness as the cheers of the crowd grew distant. A great expanse of thick gravel welcomed us toward the woods, stones sliding underfoot, almost like running on a rocky beach. The eventual woods were a relief from the gravel and the sun, but the first hills were so steep that almost everyone slowed to a walk. Walking was faster than running, actually, and wasted less energy. Five miles in, I was already staggering. Maybe this *was* too much, too soon, I thought, wincing, beginning to feel myself quail. Maybe I don't have it in me.

But it was a loop trail. Very soon, turning back made no sense. I was already in too deep for that, dripping with sweat, powering forward through the scorching heat. After miles of steep uphill peppered with relative flat, I finally turned, cresting, and began downhill. Gravity grabbed me, pulled me, plummeted me finally down. I sailed, exhausted, thrilled to be freed from the earth's resistance. And then I landed on a root, twisting, falling hard. I wiped out, sprawling in the underbrush. I had badly rolled my right ankle. It was throbbing; I was gasping from the pain. I sat in the dirt, stunned. A good five miles still stood between me and the finish line. My ankle wasn't broken, but it was in bad shape. That deep into the woods, there were really only two ways out: wait for another runner to come by, send word to the volunteers, who would then come carry me out, or suck it up and carry myself. I wiped the sweat and angry tears from my face and tried to stand. Though my ankle wobbled painfully, it held. One step, then another, slowly trying to walk off the pain. It wasn't waning, but it wasn't getting worse, and this would have to be good enough.

The trail continued winding down the hill, and I walked, steadily now, conscious of the clock running even as I softly whimpered from the pain. I began to jog, picking up speed, growing more confident. The path turned sharply—I tried to pivot with it, but twisted, my ankle buckling again beneath me. A second roll in ten minutes. "Fuck!" I cried out to no one. I had a long way to go. I didn't know how I would make it back, but I couldn't stay there.

I walked. It was all I could do. Down the switchbacks, with their loose dirt and tight corners. Slowly, deliberately placing my feet. Steadying myself by choice, not by accident. The hill stretched on, feeling even longer on the way down than on that impossible climb up it. Still, I walked, rejecting the taunt of my watch.

At last the trail opened up before me, flat, wide, straight. Dirt turned again to pavement, reliable in its hold under my feet. I jogged, and then, surprised by the sturdiness of my ankle, I ran. With just three miles left, I burst forward, pounding through the heat. I raced, hard. Jesse and Alice and the rest of the camp staff were there at the park as I rounded onto the grass. Though they were just a few feet away from me, I could hear their cheering only distantly. I powered past, my eyes fixed on one line, pushing hard through the finish.

The huge red numbers of the official clock read 2:19:24. It was better than I thought, still faster than my first half marathon almost seven years earlier. I collapsed in the grass, just grateful to have made it back, grateful that my ankle held out.

The next day, I realized my period was late. Knowing it was probably still too early to tell, expecting that it was likely nothing, I peed on a stick.

I waited, watching. Then: "Holy. Shit," I said, slowly, to myself.

I was pregnant. I had run that whole, long, hot race pregnant.

"Holy shit," I said, again, to the empty cabin. "Holy shit."

5

HER SHADOW

HER SHADOW

Awkward

When I brought my college boyfriend Andy home to meet my family during the winter break of my sophomore year, I prepared him by explaining the mess he would find there. My mom and stepdad, Mike, had torn the sunroom off our house to make way for a massive addition. This was a key part of their dream: with enough space, all four of their kids—together with whatever grandchildren might come—could be there at the same time. If there were rooms for all of us to stay in, then surely we would come, wouldn't we? As if the house was what was holding us back from being one big, happy family. They started the renovation when I was seventeen. Three years later, there remained a huge hole in front of the house, the beginnings of a foundation, and mostly a lot of cold, hard mud. Where the house had once opened onto a sunny expanse, one full side of the living room was now serving as an exterior wall, covered over with plywood.

Having just finished finals and flown from New Hampshire to Indiana, Mike picked us up and drove us home, and we parked at the end of the gravel driveway. Getting out of the truck, we turned left, away from the front walk. To dodge the big hole, we skirted the garage, then eased between the side of the house and the barbed-wire fence that kept the neighbors' sheep on their side. The wheels of our rolling suitcases didn't work in the uneven grass, so we just dragged them, thudding and twisting. Coming around the far side of the house, we saw the gangplank. I looked at Andy, cringing, grateful that this didn't seem to faze him. One long wooden slab stretched from the grass where we stood out across the muddy foundation hole, landing precariously at the front step. I went first, holding my suitcase to my chest, the board teetering from side to side.

Hopping onto the one remaining concrete step, I pressed up against the metal door, now clutching my suitcase behind me while I tried to jiggle the doorknob with my fumbling left hand. Before I could succeed, the door swung open, and there stood my mom, beaming, bouncing up and down.

"Hi! You made it! Andy, hi!" she said, waving at my boyfriend, still walking the plank.

I swung my suitcase inside, catching some insulation on the wheel and pulling it loose from the open wall just inside the door. I hugged her, tight. I was exhausted, and relieved to be home. As I pulled her in close, I felt a smack on the inside of my ankle, and what I'd momentarily forgotten came flooding back.

Her face went a little flush. "Sorry, this thing is so awkward."

"Yeah," I answered, looking closer at the gray plastic shackle on her right ankle. "It seems really heavy, like you'd be banging into things with it all the time."

She nodded, shrugged. An ankle monitor—she was embarrassed, tried to make light of it. "It is what it is," she said, her voice light.

By now, Andy had made it across the mud pit and swung his suitcase into the kitchen as well. We wheeled the luggage into my old bedroom— since my mom and stepdad were not actually married, they could not really comment on the propriety of our sleeping arrangements. This was one more layer in the endless trading of places, the slow creep of swapping roles that had defined nearly a decade of my relationship with my mother, but this week was particularly impressive. I would not be pouring out her extra-large bottles of cheap wine or stealing her car keys. I would not just fill in as her chauffeur because her driver's license had been revoked. I would do that as well, but I could only ferry her to and from work, as stipulated by her house arrest. This week we would confront the awkward, stark, and often surprisingly funny reality of my mother being a prisoner in her own house.

Just then, someone rapped on the door. My mom had already gone upstairs, so I scooted to the kitchen to answer it. No one ever knocked on our door. We were way too far out in the country; when people came, we knew to expect them, and they'd just waltz in, cheerfully hollering to announce their arrival.

Now, sliding into the kitchen, I saw the police officer who stood on the narrow cement step just outside the window. I swallowed. Jesus H, I thought to myself. Here fifteen minutes, and already the cops have arrived?

I forced a smile and opened the door. "Hi there?" It was more of a question than a greeting. I tilted my head to the side, bracing.

"Oh, hi!" he answered, confused. "Is Susan here?"

"Yeah, s-she's right here," I stammered, stepping aside as I heard her bounding down the stairs two at a time.

"Hi, Jim," she bubbled, with the infectious enthusiasm I remembered from her wonderfully sober times. "How's it going? Chilly night out there!"

"Yup, it's all been pretty quiet, though, wrapping up an easy day." He pulled out a small black kit, pulling the zipper open and lifting the lid. "Here you go," he said, handing her something that I could not see. I watched from behind as she pulled her shoulders back and then her body shot forward in one small, quick motion. One exhale.

Ah, I realized, looking across at Andy, who had appeared in the kitchen doorway, leaning his lanky body against the frame, the freckles on his face almost too cheery for this twilight zone that was my parents' kitchen. My eyes were wide. A Breathalyzer.

"All right, all good, thank you," Jim said matter-of-factly. "See you soon!"

"Yup!" my mom chirped back. "Drive safe!"

She closed the door as Andy and I watched the officer head out across the wobbling plank, fading into the evening.

My eyes must have still been wide when she turned around. "That's Jim. He has to come out here every day or two at random times to make sure I'm here when I'm supposed to be, and to Breathalyze me."

My eyes stayed wide—was this *normal?* The juxtaposition of my just-introduced college boyfriend and my mom's parole officer? Such was my mom's attitude, not looking away, not behaving like a dog with her tail between her legs, as she usually did when we were forced to acknowledge her alcoholism together. She just owned it, named her reality, and carried on. This was new. Maybe she really could pull it together. Maybe she could build this house, this life. There might be hope, maybe.

Andy and I unpacked while my mom started tossing together a dinner. Nothing fancy tonight, she said, it was already late. Still, this was a place where she could regain some of her foothold as parent—she could feed us, even if she had to clock in and out of the grocery store to do it, while someone else drove her. The ankle bracelet had a GPS tracker in it. The authorities had marked the bounds of the house and her office. If she had to go outside those places, or beyond the bounds of her rigidly defined schedule, she had to get permission. Any violation of her parole triggered an alarm.

She pulled out two frozen pizzas, slicing bell peppers and tomatoes and adding more pepperoni to "doctor them up," as she called it, then threw together the best salad Indiana could offer in December: not great, but better than what we came by at school in New England. I retreated while the pizzas baked, then later walked out of my bedroom to hear her feet slapping the bare wood of the stairs again. Most of the treads were finished with sleek pine, save the four or five in the middle, where the stairs wrapped around a tight corner. Those remained plywood. I watched as she bounded down the stairs onto the carpet, then promptly turned around and ran back up, two at a time. Her ankle bracelet shifted just slightly back and forth. I wondered if it rubbed, if she was being hurt by it. I heard the slap of her bare feet at the top of the stairs, the little jump-skip as she turned around in her bedroom, and then the quick jumps back down. She was tiny, her frame looked nearly weightless, her ponytail, blond from a box, bouncing as she whipped around again at the bottom.

"This is the best kind of exercise I've found here," she breathlessly called out over her shoulder to me, aware that I was watching in confusion. "If I don't get some kind of good workout in, I'll go crazy."

Right, I remembered. She can't go to the Y, she can't run anywhere, she can't play in her racquetball league. Her world had been reduced to this, to running up and down the stairs wearing an ankle bracelet, hopping the steps she'd never managed to complete.

Shell of a House

For years, bringing friends home had been risky. What would I find? Would my mom be the delightful, creative, exuberant—that is to say, sober—person I loved, or would she stagger awkwardly, slurring words through a sleepy smile, trying to feign sobriety? Or would she already be lying passed out on the couch, as if she had flopped down and given up entirely? I began asking these questions in middle school, then more often in high school, as her alcoholism progressed. But at least some of the time then, we could still be pleasantly surprised. Sometimes I would gamble and win, getting lucky and bringing people home to my mom's best self.

At first the building project on the farmhouse was exciting, promising even, a curious spectacle. Backhoes! Cement mixers! Once I hosted an end-of-summer barbecue for all my summer camp friends, staged around the massive hole in our front yard.

"My mom dug most of that trench herself!" I'd exclaim. "She's such a badass."

She had the ripped arms to prove it. It was only as the years progressed that the story started to flake and twist and crumble in lockstep with the construction and the slow disintegration of the dream that had been this farmhouse.

Later, one year out of college, I invited my new boyfriend, Jesse, home, with trepidation. I was choosing to trust him. We had already decided we were going to marry, but we hadn't told anyone yet. It was too much right now, too quick, and there were already three weddings scheduled for that summer: my brother's, Jesse's brother's, and my mom and Mike's. Jesse and I decided we could take our time, wait until things calmed down. But still I worried. Would he continue to see me as more than who I was related to? Could he tell I was separate from this mess? I was never sure with anyone, but I hoped, and we tried. My mother drove us home from the airport this time, her license reinstated. Still, I closed my eyes as we rolled up the final hill, nearing the gravel driveway, rounding the last curve. Jesse, though, was relaxed as we came close. I'd told him what would be waiting for us, and he hadn't run away.

Some seven years since Mom and Mike had begun renovations, real progress had been made. As we came up out of the tunnel of trees and crested the gentle hill of the driveway, I saw the house standing proud, imposing as it resided on the highest point in this part of the county. The closely mowed yard gave way to an old orchard, years since its last pruning—mostly apples, some pears—then older barns, and gentle hills easing down into rolling fields and on into woods. The house was gorgeous, majestic even.

We parked in front of the double garage and walked past fresh flower beds and young fruit trees. As we continued along the walkway to the front porch, a strange sense entered the air. Something wasn't quite right; there was a glitch in this system that visitors could never quite put their finger on. We climbed the porch steps, and the sense of oddity intensified. Then, just before my hand reached the brass handle of the front door, it hit. My eyes realized, again, what was before me, and my brain scrambled to rewire the whole scene: this house was an empty shell.

As I opened the front door, Jesse peered inside, looking through row after row of bare studs. We stepped through onto already worn plywood floors, the subfloor polished by years of mud. I held his hand, tight, as we edged past walls we could just as well have walked through. I suddenly grew more cautious, remembering I had to step carefully, lest I catch my foot in the tangle of extension cords just to my left, or stumble over the circular saw or nail gun left barely out of our path on the right. Scanning through these suggestions of walls, I saw that power tools were still strewn everywhere, work scenes abandoned, left frozen in disarray, as it always had been. Boxes of nails and screws sat open on a makeshift tool bench, a board balanced on two boxes. Three cardboard boxes were filled to overflowing with aluminum cans—Bud Light, Diet Dr Pepper.

Jesse was quiet, but his eyes were full, his gut reaction getting the better of him ever so slightly. It was impossible not to react. I was used to the unfinished state of my parents' house and hardly saw it for what it was anymore. I made my way toward the old part of the house, still livable. I cracked a joke to cut the tension, to remind Jesse that I knew that the situation was absurd but that none of it belonged to me.

The truth he and I would have to wrestle with eventually, though, was that this was my inheritance, this the dark water I'd been swimming in for years. I saw the water, I could name parts of the madness, I could call out the ways I planned to live differently. And still, the shoddy darkness, the nearly invisible walls, and the glued-together floors—this was my home, my starting place. I needed Jesse to know this about me, much as I wanted to keep it hidden away from each of us. I sighed. This was still the place I began.

Gone to Seek Oblivion

"Did you see it coming?" they asked. "Were there warning signs?"

That was what people asked; what they meant was: "Could you have prevented it? Could you have stopped your mother from killing herself, if you had showed up, done more, tried harder?" At least that's what I heard, that was how I interpreted these questions. And it was what they did mean, at least some of the time. SUICIDE IS PREVENTABLE! the billboard yelled down, taunting me. I was glad it was there, if it helped. And I loathed it.

My answers? In short, no and yes. No, I had not seen it coming; my mother had never talked to me about wanting to end her life, not ever, not once. And yet, yes, she had been seeking oblivion for decades.

That's how Jeff—the irreverent, unpredictable priest who'd led Fritz's funeral—explained it to me as we paddled together in a bright yellow kayak out around Logan Shoals. Tahoe was impeccably clear and gorgeous in contrast with the darkness we were discussing plainly for once. Jeff was also an alcoholic, but one who had been sober for decades. He remembered down to the minutiae how the disease felt inside, how it operated.

"It's not that an alcoholic wants to die, necessarily," he explained to me. "It's that we seek oblivion. It's that nothingness is somehow so much more appealing than any other way of feeling."

At least in oblivion, with deep and penetrating drunkenness—or death as its extension—you didn't have to feel anything, say anything, do anything, be alive to what you might have felt. Drunkenness was a trap door, an escape hatch from everything that was.

Ah, yes, I thought—my mother had been seeking that oblivion, skirting in and out, for most of my life. Only intermittently at first, if at all, though I was too young to know the difference. But it came creeping in, closer, closer, deeper, deeper: her appetite for nothingness, her fatal longing.

Skatetown

The tires rumbled, grinding in the gravel shoulder. Just as quickly they were back on the pavement, our old white Jetta flying down the highway past soybeans and corn. Then that awful jarring rattling again, our peeling through the gravel, this time for longer, slowing down. Then a swerve, and back on. Why was she driving so strangely?

"Mom, what's going on with the car?" I called out from the back seat, wedged between two friends from my Girl Scout troop. "Oh, we're fine, love," she sang back, sounding distant. But it continued. Pavement, shoulder, pavement, shoulder. My cheeks prickled; I was confused, embarrassed.

Some forty minutes later, we arrived at Skatetown, a tremendously exciting destination over in Marshalltown, Iowa. I tossed the odd ride to the back of my mind, found skates that fit, and took off with the other third graders on the rink. Early '90s hits blared; the disco ball spun under flashing lights. I practiced skating backward and on one leg, and twisted in circles, still confident I would be the next Nancy Kerrigan.

The evening passed as quickly as any such evening does for a child enthralled with a prized activity, the fanfare of it all diverting any attention I might have given the skating rink's café, which was actually more of a low-life bar. We piled back in the car, ready to drive home past the sea of now-dark farms to our small town, Grinnell. I had just buckled myself into the front seat when a large frame came to fill my mom's window, already rolled down for the humid night. David, the towering basketball coach who lived across the street, leaned in close. "Sue, I'd like to drive your car home." His voice was calm but firm.

"I'm fine," my mom resisted. "I will drive my own car home, thank you." Her knuckles tightened around the steering wheel, the blood draining out of them.

"No, Sue. I'm going to have to drive your car tonight."

She didn't budge, staring straight ahead. "I'm fine, Dave, please let me go."

Even at age eight, I could recognize the tension, could see their calm jockeying for what would happen next, both trying hard to have this argument without us kids understanding what was at stake.

"I can't let you do this. Please get out of the driver's seat. I will not move until you do." His voice was still quiet. He was big enough to just stand there and wait it out, insisting on his way.

My mom hung her head, just slightly, clearly embarrassed and dejected but trying hard not to show it. "Fine," she said, finally. "Liz, get in the back seat."

Both Dave and my mom were quiet on the drive home, and so were we. It was much smoother, too, as we rolled along only on the highway. The gravel shoulder rested undisturbed. Squeezed into the center seat between my friends, I could see my mother fiddling her thumb, rubbing it back and forth across her tightly clasped knuckles. Even drunk, she was reflexively trying to soothe herself. Dave dropped the other girls off at their houses, then pulled our car into our driveway. I slid out, tired, confused. I watched them from my place in the shadows as my mom said, "Thank you, Dave," barely above a whisper.

Taffy

I had elected to make taffy from scratch for my fifth-grade science project, planning to teach my peers about the chemistry involved in candymaking. It was due the following day. I had made this recipe once before, together with my brother and mom.

Timing was key: it had to be made the night before, as it didn't keep well. Late that afternoon, I reminded my mom that today was the day.

"Yes, definitely," she assured me. "Let's get to work on it as soon as we've finished dinner."

After I cleared the plates though, I couldn't find her. Checking the recipe, I began gathering the ingredients: sugar, vanilla, corn syrup, butter, cornstarch. Relief—we actually had enough of everything I needed. I remember being so hopeful.

"Mom?" I called out again. No answer. I ran up our curving wooden staircase, skipping every other step as I slid my hand up the smooth banister. "Mom?"

I stepped into her bedroom across from the landing. Asleep, still fully clothed, my mother was lying spread-eagle on her stomach, covering the bed.

"Mom, we've got to make the taffy now!" I exclaimed, exasperated.

She coughed a little, having been startled awake mid-snore. "What? Oh, that. You can do that yourself. . . . You've done it before, right?"

I was perplexed. Why was she so groggy? It was only 6:30! Why was she already asleep?

Even in my confusion, her confidence in me was a boon—if she said so, it had to be true. I still believed this. I ran back downstairs and began. I carefully measured the ingredients into the pot, mixing persistently as they heated up, trying to gauge what a sufficient but not excessive level of boiling might be, trying to remember what the hard-ball stage looked like. I couldn't find the candy thermometer. I waited a long time, stirring vigorously, trying to dodge the blistering pops of molten sugar. Juggling the pot and the recipe, I finally guessed, and poured the bubbling syrup into a buttered pan. Surely it would thicken up as I kneaded it, right? I buttered my hands and waited until it had cooled just barely enough to begin plying it. I folded and twisted it, over and over, fervently trying to force the mess I was holding to become something else, something palatable. Five minutes passed, then ten, then twenty. It was still a sticky, oozing disaster. Another ten minutes of kneading and I was exhausted. It was not going to thicken.

Washing the buttery syrup from my hands, I went upstairs and tried once more for help. My mom stirred, but I couldn't tell if she was awake enough to understand how dire the situation was. My classmates were all awaiting this clever, delicious project tomorrow. I would be humiliated. How could I fix it?

"Just wrap them up, sweetie," she offered sleepily. "It'll still taste wonderful." She rolled over and began snoring again before I could protest or persuade her to help me.

The next day, I walked into Mrs. Thomas's fifth-period science class with a tray of my own personal spin on classic taffy. I had stayed up late the night before, carefully cutting wax paper into squares, spooning the gloppy syrup into them, then rolling them up and twisting the edges shut. I didn't account for the fact that the syrup would continue to spread, wending its way out through the cracks in the papers, filling in all around the would-be discrete pieces. I had a tray of sweet slop, and it was time to present this embarrassment to my class. I clenched my teeth and tried to be persuasive, proclaiming that this was how I had meant for it to go, that it was an experiment but even better than the original. Not one of us was convinced, but my classmates were kind, and gratefully accepted the sugar, no matter its state. I was mortified. More than that, I was furious with my mother. She was wrong. I was only ten years old. I could not do this by myself.

Running Interference

The taffy mishap was just one of the early ones, though, before I really understood what was happening.

Even as a young teenager, I knew full well that my mom wanted the divorce. She tried hard to remain neutral, to avoid pitting me against my dad. Still, I knew her well enough to read her face, to catch her subtle, stifled gestures that betrayed the truth. Once, when I was older, she answered me straight: she had wanted to get divorced in Iowa, when I was younger, but then when my dad, a professor, didn't get tenure, it didn't work, we had to move, they had to stay together. After the split, my parents honored my choices around where I wanted to live, where I wanted to spend my time—I appreciated it, but maybe it was more responsibility than a thirteen-year-old was ready for. I chose her. Again and again, despite what was unfolding at her house, how the madness was picking up steam, I chose her.

By late middle school, I was pouring out bottles whenever I found them. We did not have a liquor cabinet or a wine rack. Instead, I learned to look on the floor of her closet, in her big leather work bag, under the sink in her bathroom. I had grown bolder with practice, no longer pouring out just some or watering it down. Now I dumped it all out, unafraid of her anger, and tossed the empties in the recycling bin down in the garage. She would be frustrated, but she would not direct her frustration at me. I knew that pouring it out did not solve anything or change her behavior. But it kept her sober for that day, right then, and that was better than nothing.

I was also routinely stealing her keys. I watched for the swagger, watched for her running her fingers down the doorframes to steady herself, and then I ransacked her purse, the counter, her coat pockets. I buried her keys at the bottom of my dresser drawer, beneath my rainbow toe socks and glittering tights—I was otherwise so entirely adolescent, aside from this little bit of playing the adult. Usually she didn't notice, but I could breathe easier knowing that I had them. Once in a while she looked for them, though. It was suddenly urgent, she had become agitated.

"Dammit!" she shouted into the void of the house, to no one in particular. "Where are my keys?"

I hid out in my room, cowering in the far corner of my loft bed, hoping she wouldn't ask me. She turned bags upside down, dug through drawers, pawed through piles on the counter.

"Liz, have you seen my keys?"

I didn't answer. I heard my older brother playing basketball in the driveway, and quietly went out to join him, sitting on the wall while he shot. A few minutes later she came out of the basement through the attached garage, barefoot, frustrated. "Did you take my keys?" she demanded.

I stared at her, blankly. "Mom, you can't drive right now. It's not safe."

"I'm fine! Come on, where did you put them?"

I shook my head. I was scared, but I sure as hell was not about to give them up.

Slipping

Where I could really see her veer toward oblivion, though, if only in retrospect, was when she drove alone. She managed to dodge DUIs for years, her first one coming the summer of my freshman year of high school. After I returned from Japan with the Solar Bike Team, I learned that she'd been caught. I was devastated. Officers saw her apparently passed out in her car in a parking lot, then waited and maybe, possibly goaded her into driving a few feet before arresting her. Other details were hazy, but she could argue entrapment. This pretty, articulate, well-educated white woman? A first offense? She got off.

But then the wrecks began. The Celica, a wild trade-up from the couple of old Jettas she had bought off her parents for cheap. The red sports-car reinvention of herself, a new identity following her divorce from my dad, now sat banged in and scratched up on all four sides. She'd failed to make the ninety-degree turn on the country road that led from our farmhouse to town, instead careening straight through the barbed-wire fence and down into the field. The fence remained broken for months, a harrowing reminder to me of how much worse it could have been, just a quarter mile past the sheer drop-offs by the train trestle, a mile past the gaping depths where the quarry lay plummeting down on either side of the road.

Later on, it was the SUV she crashed into our neighbor's parked cars. She'd made it down the twenty-five minutes of winding country roads, coming home from work, only to crash a tenth of a mile from our driveway. Once again, I gave thanks that the cars were unoccupied and that she wasn't hurt.

She lost her driver's license. I—just eighteen, nineteen, a senior in high school, then a college student home on visits—would drive her to and from work, glad for the freedom my driving her car afforded me. We tried to be nonchalant, as if all this were normal. It was becoming our normal, at the very least.

I was home, visiting late in college, when the doorbell rang. A police officer. Jesus H, I thought. Here we go again.

"Are you Susan?" the officer asked.

I laughed nervously. "We look alike, but no, I'm her daughter. Why? Did she drive drunk or something?" By now, I had grown weary and callous.

"Well, I don't know. Is she here?"

Weird, I thought. "No, she's at work. She left this morning."

"We found her motorcycle parked on someone's porch just off That Road," he explained. "Someone saw her slide into the ditch. I wanted to make sure she was okay, and also see what the plan was for the motorcycle."

That Road, I thought. I'd always loved that it was actually named that, printed on the sign, like it was just made for corny jokes. And she could taint even that good, easy humor.

"What the hell," I muttered. "I have no idea. I've been here all day, haven't heard anything. I can look, though." I ran upstairs, and blinked hard. There was my mom, lying in bed. "Um, Mom? A cop is here, he found your bike."

She rolled over onto her back.

"Are you okay?"

"Oh, I'm fine. I'm just resting," she answered slowly.

"Are you going to come talk to him?" I asked her, pressing. "What should I say?"

She carefully stood up and walked downstairs. "Hello, officer," she began. "Beautiful day, isn't it?" She could still flash a great smile, even when she was so far gone, completely absent behind the eyes. "I'm fine, I just laid my bike down in the curve there, some loose gravel. Caught a ride home from a kind neighbor. All good here. I'll go back with my husband and the truck to pick up the bike this afternoon."

The cop eyed her, watching for her steadiness, eyes narrowed as he tried to decide what do to. "All right, then," he started. "Just wanted to check up." Turning to me, he nodded: "You'll be here? You'll keep an eye on her?"

"Yes, sir," I sighed. I always did keep an eye on her, at least when I could. And still, she was slipping through my fingers, again and again sliding closer to the edge.

Reading the Signs

There would be more signs, more clues. The outpatient treatment she would do in Indianapolis one summer as a swap for keeping her job. The rehab counseling group she would join and return to at various points, this, too, mandated by law.

Her workplace was supportive, accommodating, more than I might have expected. She was a lecturer in accounting at Indiana University; she'd been teaching there since I was in middle school. Her department heads saw her drinking as the disease it was, and they responded compassionately. Still, she pushed them to the limit.

There was the weekend I flew home, a few weeks before my wedding, to try to keep her alive. Our family friend Leslie had called.

"You have to come," Leslie said. "Your mom is in really bad shape."

Leslie was practical, not one for hysterics. And she was clear. My brother, John, was serving in Iraq. My stepdad, Mike, was in Korea on business. Even though I was in New Hampshire, I was the one who was nearest to my mother. And I would go. But not immediately. I had given up trading my life to try to save hers. The days ahead were critical ones in my ordination process: I was to go to Boston for two days of intensive psychological testing, which was necessary, something scheduled many months before. If I bailed now, it would mean postponing my beginning seminary by another year. I gritted my teeth, talking myself in circles, wondering if this was on me.

"Okay, I'll go," I told Leslie. "But I can't get there for a couple days."

"How do you handle stressful situations? Can you give me an example?" the psychologist asked me.

He was in his early sixties and had kind eyes. He wasn't grilling me; he seemed genuinely interested in his work.

"Well . . ." I faltered. "I suppose that's where I am right now. My mother is an alcoholic, and she is in the middle of a terrible binge. I need to go home to get her into rehab. But I wasn't going to skip this part of the process."

Maybe all this was too current, too raw, I worried. My hope was that this might show I had built some healthy separation from my broken family system, while I wondered if I actually had. By this time, I had mostly stopped taking my mother's phone calls when she was drunk, curtly asking her to call back when she was sober. I was uninterested in spending time with her, even from halfway across the country, when she'd been drinking—her personality was changed that much by the bottle. She was almost never angry, but muted, slovenly, pathetic. Being with her when she'd been drinking made me feel physically ill. I had to separate myself.

I finished the barrage of psychological evaluations and flew back to Indiana, unannounced and frustrated and terribly worried. I was twenty-four years old and could only rent a car from a few companies, and only after shelling out extra cash as collateral for my presumed immaturity. I rolled my eyes at the rental-car counter and drove to her house. The dogs erupted excitedly when I opened the front door. I forced my voice to come out gentle, warm, as I called out, "Hello? Mom?" I was scared, not knowing what I'd find.

She came down the stairs, the corner treads still unfinished, in rumpled pajamas. She rubbed her eyes and immediately began to cry. I caught her as she stepped forward off the bottom step, and she sighed down into my arms. I held on tight to her small body, ravaged from the inside out. My heart hurt. Distraught, I mouthed silent thanks that she was still alive. Nothing was a given anymore.

"You didn't have to come," she said quietly.

"I know, Mom," I answered. "I want to be here. I was really worried."

It took a day for her body to begin bouncing back from this extended binge, as it always seemed to do. Angry as I was that she could do this to herself—*to me*—again and again, it seemed miraculous, what this 110-pound body could withstand, what pain it could inflict on itself. There was time that weekend to plan for her sobriety together, to get frank about hitting bottom again, to meet with her rehab counselor, again. We went to church together, at her request, and she silently wept through the service, holding my hand. She assured me that she could receive the chalice, too, that a sip of wine wasn't a problem. And we knelt there before the altar, both broken, both receiving, both holding on to some shred of hope as the oblivion, that fog of darkness, drew closer, thicker, circling around her.

I don't know if she believed in that hope back then. I don't know how much she already longed for release, for the cover of blankness and unfeeling. I knew that I still saw a way forward. And I knew that there were no longer any guarantees—not on her life.

Light and Oblivion

My mother's suicide was, of course, only one part of her. There was another side. There always is. That's why it was all so perplexing, so heartbreaking, and so utterly shocking.

The time came when I had to explain her alcoholism and suicide to my children, when they asked why Grandma Susan died. The answer eluded me, taunted me. There was no clean answer.

"Just like bodies can get sick, brains can get sick, too." This was what the experts suggested I say. "Sometimes bodies get so sick they stop working, and this can happen to our brains, too." It was true.

And.

At the same time, tangled in paradox, her mind was brilliant. Unstoppable, even in its own power to destroy her.

Who else was she? Susan, this woman who taught herself in her early twenties to make *jiaozi*, wonderfully complicated Chinese dumplings, from scratch, who learned on her own to raise ducks and then butcher them and make Peking duck for all my father's colleagues and students from the Chinese department, out in the backwoods of Maine, in the house she'd helped to design and build.

As she stepped into oblivion more often, or skirted just around its edges, still she kept working with this light of hers. Years past her death, sculptures still towered at the farm in Indiana, welded together from scrap metal during a series of classes she took at the community art center. One she called "The Dancing Woman"—rusty pipes she bent into life-giving curves, limbs painted bright blue and purple, the perfectly round head a radiant yellow. The paint was slowly flaking off now, but the art still stood, buried in cement in the earth while weeds and wildflowers grew up taller around it. She worked at carving limestone, too, eager to learn this local art form. She visited nearby quarries to pick out chunks, then tapped away with her range of chisels—a sun, a face, a dragon emerging.

This was the woman who pushed through the encroaching darkness to bring her spark into the classroom. She had stumbled quite by accident into a job teaching accounting. She was not an accountant. She had not taken a single math class when she was an undergrad at Dartmouth. When she and my father divorced, my brother, at age sixteen, did her taxes. There were different versions of the story, of course, but in essence, the accounting department at Indiana University's business school found itself suddenly down a lecturer one fall. Our neighbors two doors down were both professors and knew the person making the hire.

My mother taught herself the material, staying a chapter ahead of the students, all year long. It was wildly stressful, and risky, but it worked. She stayed. She went on to master the material and not just tolerate it, but actually appreciate its value. ("Boring accounting!" she would still exclaim, laughing. "Yeesh! How did I end up teaching accounting instead of literature or art history?") She began to introduce unconventional methods into otherwise mind-numbing lessons. Soon the students were drawing pictures of their relationship with accounting (hilarious!), writing prose, watching with glee as she taught a cost-benefit analysis with a whirling circular saw as her prop. She loved it. They loved her. Eager for more time, they would line up after class, ask to follow her to her office.

"Gladly!" she would answer. "But we're taking the stairs."

Up she would bound, two at a time, the twenty-year-olds trying to keep pace. They would fall back, panting, which she thought was wonderfully funny. She would wait for them at the top of the fourth flight, grinning.

"It's no sweat if you always take the stairs!"

For me, it was that—her laughter—that most masked her inevitable progression toward death. Hearing her laugh, I couldn't see that unfolding crash course.

Years later, when Jesse would come home to find me on the phone, he'd say he could always tell if it was my mother on the other end. Even when he was in another room, unable to make out my words, he'd know by my laughter. We laughed almost more than we spoke, she and I. When we did speak, it was often in unison. We were of one mind, and to us, the world was exceedingly comical. How could we laugh together so much while—at the same time—she sought that endless dark? It was beyond me.

6

GESTATION

GESTATION

Raising the Girl

My mom, my dad, my brother, and I were new to Iowa, having left the deep woods of Maine for the tiny college town of Grinnell, in the midst of sprawling corn and soybean fields. I was six, and we lived, for the moment, in a small ranch house, a college rental for newly arrived faculty. My dad led us into this new town, moving in his quiet way, even as a towering six-foot-one Caucasian man with laid-back brown curls, an unusual sight for a professor in the Chinese department. He laughed amiably with his colleagues back then, boyish dimples flashing, still hopeful for what lay ahead. He and my mother had had a rocky go of things in their first years of marriage, and I could sense his eagerness for this fresh start as a family in a new town, new state.

Across the street from our house was a sprawling field—Frisbee, baseball, just big, open flat grass, the edge of the campus. Railroad tracks cut through the center of the field, hauling endless chains of corn syrup tankers somewhere else, far away. John and I, independent at eight and six years old in the way New England's backwoods and small-town middle America can afford, crossed over the grass to examine the tracks. We often snuck pennies onto the rails, then retreated to our yard, waiting in the shade of the thick maple trees, watching as eventually trains would come rolling by, screeching over the tracks, leaving us giggling and anxious to race back and search for our flattened pennies. We had been at it for weeks, a goodly collection of smeared, paper-thin pennies growing, when a neighbor mentioned to us, seemingly quite offhand, that putting coins on the track could derail the train. That's not true, of course, but we didn't know it; we were horrified, silently convicted, imagining tanker after tanker splayed out across the small college campus. Would it have smashed cars? Trapped students? Caught on fire? We stopped immediately, stunned by the guilt of what could have been.

Maybe it was that early taste of guilt, the shame of what I could have made to happen, that made me ask my father the question that intrigued me. Or maybe I sensed a shift in the air, arriving there in the Bible Belt. We stood and recited the Pledge of Allegiance each morning in my first-grade class, under the stern and watchful eye of our ancient teacher. Did she notice that I pointedly went silent when all the other six-year-olds said "under God," pursing my lips, small but defiant in my stillness? How could I pledge allegiance under this God I knew nothing about? I refused. But I was hungry to know more.

I asked my father, the professor, raised Catholic, now lapsed, to tell me about Jesus. It wasn't something he talked about, but I knew that he had grown up in the church, steeped in the ways of an exceedingly Irish family. It seemed like maybe God mattered to him, still. I waited until he was saying good night, tucking me into bed in what was still an unfamiliar room. I was nestled into the bed my mom built out of leftover rough-cut pine, under the quilt she had sewn for my birthday, made from scraps of fabric—some white, some light blue, with small flowers dancing across it, encasing a tattered old blanket she had gotten for free.

"What is the deal with Jesus? Who is this person that people here are so worked up about?"

He seemed surprised, but he answered me with a story: the story of the girl rising, the one Jesus brought back from the dead. The story was disturbing and wildly powerful, but ultimately hopeful. My dad offered it as a bedtime story, quietly, matter-of-factly. A young girl got sick and died, and her parents called for Jesus. Miraculously, Jesus made her live again. He made her rise.

I was stunned. Could that really be? Did it actually happen? Could it happen again? I didn't ask my questions, but they swirled fast within me. Meek but suspicious, I could only muster a quiet "Really?"

"Really," my dad replied, earnestly.

His voice was sweet, yet he seemed a little bashful about it. He sounded like maybe he was questioning the story, even as he was still somehow hooked, riding on the deep-seated conviction of the power he had once felt in it.

There was so much I didn't know. I had not yet learned that Jesus himself had died and then risen. Resurrection was not a notion I had encountered anywhere. Easter was about dyeing eggs with that pungent mix of white vinegar and food coloring. It was about green plastic grass and chocolates and maybe even a gift, like the stuffed rabbit that arrived one Easter morning in Maine and accompanied me through the harrowing years ahead. That was Easter. Not Jesus, not love and light overcoming the power of death. Not an empty tomb, not the brave women's first witness that the Gospels recount: seeing Jesus, understanding, running to tell the others that life was somehow, inexplicably, incredibly, returning.

But here was a resurrection story for someone like me, a six-year-old child, newly Iowan. God, I heard, could be interested enough in the plight of a young dead girl to intervene. At least one time, a long, long time ago, God had paid enough attention to a little girl to see that there was more ahead of her, and stepped in to raise her back to life.

This was my solitary introduction to scripture, my earliest memory of sacred story. That one night is the only time I clearly remember either of my parents teaching me anything from the Bible. Somewhere along the line, I would absorb some of the Christmas story, the tale of Noah's ark. They did not make much of an impression.

This glimpse of resurrection, though—the possibility of life returning, even to someone like me, left me staring at the dark ceiling long after my father and I had exchanged good-nights. I lay there, wondering. Some flickering trust was planted that I, too, could be raised. I didn't know why I should ever need that, but it sounded like my life could come again, too.

Building the Kingdom

After the race through the woods of Truckee, after that positive pregnancy test, the vomiting began. I knew it would, if I was really pregnant. It always had.

A week after the test, I woke up, got out of bed, and started to brush my teeth. I couldn't even finish before I began retching, falling to my knees in the cramped bathroom of our cabin.

Yes, this was the real thing. Jesse and I were doing this again.

I lay low around camp, as much as I could. I told Laurie right away, but no one else. Summer camp was in full swing, a new crop of children arriving each week, the whole place bustling with energy and songs and games. Even at the very reasonable hour of nine o'clock, the camp's chapel gathering came far too early each morning. I gritted my teeth leading it, trying to offer stories and fun prayers while desperately wishing I was sitting on my bathroom floor. I was determined not to throw up in front of all the sweet, young campers. Hiding out in our cabin whenever I could throughout the day, I nibbled saltines, eventually graduating to waffles, a safe bet from the last two pregnancies. I slept. I stopped running, too weak to hack the trails.

I wasn't so scared though, not yet. I had never miscarried; those early weeks and months seemed relatively straightforward. But I was terrified for later. The thought of being trusted with a newborn again left me shaking. How were we allowed to have another baby? Wasn't there some cosmic law against getting another chance? I tried to believe that it hadn't been our fault, and still the guilt ran deep.

As I was busy filling my days with fighting nausea and trying to sleep and inexplicably, miraculously growing a new person, I was also working hard on my exit strategy. I didn't really want to leave Tahoe, Laurie, or Fritz's ashes and his tree, but my work at the parish in Reno left me feeling angry and empty. As had been foretold at my birthday dinner, the job at All Souls in Berkeley was indeed coming open. I worked for weeks on the application. It required long essay responses, and I dug in hard, playing with words, enjoying the writing, delighting in the chance to do something hopeful. I loved the people of All Souls, I could tell they loved me, and I so longed to be with them again.

It was an odd dance, stepping into a real search full of other highly qualified candidates, as someone already in the system. I had collaborated with various members of the search committee; it felt in some ways like I was writing letters to friends. They invited me for a Skype interview. The week leading up to the interview, however, Phil and his wife, Sarah, and their children came to be at camp with us. We had arranged months earlier for him to come and serve as my visiting chaplain that week, for his boys to be campers and for Sarah to be the camp nurse.

Big questions hung in the air between us, teasing, intimating, wondering. He could not and would not promise me anything about the job, though. I was grateful for his integrity, his determination to run a real and careful search, even as his silence was driving me mad. Still, it seemed like he was trying to drop me sneaky, hopeful hints.

One day, we sat in the late afternoon sun, planning for chapel, when he changed the subject abruptly. "Just so you know, Liz, I'm not going to be at the parish retreat this fall."

I cocked my head, confused. "Oh yeah?"

"Yeah," he went on. "It's my fortieth birthday that weekend, and I'm going to New Orleans with friends."

I stared at him, narrowing my eyes. "Why are you telling me this, Phil?"

He grinned, playful. "Because you're my friend? Because you'd want to know my birthday plans?" He offered it as a question, a thinly veiled clue.

I shook my head at him. "You are horrible, you know that?"

We went back to planning, but my head spun. The only reason he would be telling me about his birthday plans now was to give me fair warning that I'd be on my own leading that retreat, one of the biggest events of the church year, to give me more time to wrap my head around it. I sighed.

I gave him a few days to guess that I was pregnant. He'd done so immediately with Fritz, uncannily so. I was still in seminary and living next door to the church. I took a pregnancy test, excitedly saw the positive result, and a half hour later had to walk next door to help set up for our Lenten dinner program.

As Phil and I set up tables and chairs, he turned to me, out of the blue, and asked, "So, when do you think Alice is going to have a little brother or sister?"

I looked at him, shocked, mouth open. We were friends by that point, but not usually this forward, certainly not while we were working. He stopped, looking at me directly, instantly knowing—I have no poker face.

"Seriously?" he exclaimed.

I stared, still stunned. "Q-quiet!" I finally stammered, and we walked away from the parishioners.

"How far along are you?" he probed gleefully.

"I found out half an hour ago."

Now his jaw dropped. "I can't believe you!"

I grinned, shaking my head. "You cannot tell anyone!"

This time was different. No one knew what to expect from us, and it was only the thoughtless ones who wormed their way into conversations about our reproductive game plan. Even if Phil suspected, he would leave it to me.

I wanted my story out in the open, though. I wanted Phil to have my back, and I also wanted to be aboveboard in the job search. It was way too early to tell the search committee, but Phil should know.

We went walking on the beach just before dinner. The campers were all back at their cabins, and it was quiet except for the crashing waves. We walked across the smooth rocks, with Fritz's tree up above and the water stretching out beside us.

After a long silence, I started in. "I'm pregnant again," I told him, abruptly, quietly, my voice rising at the end more than I intended, as if it might be a question, I was still that unsure.

"Whoa," he said, slowly, warmly, stretching out the vowels. He could see it was complicated, raw, good. "Whoa," he said again, more excitedly. "How's that feel?"

Permission for it to be complicated. A relief.

My eyes brimmed with tears, catching me off guard. "It's really good, it's what we wanted. . . ." I trailed off. "And it's so much. It's terrifying."

He nodded. We kept walking.

"And it's kind of wild timing, too," I added eventually. "I'm due in mid-February. Maybe less than ideal?" I left off the rest, that it would be less than ideal to have a baby so soon after starting a new job.

He knew what I meant. "It's never good timing, really." He pushed away my concern. "We will—" He caught himself, his eyes flickering. "You will make it work."

I smiled at him. His poker face was much better than mine, but just then he wasn't trying hard at all.

Phil left camp on Saturday. My interview was on Monday, scheduled late in the day, thankfully, meaning I was less likely to have to leave the room to throw up. I prepared far more than I needed to, but I wanted—no, *needed*—the job. Not for my career, though that would be helpful. I needed it because I thought I could heal there in Berkeley, at All Souls. I thought I could survive there, learn to live again. Friends helped me brainstorm likely questions. Jesse quizzed me on them, helping me to think through all the different examples and stories I wanted to touch on. I was so nervous, but it felt exhilarating to be thinking about something other than keeping babies alive.

I went overboard. Because it was a Skype interview, I realized, it could be like an open-book exam. I typed notes for myself, ways I wanted to engage questions I thought the committee members would ask me. I printed them out in thirty-point type, taping them to a music stand and the bookshelf, just behind the computer screen.

The search committee was still getting set up when we began Skyping.

"One sec," Phil called from outside the camera's reach.

A moment later, he popped back into the meeting room, his back to the camera. When he moved, I saw that he'd placed an icon on the ledge of the whiteboard.

"Just to set the ambiance," he said to the group, winging a barely perceptible wink toward the computer.

It was an icon of Jesus raising Lazarus from the dead, Martha weeping and helping to unbind her risen brother at the mouth of the cave. It was the icon I had written to Phil and to All Souls a year earlier as a gift of thanks. (Traditionally, icons are said to be written, not painted, because they are considered a form of prayer, a way of sharing our sacred stories.) I had wanted to leave that place well. The people there had seen me through much. After my mom died, they had helped me to live again, to trust in the resurrection in my own body, to step toward ordination. I had spent hours and hours hunched over that slab of wood, carefully painting the bodies, bringing light to the scene, in thanksgiving for that way of resurrection. And here it was, staring back at me through the grainy screen, beckoning me home. That's what All Souls was about, I remembered, gratefully, relieved.

Resurrection. Unbinding one another. The freedom of life returning. I was not wrong to hang my hope here.

The next morning, I threw up, first thing. Still pregnant. That was the one good thing about how sick I was: it was a daily affirmation that my body was occupied, that the clump of cells was still happily dividing inside me. I puzzled over my breakfast, only nibbling around the edges, shoving it back and forth, passing time. I headed down the path to the outdoor chapel, a rustic open-air amphitheater of huge tree trunks half buried sideways into the hillside. I was dragging the box of songbooks over to set up for morning chapel when my phone buzzed.

A text from Phil. "Can we check in this morning?"

My stomach plummeted, then came crashing back up. I dropped the books, bending to heave into the sagebrush. Pregnancy and nerves did not mix well. We'd finished the interview not even fourteen hours earlier. Why did he want to talk already? What did this mean?

"I'm about to lead chapel, but I should have a little time before I have to drive to Reno. Call you at 9:45?" I texted.

"Perfect," he sent back.

My stomach twisted further as I climbed the railroad-tie stairs up to the church. I stood in the entryway, hiding behind the thick wooden doors, shaking, peering through the darkened sanctuary and then out the window to the lake. It was a day like any other, clear, lovely. I shook. I turned to take hold of the thick rope, pulling down hard with both hands to ring the church bell, calling the campers to chapel.

The minutes crept by in chapel as we sang and reflected on some story or other. I didn't know if I wanted time to move more quickly or more slowly. I still thought I might throw up in front of the campers.

After a truncated and very distracted chapel service, I dismissed the kids to their morning adventures. I walked back to our cabin, conscious of my heartbeat hammering through my chest, and closed myself in the back bedroom. Sitting up on the bed, I gazed out the window, trying to ground myself. I took a deep breath and dialed.

Phil answered promptly, his voice chipper. "How are you?"

I shook my head. He knew how I was; we'd talked just last night.

"I'm fine, Phil. How are you?" I answered flatly.

"Doing well," he returned.

I had no interest in pleasantries. "So what's up? What did you want to talk about?"

He paused. I held my breath.

"I want to invite you to come join in building up the kingdom of God here on the corner of Cedar and Spruce," he said steadily. I could hear the smile in his voice.

Blood came flooding into my face. Had I heard him right? Was this really happening? "Wow," I said simply. "Wow, thank you."

I was stunned. As broken as I was, they wanted me. All Souls was calling me home.

Into the Water

Even pregnant, even landing what I kept describing to people as my dream job, even raising Alice, this precocious two-and-a-half-year-old—even with all these good things, so much of me still felt dead. It was the kind of dead that can creep, engulfing more, claiming ever more life for itself. A parasitic kind of grief, gangrenous in its hunger to consume everything. It was enough to make me miss all of the life carrying on right around me, right inside me even, if I let it. I sensed the constant risk of getting stuck, trapped in a permanent block of grief.

I needed help, daily, stepping out and shaking loose the threat.

Laurie could help; I had known that. That had always been true. And I believed the lake could help, a depth that could hold me, catch me, envelop me. The lake could pull me out of myself, return me to the shore a little more alive.

For some time, Laurie had been taking on what she called Thirty-Day Challenges. She tried out a new practice for a month, to see how it changed her, or not. Taking things on and giving them up, both: starting a meditation practice, giving up sugar, and so on. Some stuck, and some were just interesting experiments. It sounded like a good approach to me.

In the midst of all the deadness, at the beginning of the summer, back in the middle of the waiting to get pregnant and the waiting to hear about the job, I had proposed a joint Thirty-Day Challenge: jumping in the lake, together, every day. Laurie had readily accepted.

When we started in the beginning of June, the water was still frigid— not that Lake Tahoe's water ever really warms up much. The mountain range rising on the far side was still covered in slowly melting snow, trickling into the lake. It was cold enough to make us scream and holler and jump about, and this was at least half the point.

As the weeks progressed, we fell into a rhythm. Our swims weren't generally long, at least to begin with. It was more difficult to find the time than we had expected, charging through full days of camp life, with Laurie feeding the whole camp and me alternating between throwing up, running after Alice, and trying to keep up with my work at the camp and the parish. After the dinner dishes were finished, we would find each other and walk down the crumbling cement staircase to the beach. By then the light was waning, softening into a warmth that bathed the green-and-brown hillside in yellows and pinks. The cloudy days were my favorite, the ones when fire and coals lit the whole sky in the evening, righteous, excessive, indulgent, reflecting off the surface of the lake.

Our only rule was that we fully submerge our bodies each day. All the way in, all the way under. Sometimes we swam, but when the evening air rushed cool against us, we just waded out through the long shallows until we came to a pool, barely two feet deep, where we could lie down, quickly sinking under before flashing up, whipping our hair back to the sky. Even that was enough. Cold enough to stop my breath and force me to start it again. Deep enough for me to slough off that day's deadness and leave it there, lingering in the shallows, waiting to be washed out, churned down to the depths.

Laurie and I took a photo of ourselves each day, together, at the beach. The jump-in-the-lake challenge seemed like the sort of practice that warranted proof. I needed something concrete to show that the corroding effects of grief could be stayed. I needed to see in my own eyes that there was still life inside me. Laurie and the water—they could pull that life back, make it clear. The photos surprised me. My head, thrown back in laughter. The two of us, leaning back against the boulders, absorbing their warmth, still radiating after the sun had gone. Alice, jumping into the frame, covered in sand, Laurie catching her with me, for me. Laurie held me up. The water did, too; it did not let me sink.

Thirty days came and went, and we continued, eager to see what kind of a streak we could manage together. We knew by now that this would be our last summer at the lake together, and we wanted to make the most of it. I realized I was trying to live it well, with Laurie, with the lake. I was trying to live.

Withering Tree

I walked by Fritz's aspen often. I was glad we'd planted it so centrally in camp, rather than up the hill toward the highway, where I never had any reason to go. Sometimes I walked to his tree just to be there, close. Other times I passed by it, slowing on the path on the way to the kayaks. I could also see it from down in the water. I watched its tender leaves flutter as I sat on a stump in the campfire circle each night. Jesse and I took turns dragging the hose down from a spigot at the campfire to water the tree. We waited as the water filled the berm of dirt and wood chips around the trunk, swirling the dust on its surface, sinking slowly down to the roots.

The days grew hot and we grew busier. One day I walked by Fritz's tree and saw the leaves looking limp. Some were turning brown around the edges. I ran to pull the hose down, to soak it well. It had been some time, I realized, since I'd last watered it, and I wondered if Jesse had done any better.

It was oddly satisfying to notice that I was not obsessed with this tree. I was swimming each day. I was beginning to pack and plan for our move back to Berkeley. My morning sickness was still unpleasant but waning some. I was doing good work with the camp and trying to end well at my parish in Reno. I had not forgotten Fritz—I had, for a few days, forgotten to water his tree. It was rather pathetic, the withering memorial tree, but it also seemed strangely hopeful: other things were thriving. By summer's end, some of the branches were clearly dead. When a friend who had worked at a nursery visited camp, he offered to help me prune it. In theory it seemed like an excellent idea, but I put it off. The days of his visit passed, and still I could not walk to that tree holding clippers.

That was how we left it as we packed our life back into boxes, just a year and three months after we had moved to the lake, turning around to go back to Berkeley. I watched as friends loaded our possessions into the rented moving truck, backed up our dirt driveway to the cabin exactly as the ambulance had done. I directed the helpful traffic this time, unable to do the heavy lifting, just as had been the case when we'd moved in, when I'd been pregnant with Fritz. Everything was in flux, even as we made ready to return to a known home. We finally pulled away, the truck packed, the tree's drying leaves quaking behind us.

Demanding the Coroner

It had now been more than seven months, and still we did not know why Fritz had died. All they had told us after the autopsy was that his ureters— the two little tubes that empty liquid from the kidneys into the bladder—

had been very swollen. The swelling was bad, but it didn't seem like the kind of thing that would kill a baby, the doctor had said. And so we waited. Somewhere in Sacramento there was a file all about our son's body. His body was back in the earth, but the file remained, waiting for someone to make sense of it. The hospital had insisted his body be sent there for the autopsy; it was the closest place they could find a coroner who specialized in pediatrics. What a job, I thought, cringing. It must take superhuman fortitude to be a pediatric coroner.

I had tried to push the topic of autopsy from my mind, but wondering bits snuck in anyway. How would they cut him open? What tools did they use? Were they kind? Respectful? Did it even matter if the people were gentle?

It mattered to me. I hated that they had to cut him open to have a chance at finding answers. I also hated that they had, in the end, refused to let us donate his organs. Although I had asked about it in the hospital that night and had been told there was time to make that decision later, the coroner's office eventually said that it was either/or—organ donation or autopsy—and that the autopsy took precedence. And, yes, clearly we needed answers more than we needed to donate his organs.

And still there were no answers.

Jesse periodically called to inquire. They told him that the state was quite backlogged, understaffed, and it would likely be a long time.

As my pants started to grow tight around my waist, I lost my patience. Soon I would have my first ultrasound, and dammit, I needed to know what we should be looking for with this third child, what might be wrong but could still be helped. It was ridiculous for the medical examiners not to tell us, I thought. It was irresponsible.

Jesse called again, mustering his best angry, grieving-parent voice. He explained calmly but very pointedly that I was pregnant again, and that they simply had to give us answers. They had to do their job, had to give us a report, so that we could have a chance at keeping the new baby safe.

It worked. They relented, jumping our case to the front. The coroner's report arrived in the rusty mailbox of our Berkeley apartment. Here, in the very same apartment we'd lived in before, owned by the church, we were finally going to have answers. It seemed a hollow thing to celebrate, these sheets of paper that I could not bear to read myself.

I sat across the living room from Jesse. I watched him, studying his face for clues as he sat cross-legged on my mother's couch, reading the reports slowly, intently. Without warning, he burst out laughing. I was horrified. How could something possibly be funny in the coroner's report about our son?

"What?" I exclaimed.

He kept laughing.

"Jesse, what is it?"

He tried to answer me, but he was still laughing, bending over now, wiping his eyes. He finally caught his breath. "It's the toxicology report," he explained. "It's where they look for drugs and alcohol and other substances in his blood."

"So?" I asked.

"The only thing present," he said, beginning to laugh again, "was caffeine."

I smiled. "That actually is pretty funny. Not at all surprising, but funny."

Jesse smiled back.

I was grateful for the surprise of levity. "Poor kid must have been buzzed by my breast milk. I can't believe he always slept so well."

Jesse went on reading the report. There were answers, ultimately. The ends of Fritz's ureters had been partially covered by tiny flaps of skin, a simple congenital abnormality. The flaps could have easily been removed had anyone known they were there—but they weren't big enough to see on an ultrasound. The errant flaps allowed most of the fluid from Fritz's kidneys to pass normally into his bladder, but some of the fluid backed up. Eventually, it got infected. The infection then progressed into his kidneys, they said, and finally into his blood. He had urosepsis: essentially, a urinary tract infection that jumped into his blood.

It was so simple, so preventable, yet also impossible to detect. Because he was so young, he hadn't shown the typical symptoms. No fever, ever. His oxygen levels were fine. That's why the urgent care doctor couldn't tell.

But we had an answer now. Awful, but simple and clear. It was neither the madness of SIDS nor the horrible label "inconclusive cause of death"—the one that would have left us squarely in the unknown, the inexplicable. We could work with the information in the coroner's report; we could look for those awful flaps in the new baby. The answer gave us a chance.

Endless Scanning

The scans began early and continued often. I was working with midwives again, planning to deliver at home again, and deeply relieved to be back in Berkeley, with the same midwives who had delivered Alice, whom I trusted completely. And we were much more cautious this time.

I had begun my dream job as the associate rector at All Souls, which came with the added bonus of real, excellent health insurance. I explained to the first ultrasound technician what our situation was, and within ten minutes, the neonatologist had taken her place. He scoured the images of my tiny baby, my abdomen only just beginning to swell. It was too early to see anything definitive, but he assured me that by twenty weeks, he should be able to tell.

I returned then, halfway through, with Alice and Jesse in tow. Alice struggled to make out the grainy image we kept insisting was a baby.

"You want to know the sex?" the tech asked.

"Absolutely," I responded without hesitation. I may be the least patient person I know.

"You're having a boy," she said gently. Maybe she had read our complicated chart. Maybe she was just tender.

A shiver ran down the back of my neck. Another boy. I hadn't known what I wanted, or if I cared. But another boy, I thought. It was Sam. He was actually here.

The head neonatologist once again replaced the tech, swiveling on the low stool, and began taking images of his urinary tract from every angle.

"A normal ultrasound machine wouldn't be able to detect something as small as the ureters," he narrated. "But this one, it's much stronger, it would show up here."

I began breathing easier. They could catch it this time. The doctor talked his way through everything he was looking at, naming off how each body part looked absolutely normal. It was generous of him, I thought, to give me all those assurances.

He spun on his stool to face me and handed me a towel for my slippery belly. "Your baby looks great," he said. "Everything is developing perfectly normally."

I loved that word, *normally*.

"As far as I'm concerned, I don't need to see you back for another six to eight weeks. And," he went on, "I can imagine you might be feeling pretty nervous. I'm going to email you so that you can respond directly to me—it's a way to sort of hack our appointment system—and if at any point you want to have another ultrasound, you just let me know. We can do them every week if you need to. I'll make your insurance cover it. The important thing is that you be able to relax."

I looked at him, eyes wide. "Thank you" was all I could muster, grateful that he understood.

Prenatal care was a mixed bag, though, and unpredictable.

My midwives worked in a team: two of them, plus some apprentices. We switched off who I saw at a given appointment so that I would be well connected to them all, and comfortable working with whoever was on call when the baby came.

Michelle was my favorite: strong, smart, and still so gentle. She had delivered Alice, and she was unafraid of hearing about Fritz, of that whole part of my story. She knew I was terrified, and she was ready to talk about that, to invite my fear into the room. She wanted to learn all about him.

The other midwife was impressively experienced. Leah had delivered more than three thousand babies over the previous thirty years. She knew her stuff. And I felt hopeful: Michelle asked me one day if I had known that Leah had lost a baby, too. I hadn't, but this seemed to bode well. She would understand me, I thought.

I asked Leah about it at my next appointment. Her baby had been older than Fritz, ten months. They had gone camping as a family, and when they woke in the morning he was dead in the tent, just like that. They called it SIDS. She went on to have more children after him.

A month later, I was lying on my back as Leah kneaded my stomach, measuring the baby, checking his position.

Without warning, she launched in. "Have you considered the possibility that this baby might be Fritz returning to you?" she asked.

I gaped. Had I heard her correctly? Had she really just asked me that, in all earnestness? She hummed along, continuing her work. The apprentice stood with her back to us, I couldn't tell her reaction.

"No," I finally answered, firmly. "No, I hadn't considered that possibility. I am pretty sure that this baby is his own person."

I was reeling, offended, but more than anything, hurt. Leah was supposed to get it! I had known she was kind of woo-woo, but now she was suggesting that this baby was Fritz reincarnated? It was too much. This was a new one, though, a totally Berkeley spin on the wild things people had been saying to me about my dead son. I knew my baby would be safe if it worked out that Leah delivered him, but I began hoping fervently for Michelle to be the one on call. I wanted him to be caught by someone who understood him to be his own person.

The baby was kicking now, and I could eat again. Each morning still began with me on the bathroom floor, as a matter of course, but I was feeling pretty human the rest of the time. My body knew how to do this. It was familiar territory. It was my heart that was reeling, staggering, unsure. If he was still for too long, I would jostle my belly, waking him, bothering him. Move please, baby. Please show me you're well, baby, show me you're fine. I was sure it was obnoxious of me, but I needed it. I needed this boy to stay alive.

7

INCARNATE

IИCVᴚИVTE

Tending the Body

When I received the documents regarding my mother's death, Jesse and I had already returned home to California from her funeral, absorbed her furniture into our apartment, started back to work and school. Life was attempting normalcy.

At first, I hadn't even known the documents existed. My mother's hospital records and coroner's report were not offered to me, by either officials or family members, the prevailing assumption being that they would be too much for me. I learned only from casual conversation with my stepsister that the records existed and were available; she had assumed I knew.

"Do you want them?" she asked, maybe surprised, a twinge of concern in her voice.

"Yes, of course I do, please send them!" I insisted, incensed that she had

203

received them before me. I expected the documents to be gruesome. Still, I had to read them.

They arrived by email in October, a month and a half after my mother had died.

The more I learn about death, the more I wish I had forced the powers that be to delay my mother's cremation, to wait for me to get there. I had wanted to see her body; I wanted to weep over her and kiss her forehead and hold her hands. I did not know at the time that I could have demanded that. She died, and then it sounded like all the arrangements were in motion, like there was nothing I could do to stop the process. I suspect now that everyone was trying to protect me; I did not know I had agency in the matter.

The hospital records and coroner's report were the closest I would come to seeing my mother one more time. Through these pages I could reach out to trace the body that carried me, kneeling in reverence before the crushed womb that was once my home.

Holding my laptop, I sat on her couch—now transported to California— and cautiously opened the PDFs, obviously scanned from poor, grainy photocopies.

"Do you want me to read them with you?" Jesse offered. He watched me, with some mix of concern and curiosity. Was I really up for this? Was this actually a good idea?

"Not yet," I said firmly. "I think I need to do this myself." I couldn't pay attention to anyone else right then, not even to someone caring for me. I needed to give all my focus to my mother's body, six weeks too late, separated by half a continent and the ruthless fury of the crematorium. My eyes darted from one line to the next, devouring information as I carefully scrolled, trying to see what had actually happened that August morning.

My mother didn't die right away. Everyone had told me that she did. I didn't know what information they'd had at the time, since it was all so scrambled at first. And I suspected it may have also been a nod toward solace, reassuring me that at least she had felt no pain.

This was not true.

Her end was far worse. She jumped at 7:18 a.m., the official documents said, and landed in the courtyard between the parking garage and an adjoining hotel. There had been three witnesses, two in the garage, one down in the courtyard below. When the EMTs arrived, minutes later, she was alert. The words in the hospital report were straightforward: "Appears to be in severe distress." She was screaming in anguish, incoherently, I learned, as she writhed on the ground.

I forced myself to imagine the scene: ambulance and fire truck filling the small downtown side street, paramedics piling through the hotel and parking garage to where she lay in the courtyard. Cop cars blocking traffic, redirecting cars up toward the courthouse. People arriving at the parking garage from another street, intending to begin their workdays but finding a suicide scene. I wondered how much blood spilled on the pavement. The report didn't say.

The EMTs took her first to the hospital in Bloomington, where she had been just the night before for a routine check as part of her DUI. They worked to intubate her; she resisted, but they succeeded. They pushed propofol to sedate her, because she was flailing, thrashing, making their work harder. They x-rayed her bones, revealing that fewer were broken than I had imagined. Her pelvis was shattered. Her heel was broken, and her humerus. She was small but tough, I thought, to jump from that high and not even break her legs. This was so like her. They did CT scans with her pelvis wrapped tight in a bedsheet, a futile attempt to stabilize it. Massive internal bleeding, as expected. They gave her four units of blood. I made a mental note that I should donate again when I was done breastfeeding, grateful to all the strangers who tried to save her with their own blood.

And then they realized the limits at the local hospital. Her bleeding was too extensive, her pelvis too crushed for them to help her in Bloomington. At 10:30 that morning, they loaded my mother into a LifeLine helicopter, flying her to a trauma center in Indianapolis.

My mother died in the air, at 10:45 a.m., nearly three and a half hours after she'd jumped.

Thomas in My Stead

The first name of the person who performed the autopsy was Thomas. I tried to remember what *DO* stood for, the letters that followed his name. I googled the letters, then googled his name. He was a doctor of osteopathy. In my haze, it didn't occur to me that googling him would also show me his face. I closed the browser quickly, afraid to see the person who got to do my part, being the last one to care for my mother's body. I didn't want to know, I thought. But soon my curiosity got the best of me, and I searched his name again.

Thomas was younger than I expected, I guessed probably thirty-five, going by the year he graduated from college. He was already beginning to bald, but he shared a wide smile into the camera, his dark eyes shining, dimples softening his young face further. I glanced through his CV. All the way at the bottom, below all the education and fellowships and employment, was a list of his favorite pastimes, which included fishing, playing board games, and spending quality time with his wife and kids. My shoulders dropped, loosening. I trusted this guy. He seemed warm, I told myself, hoping he'd been kind to her.

I began reading. Thomas received my mother's body unclad. Rigor mortis had not yet set in, he wrote, and the body was still warm to the touch. Oh, how I wished they were my hands, receiving that lingering warmth, the last vestiges of her life still departing. *Unclad* only meant she wasn't wearing clothes, I soon realized, but there were things all over her body: a pulse oximeter around her left pointer finger, a bandage on her left wrist, a pelvic harness for stabilization, defibrillator pads on her back and chest, a blood pressure cuff on her left arm, multiple EKG pads, an endotracheal tube, an oral gastric tube, an Ace bandage on her right upper arm around the fracture, chest tubes, arterial lines, a soft cast also on her right arm, a white bandage on her foot, and a medical ID bracelet on her left wrist.

Defibrillator pads, I read again. I imagined them adhered to her chest, where I had nestled every night as a child, listening to her read, calming myself to her heartbeat, slowly falling asleep. They tried to jump-start her heart when she died, one last-ditch effort to bring her back. The reality of her death was still setting in for me.

Thomas wrote that my mother was five foot six. It was not true. I loved her body, knew her body in a way that no medical expert could.

"She was five feet and one inch tall," I said out loud. I wanted to submit edits, make this final record accurate.

The cause of death was simple, and obvious: blunt force trauma to the back and pelvis, due to jumping off a building. Manner of death: suicide. These rulings, these descriptions, these were not why I came here, why I opened this report. I wanted to see her, to imagine her even at her most broken, to love her even there, even like that. I wanted to tend her body.

Thomas got to touch her body, examine her wounds, ask the questions. Thomas, in the Gospel of John, is the so-called doubter, the questioner, ultimately the believer. But this body was dead, without question. It was this doctor's job to ascertain the death, to describe it, to classify its manner and cause, to catalog it. Still, John's story of Thomas's reaching out for Jesus stuck with me, moved through me. He understood that Jesus's actual body mattered, that his wounds were important even in his rising. We almost never talk like this, sharing the real details, the full truth, about our bodies—especially not when they are broken. It's considered impolite, maybe even gruesome, shocking. I understand why—but that same arresting intimacy is the primal expression of our care, of the love I longed to offer my mother's body one more time, to care for it, to reach out and behold it, saying that everything that happened to her body did, in fact, matter. I believed that, but now I could only share that love through words on a page.

I glanced at the bottom line, included almost as an afterthought. Her toenails, Thomas noted, were painted purple. Yes! This was what I wanted to know. I exhaled, smiling, beginning to laugh, tears streaming. This was my mother: unable to beat back the demon of booze but dying still with purple toenails. It was bittersweet. It was gorgeous, the playful sass of her; this was the Susan I loved.

She Already Tried

I've said that my mother's suicide was an absolute surprise to me. It shouldn't have been. I read deeper into the hospital records, going back in time. Down below all the EMT reports, the CT scans, the helicopter ride, and the toxicology labs were older records from the same local hospital.

On July 9, not seven weeks before her death, she had been admitted. On the intake form under "Social History" was "Occasional use of alcohol"— that was one way to put it, I thought.

I knew that she had gone on a bad bender back in July. She was supposed to be teaching a summer session class at Indiana University and instead got blasted. I knew that my brother had gotten her into a rehab center but could only request a seventy-two-hour hold; after that, it was all up to her. Rehab centers were of no use to her, she told me later. She had already learned what she could from them. She knew what she had to do; she just needed to go to meetings and stick with her plan. I didn't believe her, I thought more help might make a difference, but I was as powerless as she.

I read on. The July 9 admission came after a stranger found my mother facedown in a random driveway. She had with her one bottle of Listerine and another of vanilla extract. The stranger called 911, and at 1:59 a.m., she was taken by ambulance to the hospital. In those early hours of the morning, conscious but still drunk, she admitted to drinking a bottle of vodka, too, with the intent of harming herself. The doctor recorded the event as a suicide attempt but noted that she "would not admit why she wants to harm herself."

Her jump from the parking garage wasn't just an impulsive choice after all. I turned this new, ghastly information over in my brain. She had been working toward oblivion for years, I knew. But that she said so, said it aloud, to another person? This was more grim and heartbreaking than I had imagined. She had been looking into that chasm for some time. She had tried to put on a good face for me, even as she was trying to find her way through the anguish, her way to end.

It was what she had wanted, and she had already tried.

8

BIRTHING

BIKLHINC

Isn't It Sweet?

In the fall of 2014, we had begun to settle back into Berkeley, into our old rhythms. We were even living in our same old apartment in the parish house, the same apartment where Alice was born, the one my mom had helped paint bright white and lavender and two shades of green as Jesse and I got ready to become parents. The old white building was more decrepit now, three years on, paint chipping further off, wiring and plumbing finicky at best. But living here was part of my compensation for working at All Souls, and we certainly couldn't afford anything market rate in Berkeley. Even better: I no longer had any kind of commute; I just walked out along the wooden balcony, running the length of the building, down the mossy wooden stairs that bowed underfoot, through the fog, and across the broken cement of the parking lot to the church each morning. In September the days grew hot, the fog long gone by evening. Our house sat right on the corner of Cedar and Oxford, two fairly busy streets, corridors up through and parallel to the Berkeley Hills, and their pavement continued radiating the day's heat well past dusk.

Alice had just turned three. One evening I was carrying clean laundry up from the dank laundry room in the basement, with Alice tagging along. The basket felt unreasonably heavy against my swelling belly—everything felt heavy, being pregnant again. It was dark out by now, the moon and the streetlights lighting our way past the overgrown jasmine and rosemary.

To reach our back door, we rounded the cement stairs, which were ever so slowly crumbling away from the old building. Alice hung on to my pocket, swinging through each step. She stopped halfway up the six steps to the landing, turning around and looking up at me.

"Mama!" she yelled, begging my attention, though I was right beside her. "Mama, isn't it sweet that Grandma Susan is holding baby Fritz?"

I set down the basket, steadying it from toppling down the dusty stairs. "What's that, sweetheart?" I had heard her but couldn't quite believe that I had. Her words had come out of nowhere.

"Isn't it sweet that Grandma Susan is holding baby Fritz?" she said again, clearly, and adamant. "Isn't that sweet, Mama?"

She still couldn't say her *r*'s properly; they came out as lovely cherubic *w*'s: *Guwandma* Susan is holding baby *Fawitz*.

"Gosh, yes," I stammered. "Yes, love, that's wonderful." I didn't know how she could have come up with this. I certainly hadn't told her that all dead people hang out together, or that her grandma and brother would have found each other on the other side.

"Yes," I said again, "that is really sweet. Thank you for reminding me of that. . . ." My voice trailed off. She didn't need to hear the rest, not yet.

Maybe when Alice was older, I would tell her that I didn't trust my mom alone with her, that Jesse and I had jigsawed our schedules so we wouldn't have to leave our new baby home alone with her grandmother. If she drank when John and I were little, why wouldn't she with Alice? Still, I'd agonized over the simple decision we'd made not to trust her. Was it overbearing, too controlling? Should I lighten up and let grandmother and granddaughter enjoy each other? I could not settle easily, no matter the choice.

But now? A strange comfort came over me. My mom was free. Wherever she was, however she was, I didn't believe she was still drunk and doomed and out of control. Wherever she and Fritz were, she could hold my baby, somehow, in my stead. Finally, it was a good thing for her to be with my child without me.

I was still standing, stunned, on the concrete stairs, leaning against the old wicker laundry basket, which had also been my mom's. Alice had already started up the next flight of stairs into our apartment, out of sight, her usual clamor rattling behind her. She had simply been narrating her world to me. Her world included such obvious things as her dead grandmother and dead baby brother, snuggling somewhere beyond us.

It was sweet, she'd told me, and it was.

Birthday Cake

I wondered if Karen, the midwives' apprentice, had told Michelle, my favorite midwife, about the strange reincarnation conversation I'd had with Leah. If so, did Karen let on how horrified I sounded at the senior midwife's suggestion that my new baby might be Fritz reincarnated and returning to me? It seemed possible that she had. And Michelle herself was intuitive and generous. My anxiety rose higher as the weeks ticked by and my belly grew rounder.

Michelle paused during one of our weekly routine checkups. Taking my shoulders in her hands as my legs dangled off the table, she made a promise: "I want you to know that I'll be the one to deliver your baby, no matter who is on call when the time comes."

The words settled on me, pouring comfort through layers of fear that resided even deeper in me than I could have known.

"Really?" I managed. "You can do that?" I didn't know how the midwives organized themselves exactly, but this seemed like a significant gift to offer. Michelle had little kids of her own, and her nights off were precious.

"I will be there," she said simply. She wasn't going to tell me what sacrifices she would have to make for it to be so. It just was.

"That's what I want," I said, my voice cracking. "I really want it to be you again."

I lived in fear now. There was no fighting or escaping it. I was restless, making this baby dance for me, asking him endlessly to show me he was alive, pushing on my belly to make him wriggle. I tried to harness myself toward strength again, too. In my third trimester, I was feeling well enough to run. I had been frustrated for the first six months, not being able to run. It wasn't just being sick to my stomach, but feeling weak, cooped up. I strained to remember how to breathe without running. It was even harder to sit with all my fears.

Fritz's first birthday neared. I had to be able to run through it, at least a little bit.

How do you celebrate your dead son's first birthday? Jesse and I had no idea. We had to follow Alice's lead. At three, she was unafraid. She still didn't know how awful this all was, except for how oddly his death made us act. She opened her closet and rocked back on her heels to tug out the box of party supplies. I watched from the doorway, slumped against the frame, as she flung off the plastic lid and began digging through the contents. I hadn't planned to decorate. She disagreed. She found the string of tie-dyed banners we hang up on birthdays and threw them in my direction, then continued searching. She emerged, triumphant, holding a small birthday balloon on a stick that she had convinced me to buy from the checkout lane of some grocery store ages before.

She sprang to her feet, jumping and spinning, beginning to sing: "Hooray! Yippee! I'm going to wave my flag around for dear life! It's Fritz's birthday! We're going to have cake today, today!"

It was a good day for her. This was her normal: a dead brother. She knew that people celebrate birthdays with cake. That could be our starting point. She and I made a chocolate cake, and we ate great thick wedges, the ganache oozing down. Alice sang "Happy Birthday," but I could not. I could only watch, weeping as she sang, weeping as she blew out the lone candle. My slice was salty, wet with tears.

At the same time, though, this new boy kept growing. The generous neonatologist's scans continued, each one assuring me for a couple of weeks that he remained healthy. Everything looked totally normal, they told us, though nothing about my life felt normal anymore.

I kept running, slowly. I was making a strange, short pilgrimage, I realized, stepping through the days when Fritz had been alive. It was its own brief season, upon which was overlaid Advent and Christmas and New Year's and all the mayhem those days bring. For forty days, I could trace where we had been with him, track those days and places, feel in real time how short his life had been. It was like a strange Lent for me, those forty days. It marked the gift of life, stark only in its punishing brevity. One week old, I remembered. Almost a quarter of his life gone, I hadn't known. Christmas, with only two weeks more to live. Then so quickly, January 9: time's up. I dreaded his death day. As it neared, I plummeted in every way, my eyes clouding over, my muscles saturated with adrenaline, and my heart pumping fast, even as it was already overtaxed sustaining another baby within. I ran again. I had no choice but to run, if I was going to make it through the day.

And then, like clockwork, quite beyond my doing, another day came, and another. I'd survived the first pass through the anniversary of my baby's death. I was astonished. I was still standing.

Birth Days

My own birthday loomed, the epilogue to my pilgrim's way through Fritz's life. After his death day came my memory of the purgatorial weeks of planning, of waiting for people to gather, and then of driving to collect his ashes on my birthday. I would never be the kind of person who would coyly fib that I was turning twenty-nine again. That singular twenty-ninth birthday had very nearly been too much for me. Just as I hadn't known how to celebrate my dead son's birthday, I wasn't really sure how to go about this one of mine, either. I firmly believed that any birthday was important to celebrate. It was very good to get older. But I wasn't the person I'd been before, and the typical shenanigans for a thirtieth birthday party, whatever they might be, would feel hollow.

The idea came out of nowhere. I'd enact a spoof on the wild 12K race in San Francisco, Bay to Breakers, in which people run in zany costumes: hot-pink gorilla suits, inflatable pool toys, full body paint, elaborate centipede costumes connecting big groups of runners together as one flamboyant idea. Plenty of people run in nothing at all. The twist for mine would be cake—Bay to Cakers. It was a simple enough invitation: come run a 5K with me at the Berkeley marina, bring cake to share, or at least your appetite. At thirty-seven weeks pregnant, I didn't need much of a costume. I was already a ridiculous sight, trying to twist my legs outward to run-waddle around my now full-term baby. A tie-dyed maternity shirt, the spiral centered on my belly, was plenty.

A jumbled group of friends gathered on my thirtieth birthday. Some I'd known since middle school, others from college or seminary. There were a few parishioners, some of them teenagers from our youth group. One small dog, two big ones. We ran two laps around César Chávez Park, an old landfill turned into grassy fields next to sailboats at the marina. As the sun began to burn away the fog, the Golden Gate Bridge emerged from the dazzling haze across the water. I was the last one to finish, by a significant margin, glistening with sweat. I was also more triumphant than the rest of the runners: 3.1 miles was a real feat, made sweeter as I was cheered across the finish line by my exuberant three-year-old and my odd collection of friends. And I was grinning, sincerely, pumping my fists in the air. I had survived one year to arrive at this birthday—thirty!—and it was not to be defined by ashes. We sat down on the rocky shoreline and dug into all kinds of different cakes.

My baby's due date came and went, but I wasn't surprised. I had been preparing myself for the long haul. The extra twenty days I spent carrying Fritz were burned into my memory; I would not set my hopes on an on-time arrival. Besides, there was too much work to do—getting half of my job parceled out to willing volunteers, bringing the priest who would be subbing for me part-time up to speed. I was preparing for birth, down to the wire, just as the congregation—as a body—was preparing for Lent. We feasted on Mardi Gras, carried on together, then moved out into the courtyard to burn last year's palms late that night, creating the ashes for the next day. Gathering again on Ash Wednesday, we marked each other's foreheads with that blackened sign of the cross, a reminder of our mortality standing in stark contrast with the new life that was so ready to be born of me. Death was present, even now, even past my due date. I knew as much this time around. Nothing was a given, nothing was to be taken for granted. This new life still came in the shadow of death. The following night, Thursday, the creases of my thumb still blackened from the ashes, contractions began.

Jesse and I had taken our old bedroom back when we'd returned to this apartment, the lavender one. I dozed in between the contractions through the night, waking in the wee hours not for the new baby but for my first child. I sprang up and moved as quickly as I could, which was of course quite slowly, across the hall and into the bright light of the bathroom: Alice was suddenly vomiting all over the black-and-white tile, stricken without warning by a stomach bug. Jesse washed the floor while I helped her back to sleep in her bedroom, trying to still my writhing as a contraction hit every now and again. An hour later, at 4:00 a.m., we were all awake once more. Alice had thrown up again, this time right in her bed. My contractions were coming fast. It was time to divide and conquer. Jesse bathed Alice while I took to the living room, needing to stand now, beginning to sway through the contractions. This was really happening. I started calling my people.

First the midwife; then Laurie and my mother-in-law, each of whom was driving from three hours away; then my brother-in-law.

My other births had been intimate, just Jesse and the midwives and me. This time, I felt I needed all the help I could get. Fear kicked up in a way I had not experienced before nor have since. I didn't want to be alone in that. What if there was a complication? What if he didn't make it? I knew I could get him out—I knew my body was capable of that. I also knew I couldn't control the rest, that I could not protect him from everything. My body was already rolling toward birth, while I was becoming increasingly paralyzed by fear.

Michelle arrived at our house while the streets were still quiet, well before dawn. She greeted me warmly, taking in the scene: Alice, her hair freshly shampooed, her stomach inexplicably settled, now sat in the wooden chair I was leaning on at the dining room table. She was facing backward to hold my hands, sweetly encouraging me. Jesse was filling the birthing tub, just behind me, where the dining room portion of the room transitioned to become the living room, surrounded by an L-shaped couch on one side and my mother's fancy sofa bed on the other. My philodendron circled the room, lapping itself, same as it had multiple times around our even tinier main room in the cabin. I was moaning loudly from a deep and faraway place, unaware of any of these surroundings. Michelle got to work, setting out her instruments and supplies across the large oak table and then helping me onto my mother's couch, laying me back to check me. There was no question that this baby was coming, but I still had a long way to go. Five centimeters, she told me, her voice apologetic. My heart sank.

Minutes stretched into hours. Dawn broke, and with it the sound of morning traffic at the busy intersection three stories below. My people began showing up. First Jesse's brother, Dan, and his wife, Annie, with their eighteen-month-old daughter in tow. Then my mother-in-law, Cheri, down from the foothills. Each brought new waves of energy, relieving the team that had already been with me. Finally, Laurie made it—driving down from Tahoe in record time, and I could not have waited longer. I needed her close at hand. I wasn't making much progress, but with Laurie there, I became hopeful. After several hours Michelle offered to try breaking my water, in the hopes this might speed things up.

I had been laboring in the birthing tub, remembering keenly how good the water had been with Fritz. But six hours in, I still wasn't getting much further along. Michelle and Karen, the apprentice, coaxed me out, convincing me to move and sway and try other positions. Finally, I began to push, lying back on the couch. My mother's couch, covered in layers of old towels. It wasn't working.

"I know how to do this," I yelled at them, near tears, "and it's not fucking working!"

They helped to turn the baby more, helped me turn and flex and harness more of my strength.

"Fuck!" I yelled again. "This is fucking awful!"

"Do all priests cuss this much?" Karen asked, wide-eyed but grinning.

"They fucking do when they're giving birth!" I shot back.

I leaned back into Jesse and bore my eyes up into Laurie's as she stood a few feet away. I didn't want to be here, but she helped me remember that I was whole, that I was enough. I could tell she thought I had the strength to go on, and tried to trust her. We inched forward, the baby and I, as I yelled and thrashed and tried to focus.

Finally, his head slowly emerged.

"One more!" they said softly. "One more push!"

I heaved, wrenching, curling forward. Then he was out, into Karen's hands, placed on my chest in one swoop. I held my breath, waiting for his. I was petrified, frozen. I waited. The room was silent. No one moved.

And then he cried. Sam *breathed*. He was fine.

Jesse knelt close, kissing my wet forehead, meeting Sam. Laurie held Alice next to us, tears welling in her eyes, locking with mine. She understood, as I did, that nothing was guaranteed anymore.

On this day, too—February 20, 2015—there would be cake: a 0th birthday cake. It was a heaping chocolate layer cake, topped with a zero candle. (The candle was meant for decadal birthdays, I assumed.) It was something we had begun with Alice and then repeated for Fritz—not knowing, of course, that zero would be the only birthday Fritz would have. There was no telling how many birthdays Sam would have, either, which seemed to be even more reason for the celebratory cake right now.

Three weeks later, in the midwives' office for a postpartum checkup, I asked Michelle about the silence just after Sam was born, about my terror in that moment. What had that been like for her? How long had it really been before he'd taken a breath?

She smiled. "That? It was totally normal," she said. "I knew he would breathe. It wasn't long at all."

Running After Sam

"It's still really early to be running, Liz," Michelle said gently.

It wasn't an admonishment, exactly, simply a strong word of caution. I was in for another postpartum checkup. Sam was one month old. We were hitting the critical point, the days counting up closer toward forty. It didn't matter that all his tests were coming back perfectly—the extra ultrasounds on his own little belly, at three days old, then two weeks, the neonatal urologist calling us personally to talk through the results. I appreciated the string of good news, but I wasn't calmed much by it. It didn't help that they kept hedging: "One more test, no, just one more; oh, actually, we'll need to see him back again at six weeks." Still no definitive answer that he was healthy. Just the assurance that, so far, things looked fine. It wasn't enough. I needed to run.

"I'm just afraid you might hurt yourself," Michelle went on, kneading my belly. "Your uterus has contracted really nicely—no small thing for a third baby—but your abs are still spread pretty far apart. It's called diastasis recti, and it's really common after multiple births."

I looked at her, longing for a different answer.

"Here, let me show you." She took my fingers, placing them just above my belly button. "Now curl your head up," she said, and pushed my fingers down. "Feel that gap?"

I did.

"There isn't normally a space there. You'll need to bring those muscles back together before you can really run safely."

She pointed me to some simple exercises that would help, essentially very toned-down versions of crunches, and encouraged me to pace myself even with these. I was grateful that at least this was a tangible step in the right direction, something I could do toward running. Michelle also knew I didn't always follow directions so well.

"If you have to run, just go really slowly," she added. "Don't go far. Please listen to your body."

I smiled. I *was* listening to my body. But it was more than muscles; there were other parts of me I had to keep safe, too. I was also still afraid, confused, sad. I had to put the darkness somewhere. I needed to put it into running.

Holy Romper

We baptized Sam as quickly as we could without acting as if he were about to die. Tradition holds that any baptized Christian can baptize someone in the case of an emergency—certainly I could do it as a priest. But we also believe that it's something to be done in the midst of community, with all the people promising to support the newly baptized person throughout their life. And we traditionally do it at particular times of the year, on big feast days, when we can really turn our attention to this mysterious and wonderful and rather strange thing we mark together, when God shows up in a new way for us. Easter was the next date after Sam's birth when we would be celebrating baptisms at All Souls—I'd signed him up before he was born.

It's not that I thought babies might go to hell or some unfortunate purgatorial holding zone if they died before being baptized. An early baptism wasn't any kind of quick insurance policy. I'd always found that line of thinking ridiculous, and even more so after Fritz died. There was just no way that God would refuse anyone, I thought, much less a tiny, blameless baby.

And yet: I really, *really* did not want to baptize another dead baby. I was glad that I had done so with Fritz; it was better than the alternative of not doing it at all. And I was going to do anything to keep from going through that again with one of my own.

I spent a good chunk of time on maternity leave sewing Sam a tiny romper for the day, even though I had quietly mocked such frivolity in the past. I had some raw silk, ivory, left over from when I'd sewn my wedding dress. Laying the pattern pieces out creatively—very much like my mother in this—I had just enough of the remnants.

The sacrament was not about the clothes or the party or any of that. It was about claiming this baby as God's own and sealing him into the Body of Christ, this community, and promising to try to do right by him. And I couldn't shake from my head the images of the last time I baptized a son of mine: stark in the fluorescence of that ER, water poured out of a banged-up lavender-colored water bottle, with him dressed only in a green diaper, intubated and still covered in tape. This time, we would celebrate, fully.

I finished the collar edges by hand the night before, and sewed buttons onto the faux vest on Easter morning. It only barely fit Sam; he'd grown so much since I started three weeks earlier.

Phil had given me the choice: Did I just want to be the parent that day, or did I want to be the priest, too? I was still on leave, so I wouldn't vest or preach or lead anything else. But I could do the actual baptism if I wanted to. I did. I had to. I had to baptize both of my sons myself.

Even as much as he had grown, Sam was still tiny and floppy. By Easter Sunday, he was now only four days older than Fritz had been when he died. I juggled between nursing and changing diapers and managing Alice's energy through the service. It was harder parenting in the pews than leading up front, I thought. But we made it, and halfway through we all processed to the font at the back of the church. Someone handed me a stole and the microphone pack, which I fumbled to put on while still holding Sam. I had only ever used the mic with a robe on, and without a newborn in my arms. Absent a pocket, I clipped the mic pack to the waistband of my skirt. Phil had already started into the thanksgiving over the water, a long and involved prayer chanted while filling the white marble font and blessing the fresh water. Something felt off. I was sagging. But Alice was in Jesse's arms, watching—it wasn't her tugging at my hem. I shifted my weight to the other leg, but then felt the mic pack drop farther. It was the elastic in my skirt— too loose, too big. Already I was smaller than when I'd bought the skirt soon after giving birth. My rear end, I realized, was hanging out.

The long prayer continued. I jostled Sam into the crook of my left arm, snagged the mic pack, and hiked my skirt back up. Partial success. Except I still had no pockets. Looking around and running out of time, I shoved the mic pack onto the back side of my stole. It began sliding around my neck, under the new weight. I straightened the stole and pinned Sam against it, holding it in place, which was going to have to do.

And then it was my turn. I stepped up to the font. This was the font in which I'd hoped we would baptize Fritz. It still hurt, that void, but it was right to be here now, be here with all these good people surrounding us. They fell quiet. Looking around, I saw tears in parishioners' eyes. They knew how complicated this was, how overwhelming, and—even in the deep joy of it—how sad, how much everything of life was coming at once.

I held my small son over the font, his body filling only the length of my forearm. I cupped my right hand, dipped it into the water, and carefully poured a little onto his head. It trickled through his fine hair and back into the font. His arms flailed but he did not protest.

"Samuel Erik," I began, tears pushing at my eyes, my throat tempted to warble, "I baptize you in the name of the Father"—another cup of water from my palm—"and of the Son"—a third pouring down—"and of the Holy Spirit."

"Amen," the people all said. It was a measured response, though, not the usual exuberant shout. Their voices were solid, clear, and present but no more. They affirmed this moment in its tenderness, joining me there.

When?

For weeks, since before Sam was born, Alice had assumed the new baby was going to die, as Fritz had. But she wasn't worried about it.

"How long will this baby stay with us?" she would ask, kindly, calmly, expectantly.

One day, when Sam was two months old, Alice stood at my knee, petting his fine hair forward. I was nursing him, trying to split my attention between the two of them.

"Why is he still here?" she asked, clearly surprised that he was now older than Fritz had ever been.

"Sam's healthy," I said simply. "He's getting plenty to eat, and there's nothing wrong with his body the way there was with Fritz's. He isn't sick."

Alice persisted. "But when is he going to die? When will the next baby come?"

She had only one model for how all this worked. A baby came, stayed for a little while, then died and we got another. She expected we'd be repeating the pattern.

As much as she had demanded we tell her the story of how Fritz died a year earlier, now we had to tell her the basic biological story of how most babies survive, that we could assume that Sam would live and grow, and trust that. I wasn't sure that I did trust it, not really, but I wanted Alice to.

She still seemed suspicious, but the wooden train set began to seem more interesting than my refusal to give her a clear, short life expectancy for her youngest brother. She demurred, for the time being, not yet convinced.

Sick Kids

"I am more neurotic than I used to be," I often joked, this being *such* an understatement.

So far, Sam had slept well in the co-sleeper, a three-sided bassinet that attached to the side of our bed. Sometimes he made a funny whistling sound while he slept. When he did, Jesse and I lay side by side in the dark, listening when we should have been sleeping.

"Do you think that's normal?" I asked.

"I don't know," Jesse replied. "I don't remember that with the other two."

"Maybe he's just snoring?" I offered, more a question than a suggestion. "He seems fine."

"Yeah, he does," Jesse agreed. "But . . ."

We didn't usually finish the sentence: But then again, he might be about to die. We were both thinking it, so we didn't have to say it out loud. We listened to him squeak, keeping ourselves wide awake, vigilant. It was impossible to sleep deeply with him next to me.

Jesse tried to describe the whistling sound to our pediatrician. She had been so patient with us already; she didn't mind that we were obsessing, that I was neurotic—all this seemed reasonable to her. She was not concerned with the strange sound, since Sam seemed otherwise fine, and was sleeping, and clearly well oxygenated.

"Yes, he is warm and pink and plump," I acknowledged. "Okay, we will try to calm down."

Yeah, right. Fat chance.

Then sometimes Sam just wailed. We tried everything. Clean diaper. All the milk he wanted. Fresh air, songs, warmer clothes, cooler clothes. Mostly he was a calm and happy baby, as his brother had been, and the days were rare that he was inconsolable—which made them harder, made them seem an aberration, a legitimate cause for alarm. When I had tried everything I could, sometimes I just gave up, passing him to Jesse, asking him to please go somewhere else and to please shut the door. Then I sat, clutching my knees to my chest, unable to take in what Alice was showing me or asking me.

I sat, trying to wall out the wailing, trying to block it from my mind—which was impossible. I looked at the clock, checking how long it would be until it was a reasonable time to pour myself a glass of wine and then refill it until my fear was somewhat numbed. I recognized the danger of this mounting habit of mine, but I didn't know what else to do, how to abide the fear that came when he just cried. Deep in my being, Sam's inconsolable wailing meant one thing: my son was about to die. I could not stop death then; I knew I could not stop it now. I closed my eyes, holding my breath.

Time stopped, then somehow started again. Jesse eventually emerged. Sometimes Sam was asleep, sometimes he was ready to nurse, sometimes he just seemed to have needed a good cry.

Still the adrenaline pumped. I was hyperalert, on guard.

It was worse when the kids were sick. Alice came home one day with a new bug from school, as she had done every other week all year. Mostly it had just been snot and coughing, but this time it came with a fever. Even though Fritz hadn't had a fever, a spike in temperature made any situation seem more dire. Every half hour, I reached for the high-tech forehead scanning thermometer we bought when Fritz was briefly sick at two weeks old, when we thought it was the conscientious, but probably unnecessary, thing to do.

Now the thermometer was just a nuisance for Alice. I was grateful that she could speak, at least. At more than three and a half now, she was perfectly articulate.

"Does your stomach hurt?" I asked. "Is it hard to breathe? Do you think you're peeing less than usual? Does that hurt?" I pressed where I thought her appendix might be. "How's that?"

"Mommy!" she yelled, breaking through her lethargy, eyes as daggers at me, her pupils big and mad. "Will you just leave me alone?"

"Yes, love, I'm sorry." I gently tucked her into her bed. She rolled away from me, closing her eyes tight. I kissed her head and stood, watching the covers rise and fall ever so slightly.

"Just leave me. I want to sleep," she whimpered quietly.

I took a deep breath and left the room. I would be back in a half hour, maybe less, thermometer in hand.

I paced the apartment. I snapped at Jesse, though he had done nothing. I snapped because Alice had a fever and a cough. I snapped because I was certain she was about to die. I finally poured myself a mug of wine, but it did not help. Nothing comforted me. There was no soothing my fear.

I could take her to the doctor—I did it more frequently now, unlike when she was a first and only child. But that was part of the problem: it would not matter if the doctor said that she was fine. That one crucial time a doctor said a baby of mine was fine, he'd been dead five hours later.

Nursing Sam in the living room, I fiddled with the thermometer, trying to decide when I could bother Alice again to momentarily ease my fear. I wondered if I would always be this fearful. I wondered if my children would hate me for it, if they would think I was crazy. I didn't know how to calm the anxiety that eroded my own breath. I didn't know how to trust that these two children of mine were, in fact, living and growing, better than fine. They were thriving.

Racing Again

Through those early months of postpartum running, I went slow. Really, really slow. It felt like my insides were going to fall out of me, like my legs were dangling several inches out from my hip sockets. Fine, I thought. Maybe Michelle was right; maybe it was too soon. But by summer I could really run again, relieved to be able to put all my feelings somewhere. I dug in harder. I signed up for a race: the Berkeley Half Marathon, in November. Sam would be nine months old by then, so it seemed doable, if maybe a stretch. I plodded, slow but determined, as the months ticked by. Jesse and I were beginning to get the hang of our new configuration of parenting and work and grief, it seemed, and I was beginning to get my legs under me again.

There was little sleep the night before the race: Alice with nightmares, Sam still nursing frequently. I longed for Jesse's help, but he was out of town. I woke weary and aching, rushing to get ready. Trying to be positive, I left careful babysitting instructions with Jesse's mom, then snuck out of the house with the kids still asleep.

The gun went off and the crowd of runners, thousands strong, carried me along for a couple of miles, but the first hill demolished my spirits and I was hurting. I kept going but cursed everything.

"This fucking sucks!" I spit through my teeth.

The friends I was running with pulled me forward, one with constant comedic relief offered in a thick French accent, another, Caroline, with her ruthless coaching. Endlessly encouraging, she passed the miles telling me to keep going, telling me to go faster. I just hurt.

It was an awful race until the very end. I found some last reserve of energy and pushed, hard.

"Faster, Liz, run faster!" Caroline yelled from up ahead.

"I'm going as fast as I can!" I yelled back, not sure if it was true, but I was angry and in pain.

I finished, though, and nearly collapsed, staggering, leaning on Caroline's shoulder, first through the line to have a medal placed around my neck, then on to the med tent. They gave me a cup of Gatorade, then another. I shivered in the emergency blanket Caroline had wisely tied around my shoulders. I sat, stunned, unfeeling.

I caught my breath and finished my Gatorade, and then it was time to go. It was Sunday, and I had work to do, a service to lead. I limped back to the corral of bikes, retrieved mine, and slowly rolled home, grateful that pedaling seemed to use different muscles than the running had. I staggered up the stairs to our apartment, showered off the race grime, and then sank into my glider to nurse Sam and gulp down the smoothie I'd made the night before.

And then it was time to go, again. I passed Sam back to my mother-in-law, trying to ignore his cries as I threw on my clerical shirt, fastened my collar, and stepped into my slacks. My feet were raw. I slipped on the most comfortable of my work shoes. I flew out the door, down the balcony, and across the parking lot. I could not run up the stairs in the church two at a time, or at all. I stepped into the sacristy to find the whole altar party waiting. I had eight minutes to spare.

"Good morning," I said, exhausted, relieved, my hair still dripping. "Let's do this."

I rushed to fasten the snaps and ties of my robes, threw on my microphone, and set off. It was tight, but I was just making it.

My body ached as I presided over the service. Orans, the priest's primary position in offering prayers, with hands open and arms outstretched, was punishing. My mind slipped away for stretches, then returned as I tried to find out where we were, rushing to find what was next. I wasn't delirious, exactly, but I was not far off. I made it through the service. Then it was on to a newcomers' luncheon.

Can you imagine? Sitting down to a lovely lunch with thirty people considering becoming members of the parish, in a gorgeous home up in the Berkeley Hills, the living room windows looking out to the Golden Gate Bridge. My hair was dry now, but I was famished, and my body was beginning to stiffen. I poured myself a glass of wine, trying to loosen up, then soon poured another. I tried hard to make pleasant conversation, asking questions, trying to absorb the answers. Then came the worst part: Stump the Priests. It's a game we often played at these gatherings, a chance for everyone to ask any question they want to, anonymously, about the church, or religious life, or anything else. Phil and I took turns answering. Coherent sentences were elusive this time, exhausted and tipsy as I was. I tried to make the pauses look deep and thoughtful. I gave up and kicked some of the harder questions back to Phil.

It was a hard day, a largely miserable one, not one I would repeat. Yet I also felt triumphant, creaking up the stairs late in the afternoon to our apartment, where I would have crashed had it not been for the young children eagerly waiting my return. At least I had done it, ill-conceived as this day had been. I was still trying to convince myself that I could do hard things, that I was succeeding at racing and nursing and working, all at the same time. I was still trying to convince myself that I could do the hardest thing: surviving.

Recuperating that week, I slowed to a jog. Then I began training again in earnest, running hard through Fritz's second birthday, running again through the days of his life. I needed to be stronger, faster, to compensate, to be able to live without my two-year-old.

Wet Nurse

On January 9, the two-year anniversary of Fritz's death, I headed out to run the Inspiration Point Trail, up in Tilden Park, high in the hills above Berkeley. As I passed the weathered wooden signs, I wondered at the trail's name, in that it so completely restates the obvious.

It was cool and foggy, light rain falling. I planned to do twelve miles to train for the homegrown half marathon I was planning for my birthday in a couple of weeks. But quietly, I knew that I might keep going. I might not stop today. The running felt wonderful, exhilarating. Two years on, and it remained challenging to sit still in my grief. When I ran, though, I could feel Fritz in my breath, my fingers, my heart. My heart seemed to be swelling even in its changed, concave shape, the form that betrayed his absence.

As I began up the last big hill, the last half mile to the end of the four miles of pavement, my vision shifted. I saw her. Mary, the Mother of God, came to me, her arms open, outstretched. Deep in the pit of me, I was still distraught that I could not feed my sweet boy, that I could not take care of him or protect him. But in this moment, moving through the fog, I saw something else. I watched myself handing Fritz into Mary's open arms. This was the vision. I was suddenly overcome.

"Mary, nurse my son! Take him, feed him!" I cried out, still running through the rain.

And she did. He latched easily as she cradled him. He gulped and drank, delighted.

Mary, Fritz's wet nurse. And why should it be any other way? Of course there would be breast milk at the welcome table, in whatever great beyond lies waiting for us on the other side. And of course this sweet Mother of God, who knew the death of her own son, would be there to take mine, too.

It was a gift, a relief. As I pushed on through the fog, the vision closed, but the sense of it lingered with me. I was overwhelmed with gratitude for this saint who was pouring out life for me, from her own self, bearing a sister up from across time and space and mystery.

Weeks and months spun by, and still I ran. I began working with Ruth as my running coach again, training with more discipline, trying to heed her urging to take it easy sometimes, to take my watch off and stop worrying about times.

"Just have fun," she would say, "just enjoy this run, nice and easy."

My brain struggled with her counsel. Running wasn't so much about fun for me, it was about being strong, about surviving. I was still reluctant to ease up. But she was right, again. Easing up made me faster.

I ran another half marathon, then began digging in, stretching further. On a whim, I told Jesse and Laurie I was going to run a marathon this year. They raised their eyebrows. I began researching races, looking at dates and elevation gains. I signed up for the San Francisco Marathon, surprising us all. It was easy to get to, a good date, impossible hills. It would do. My long runs on Saturday mornings got longer and longer, each one surprising me more than the last, each one a new record for how far I could go on my own two feet, each one giving me more and more time to settle in and think, and breathe, and pray. I could relax into the distances; fifteen miles, eighteen miles, twenty miles: this was too far to push hard the whole time. I was moving, steadily. I was doing this: surviving.

Bread and Ashes

Soon after my vision of Mary and Fritz, I gathered around a sprawling dining room table one Sunday morning in February 2016. I was there with the vestry of All Souls, the parish's group of twelve elected lay leaders. We were tucked away up in the hills of Sonoma County, our meeting space dwarfed by towering redwoods and flooded by the morning light coming through a wall filled end to end and all the way to the ceiling with rickety windows.

We were making Eucharist. We reflected together on the Word, and we shared peace and offered prayers. And then we broke bread.

At least I tried to. It was more challenging than usual.

We were on retreat in the village of Camp Meeker, and together we were consecrating the basic stuff of life. A glass of wine, saved from lighthearted fellowship the night before. Some bread that I had brought to the retreat house from the Cheese Board bakery down the hill from my home.

It was a whole loaf, actually, a hearty round. And when, having blessed it, I tried to ritually break it, I could not. This bread was big, and the crust was thick. I wrestled with it, first quietly bemused, but then one person let slip a stifled laugh, then another. Soon all of us were chuckling as I struggled to finally tear it apart, long past the solemnity of that usually quiet moment.

It was simple, and it was funny, and we were broken open into unexpected laughter and, with it, joy. There was no question that there was enough, that all would be fed. And there was a lightness in us, mindful of being here and alive together.

I tore off a hunk of bread for the soul on my left, who shared it with the next, and the next. The bread was passed, connecting the circle, which had now gone quiet again. I looked down, and was taken aback: in the midst of all this joy, I registered my hands. Having wrestled with this loaf, I saw my hands covered with ashes and was transported, one foot remaining in that sunny room, the other standing in the darkened camp kitchen at Tahoe, weeping into the flour, as if it were my son's ashes, to make our communion bread for his funeral.

I was there again, now, here.

It was a thin place, crossing time, the holy cutting into our midst. Mortality loomed close at hand, Fritz's and mine, the valley of the shadow of death encroaching, beckoning.

I closed my eyes, rubbing the flour between my fingers, pushing it into my skin. I stood still, shaken, lifted into another world as I heard the bread still circling the table, the cup of wine following it. The taste of the bread, sweet and yeasty, remained on my tongue. It was the taste of the fullness of life, the taste of laughing with these good souls, but it brought close the knowledge of our death.

We finished, and packed up from the Eucharist and the weekend, the thin veil slowly fading into opacity, my feet growing more grounded in the present place. But I had seen his ashes, I thought to myself. I had held them once again.

I sang, just under my breath, walking beneath the redwoods, not knowing what else to do. *If we live, we live to the Lord. If we die, we die to the Lord. So then whether we live, or whether we die, we are the Lord's.* (Romans 14:8, NRSV) It's a chant, circling around on itself again and again, insisting that this is the truth, that we belong to God. We live as though we belong to God; we die as though we belong to God; it is true that we belong to God.

Back in Berkeley a few days later, on Ash Wednesday, I preached this story of bread and ash with trepidation. I told my parishioners about my twenty-ninth birthday party, too, about the celebration intertwined with the mourning, how it all happened at once.

I hoped it was all true. I preached it to myself. It wasn't good news, really, but it was grounded in hope. I reached to usher us into another Lent, to begin well, to show up.

"This is Lent, friends," I told them, closing:

> We come together and we mark ourselves with the depth of our being—all we have been, all that we shall be. We do this not to be miserable, or fearful, or resigned to death. Rather, we lift our

eyes squarely to the reality of our short time on earth, because we are here *now*. We do so because we choose to live and die to the Lord.

We enter into Lent because when we see our hands, covered in ashes, we trust that we are still fed. Even in the face of death, we choose to really live—to feast, to share joy, to love.

This is Lent. Our hands are covered in ashes, even as we hold this bread of life.

It is enough. It is good.

I stopped speaking and sat down in the front pew, staring at my hands. They were just my hands now, bathed not in human ash, but rather the blackened ash of palms, from the foreheads I had blessed with mortality earlier that day. For now, my hands were just themselves, alive and ready.

The Box, the Font, and Ruthie

It was Maundy Thursday, six weeks later. Fritz had been dead two years and change, but it was my third Holy Week since he died. The previous year, I'd been on maternity leave with Sam; the year before that had felt like a joke of a ritual in Reno. We had washed one another's hands instead of our feet on Maundy Thursday in Reno. Why this break with tradition, with the commandment given by Jesus? Because feet were deemed too vulnerable, too intimate. I had scoffed, frustrated. In Reno we had also lit the new fire of Easter, the symbolic light that crashes into the most oppressive darkness, on Saturday evening, far too early, and inside the building, still awash with light from the setting sun flooding through the stained-glass windows. The fire was fueled with alcohol and salts, held in a 1970s casserole dish with burnt-orange and olive-green flowers painted on its side. I had largely ignored the whole thing, dismayed by the meager attempt at honoring resurrection as an actual possibility in our midst.

At All Souls it felt right to me, real and gutsy. I was afraid of making my way through Holy Week this year, but also excited and—maybe—ready.

Thursday came. We prayed and sang. We took turns washing one another's feet; we actually scrubbed them, intently. It was tender and uncomfortable and sweet and good, this intimacy. At the end of the service, the sky outside now dark, we stripped the altar. The choir had already processed to the back of the church, the lights nearly out. They began chanting Psalm 22 in a lilting lament:

> My God, my God, why have you forsaken me?
> and are so far from my cry
> and from the words of my distress? (Psalm 22:1, BCP)

I joined with Tripp, who had preached that night, the friend who knew that grief will *fuck you up*. Carefully, we removed every bit of adornment from the altar and the area around it—the candles, the icons, the linens, the brass crosses, all of it.

The Psalm continued:

> O my God, I cry in the daytime, but you do not answer;
> by night as well, but I find no rest. (Psalm 22:2, BCP)

We carried everything away, back to the sacristy, out of sight. When the simple wooden altar was totally bare, we poured water across it, washing it clean. I scrubbed it, as I had scrubbed feet earlier. Then I took a clean towel and dried the altar, carefully and thoroughly, as we had dried one another's feet.

We left the altar stark and vacant, the blond pine only dully visible in the dark. What was usually a place of joy and feasting was now empty, barren. These ritual tasks complete, I extinguished the one last flickering flame. It was a tall votive candle that burns perpetually, except for this night. Its light tells us that somehow God is present because the consecrated bread and wine are present, reserved there in the ambry, the little nook built into the wall that holds blessed bread and wine and oils atop a tiny carpet of well-aged red velvet. I removed the sacrament now, leaving the ambry door ajar.

The choir chanted on:

> I am poured out like water; all my bones are out of joint;
> my heart within my breast is melting wax.
> My mouth is dried out like a pot-sherd;
> my tongue sticks to the roof of my mouth;
> and you have laid me in the dust of the grave. (Psalm 22:14–15, BCP)

And then we walked. I was carrying the small silver box from the ambry. It is more common for a ciborium—the metal vessel for the blessed bread—to be round, often looking like a chalice with a lid, but this one was decidedly square, the silver thinning in places but still catching the faint glow coming through the skylight above. Cradled within it, beneath the tightly closed lid, was the bread, the Body of Christ. I processed down the darkened aisle. I knew Tripp was behind me, but I could not hear him. I seemed to be all alone. My mind flashed to another place.

My body knew this walk. My hands remembered the corners of this box. My arms remembered the weight of holding this nearly empty box carefully in front of me, leading me forward to the place I hated to go. I remembered the last time—the only other time—I had walked clutching the box of a lost son in my hands. I was there again, walking through wood chips, the afternoon lake glistening before me. This time, though, all was dark.

Slowly, quietly, rhythmically, I walked without the light of the paschal candle, without Jesse and Alice at my side. I arrived at the back of the darkened church, and two young acolytes joined on either side of me with lit tapers in simple wooden candlesticks. Out through the heavy copper doors we went, down the street. People piled in behind us, following, on into the chapel. We packed this small bunker of a holy space, the thick cement walls enclosing us on all sides, like a cave. It had been transformed into a garden for the night, plants and flowers covering and circling the altar. I placed my box there in the midst of them, a candle snug at its side. This cave was a place to wait. A hundred people squeezed into the chapel, built for thirty-five, maybe forty. We kept watch, we prayed, we sang, our voices rising full: "Stay with me, remain here with me, watch and pray. Watch and pray." We chanted the words, rich in layers of harmony, again and again. Fat tears rolled down my cheeks as I kept vigil for our lost sons, for Mary's and for mine.

Folks eventually trickled away into the night, but there was no end to this service; it is one long liturgy, stretching across three days to Easter.

We returned early the next morning for Good Friday. Good Friday was easy. I got the grief of it, the guilt. This was still where I lived. It was a relief to have others catch up to this place with me for a day.

And then we waited. Jesus was in the tomb, betrayed and slain and abandoned again. We waited through Saturday. It was fully dark by the time we came together again for the Easter Vigil. Wood had been stacked carefully for a fire, and when Phil and the acolytes and I emerged from the church, the crowd drew close. It was too dark to see who was there. Phil struck a match, waiting, watching, as it slowly caught. The song began, just a few voices at first, then more and more joining in as the fire started to burn. It was a soulful chant, still dark, so real, entirely hopeful: "Within our darkest night, you kindle the fire that never dies away, that never dies away." Again and again we sang it, the flames jumping two and three and now four feet high as the wind picked up. "Within our darkest night, you kindle the fire that never dies away, that never dies away. Within our darkest night, you kindle the fire that never dies away, that never dies away."

How much did I believe this? I wondered. I'd been singing it for more than a dozen years at this point, long before I knew how lethal the darkness could become. The song flowed through my body, jumping with the fire's sparks. Phil dodged the blustery flames, attempting to light the new paschal candle without catching fire himself.

We came inside, filling the darkened church with candlelight, filling it with wild stories lifted up as the arc of salvation history. Of creation groaning in its goodness, at the beginning of it all. Was it? Was it good? Then of Shadrach, Meshach, and Abednego in the fiery furnace, emerging not even singed, not even smelling of smoke. Of Jonah, spewed out from the belly of the fish, of deliverance across the dry floor of the Red Sea. Can you believe it? Could I? Then came the rattling bones. Ezekiel, my prophet. The bones tapping, wriggling back to life in his prophecy. Even these dry bones can live, he shows. I breathed the story in, reaching.

We came to the font. This was the night we would baptize Elias, the son of Tripp and his wife, Trish. Elias was about to turn one. Our families' lives were intertwined. Day after day in his early life, I had pumped and given Elias my milk. I had too much for Sam, as I had had with Alice and Fritz. Here was another son I fed when I couldn't feed my first.

Agitated, I wrestled some invisible angel as we stood around the font. This celebration was good and right. And yet I couldn't shake the memory of what *hadn't* happened at this font: Phil on the other side, standing as a godparent, vowing to Fritz.

Instead, Fritz was present in the Litany of the Saints. After the baptism, we went out into the night, singing to the holy women and holy men who had left us, who interceded for us, whom we bade to come rejoice with us. Teenage acolytes led the unusual parade, swinging incense, carrying the cross and torches. The choir followed, then the two hundred faithful who had come to spend hours at church this late Saturday night. We walked down the sidewalk in North Berkeley, dark, empty, and quiet, except for us with our candles and our singing. "Come rejoice with us," we chanted, bidding saint after saint present: "Mary the Mother of God, Paul of Tarsus, Teresa of Ávila. Come rejoice with us. Martin Luther King Jr., Jonathan Daniels, Francis and Clare, Hildegard and Brigid. Come rejoice with us." Having crossed intersections and circled back to the church, we entered the narthex, both the light of our candles and our voices swelling. There we called on the saints we had known in our own lives, the ones who had died this year, the people we loved and saw no more. And Fritz. He wasn't sitting in the font. Yet he came, present, in the peels of alleluias, in the death rising.

Easter morning came predictably, the sun cresting the hills far too early after the late-night vigil. I was exhausted in the glory of it all, my eyes bleary with the blur of pastel dresses and smart neckties. I presided, made Eucharist with this throng hundreds strong, then went to share it out with the masses. I was giving out bread, again and again. I moved down the packed altar rail countless times, filled with all the folks we wouldn't see again until Christmas.

A one point I knelt down to place the bread in a pair of small, outstretched hands, one cradling the other. I looked up to meet the eyes that belonged to these hands and saw Ruthie, no longer a baby, but a toddler, strong from her start with my milk—with Fritz's milk. I hadn't seen her for a long time.

"The Body of Christ, the bread of heaven," I said, swallowing hard.

She looked me in the eye. "Amen," she answered, seeming to agree.

Meeting Ruthie at the altar rail there, quite by surprise, pulled me to notice that we were beginning to come full circle, that I was beginning to lap myself here on these circuits of years, of death anniversaries, of feast days. Ruthie was Fritz's milk sister, to use her grandmother's term. But here she was, standing to take communion, responding to the gift as a verbal human being. I myself was no longer carrying the box of a lost son, but instead remembering that son and chasing after another. We were deep into Easter, right here, in the present.

9

SOBER

SOBER

A Loaded History

I have always had a fraught relationship with alcohol. It entices me. It scares me. I have scorned it, blamed it, used it, longed for it.

In high school I swore I would never drink. It just didn't seem worth it, I said. I obviously had terrible genes, so why would I want to play with fire like that? I loathed what alcohol had done to my mother; I hated it for the ways it stole her from me again and again.

But by the winter of my freshman year of college, I had changed my tune. I was dating a junior, Andy, who knew my family's messiness, knew my mom, and still didn't flinch. He also made gin and tonics seem classy and responsible, and they were that for him. I could handle this, I thought. I still resented alcohol, but I equally resented that my mother's alcoholism should bar me from joining in normal college fun.

The boozy culture at Dartmouth was a terrible metric for someone trying to learn responsible drinking. While I was a student, the sports teams had the lackluster nickname "Big Green" but no official mascot, so the satirical college newspaper crew took it upon themselves to create a livelier option: Keggy the Keg. He showed up in a remarkable larger-than-life costume at sporting events, to cheers and chants of "It's drriiinnnkking time!" A near ubiquitous turn of phrase on campus was *boot and rally*—a celebratory exclamation summing up the practice of drinking until one booted, that is, vomited, and then rallying, going back out to drink more. It was horrifying to me then. In retrospect, it strikes me mostly as sad.

But learn to drink I did. Many of my classmates outpaced me, but I developed a taste for it. Studying abroad in Argentina carried particularly good opportunities for growing more comfortable with alcohol. The wine flowed freely there, as did wild cocktails, the contents of which I couldn't actually understand from the menu. I was free, I was empowered, and I was convinced I was invincible. One night out in Patagonia, I threw up first on the dance floor and then on the street while a classmate helped me back to the hostel. The next day was wretched. My head pounded in the bright sun. We went to a Catholic church, Palm Sunday. I was hungover, and so guilty.

Seminary was a place with lots of easy booze, too. Weekly "Community Nights" ended with a walk down the street to share pitchers of beer and enormous glasses of wine. Special events had open bars. I drank, I drank too much, I fit right in. It wasn't until Fritz died that drinking took on a different role in my life.

Numb

That spring after Fritz died, I just couldn't handle more, especially by the end of the day. I couldn't think more. I needed to stop feeling. A glass of wine took the edge off, a second helped dull it further. My mother-in-law's brandy was faster.

I drank almost nightly. Never too much, ostensibly. Enough to make it through, I told myself. I deserved it; it was understandable.

With three pregnancies in short order, however, I took big chunks of time off from drinking in my twenties. There was no question, no challenge, other than that people guessed I was pregnant before I wanted to share the news, on account of my not drinking. After Sam was born, though, I returned quickly. Everything irritated me. I was beyond exhausted: a preschooler and a newborn; work; running; and on top of all that, grief and paralyzing fear.

Wine, yes. A mojito? Better. Fine Bulleit bourbon, in anything? Delicious. It went down smooth and I felt classy, like I was just a little bit freer. That was the story I told myself. I was a liberated woman, independent, free to do as I pleased.

Jesse didn't love it. He's always been more health-conscious than I, fighting off sugar and fried treats and rarely drinking even a taste of alcohol. It was expensive, my body didn't need it, and I was nursing—that was his take.

"I feel like hard alcohol and breastfeeding don't go together," he said one night, not criticizing exactly, but questioning and concerned.

"Well, I'm drinking it *after* I've nursed him. I don't drink that much," I shot back, defensive.

I googled ferociously. Most sites agreed with him. But finally, there it was, a couple of lines in an article from La Leche League, suggesting that what I was doing was fine, that the admonishment not to drink was just one more way the patriarchy was controlling women. I sent the link to him, feeling vindicated.

Mostly, though, I was relieved to have the permission from an expert. I didn't want to have to feel everything that was rising in me daily. I needed to be able to turn it off.

I was afraid that my living kids would die. I was angry at all I had been dealt. And I felt so very alone. Drinking didn't make that go away. But with a drink in my hand, I didn't have to feel as much. I could just be cranky and short-tempered instead, snapping at my family for existing while being terrified that suddenly they would not.

Big crowds were the worst. Conferences, in particular. "How many kids do you have?" strangers would ask. They always did, over and over. "How old are they?"

I fumbled, hemming awkwardly. Would I be honest? It was exhausting, telling people about your dead baby when they were just looking to make small talk. But leaving Fritz out felt like a betrayal. Each time I chose that easy way of deleting Fritz, I felt like a fraud, and hated myself for it. These places were lonely—filled with people, but mostly ones I suspected wouldn't get it. Alcohol smoothed over the angst. It didn't matter how I answered the question. Whatever I said, however anyone responded, it wouldn't penetrate me—neither the horrified apologies of "Sorry, I just can't imagine" nor my remorse when I chose to lie. I could just be. Numb, flowing, easy, asleep.

But it was never enough. The fear, the horrendous grief, always snuck back in. I drank more, staving off these feelings. I wanted to be invincible. I knew I was not: not against the alcohol, not against the grief. Still, I tried.

At one conference in 2016, two and a half years after Fritz's death, I was traveling on my own for one of the first times since having kids. I was free, and I was so, so alone. We had a night off midweek, and some of us gathered for a barbecue at a local participant's house. I drank. We tried to get the grill going. People asked those "how many do you have" questions. I drank more. Eventually, hours in, there was food, but I was already far gone. And still I drank more. I kept telling myself it was about being free, while knowing I was buried under more than I could handle.

It was a sickening night. I threw up out the car window, then back in my hotel room. I was a mess, passed out in my clothes. I woke at four in the morning, suddenly aware of what had happened and horrified with myself. I cleaned the vomit from the sink, took a shower, and went back to bed. This could not be who I was. I woke again to a fire alarm blaring at five. Shaky, my head pounding, I stumbled out to the parking lot. Cold, groggy, and annoyed, I milled about with the other conference center guests. I walked over to the car in which I had ridden the night before and saw my vomit streaking down the passenger door. Again, I was horrified. When the alarm was finally turned off, I went straight to the bathroom and gathered wet paper towels. I returned to the parking lot and carefully washed my mess off the car, hoping no one saw me. I slunk back to the front doors: locked. Fuck, I thought. *Fuck.* They kept them locked overnight and wouldn't open them for another hour. I shivered, but I figured this was what I deserved. And then someone was there, opening the door. I was saved, for now. I returned to my room, grateful that I hadn't had the presence of mind to lock it, because I hadn't taken the key with me.

I slept, rising just in time for the first meeting of the day. Breakfast would have been no help to me. I was miserable all day: sweating, nauseous, mortified. I tried to smile and play it cool. I wanted neither pity for my mistakes nor the embarrassment of owning up to them.

Once my hangover subsided, I was simply scared. Who and what had I become? Was this me, someone who threw away precious solo time to drink myself sick? What was I running from? The rest of the week was a blur of guilt, of beating myself up, of wondering which way was forward.

Maybe I would quit, I thought. But by the last night there, I had already changed my tune, found fresh rationales, more drinks to enjoy.

Returning home, though, I didn't drink for weeks. I rolled back and forth, going greater stretches sober and then drinking more than I could handle, more than made sense for my family, and still it was not enough to make the grief go away. Nothing could make it leave me.

I thought about alcohol often. When I would be able to get it; if I should buy more on this trip to Trader Joe's, just in case; how much there would be at the party; whether I could snag the last quarter of that bottle of wine before someone else got to it at dinner.

And I fretted. Was I turning into my mother? How would I be able to handle grief without alcohol?

I wasn't my mother. But slowly, painfully, I was realizing that I could become her. It was nowhere near that bad, not yet. And her end was not a given for me. But her oblivion could be mine. I had the affinity, was seeking it, in small doses, not because I wanted the oblivion, but because I felt I needed a buffer from my grief.

Somewhere deep within me, I knew I needed to quit. But I wasn't sure I could, or if I would. Sitting in church Sunday by Sunday, I listened to the other preachers and heard clearly the call, an invitation to another way of life. They weren't talking about drinking, not directly—they were unpacking the inherent value of life, the need for integrity, the way to move through this world in right relationship—but that call was being handed to me, again and again: it was time for me to give this up. I didn't know how that would happen, or what it would look like. All I knew, in that moment, was that it needed to be.

Mary's Sacred Heart

Running the ridge above Berkeley, looking westward toward the Bay and eastward toward Mount Diablo, I remembered that this was how I prayed. I forgot so easily, and so often. I began pounding my prayers. With light feet, knocking the weathered pavement, looking for an opening, over and over.

I was just starting up the last, long hill, the trail ahead wrapping, carving upward around it. Going under the twisted old live oaks, I felt pressure in my chest. I felt it swelling. I checked my heart rate monitor, perplexed. But my heart wasn't beating faster. It wasn't that I was working harder going up the hill; I had only just begun. I kept running, noticing, listening to the sensation. It began to feel like a heart—but another heart, a new one, extra. And it took on a new shape. It didn't feel like a biologically human heart, muscle and pumping and valves and sinew, but rather the classic, rounded Valentine's heart, filling my chest, surrounding my own, still swelling. This heart was warm, intense, glowing. My chest was filled with light, light that was now seeping into my lungs.

I continued running slowly up this hill, through the thin place where, in wind and rain and fog some ten months earlier, I'd been given the vision of Mary taking Fritz to nurse. I turned the bends, kicking my run into high gear, pushing hard, still paying attention to this strange heart. In the flash of a moment, I received that it was Mary's Sacred Heart. Is that a thing? I wondered. I had no idea, except that Mary's Sacred Heart was in me now, no knowledge of how this had happened except that Mary's Sacred Heart had just been *given to me*. Rounding toward the top of the hill, I closed my eyes, and where the gray sky had been, a heart glowed orange, as if I'd been staring at a brightly throbbing light instead of the dull golden brown of the East Bay hillsides in fall. The swelling heart felt like armor, encasing my own heart, impenetrable, keeping my heart safe, strong.

As I crested the hill, I asked, "Mary, why did you give me your Sacred Heart? What do I do with it?"

Immediately, before I had even finished uttering these words, the answer came: "Let it break."

Holy shit, I thought, reeling, turning around at the end of the trail and heading back down. That didn't come from me.

"Here is your armor, shielding your heart," the answer said. "Now let it break."

What?

I turned this over and over in my mind, running out the long hill, letting gravity have its way. I listened to the wind, to my footfalls on the cracking pavement, one after the other after the other. I drank water and ate a few bites of a snack, depleted by the run, the hill, the vision.

And then I started back up from the valley, slowly rising again to the ridge. Running past the lazing cattle, I confessed, frustrated, "Mary, I don't want to have a broken heart."

And back came her response: "Neither did I."

I ran the three and a half miles back, chewing on this vision, turning it over again and again. I needed to stop fighting my own broken heart. It was all right that I was broken, and I could settle there, stop punishing myself for it. I needed to just survive like that, *broken*. That's what I was. I needed to let it be, all of it, all broken, broken for all time.

Thirty Days

What would it mean to quit drinking if I wasn't the sort of alcoholic my mother had been? If I hadn't hit a rock bottom like hers, but saw it threatening in the distance? What did sobriety mean, and what did it require? I didn't know. I was terrified. People had talked me out of quitting before.

"You're fine!" they assured me. "You are not your mother. You are being too hard on yourself, Liz. Relax!"

But I decided that I would quit for myself, and for myself alone, regardless of what others said. A Thirty-Day Challenge, to start. I wanted to reach for a hundred days, I wanted to reach for always, but those goals seemed too lofty—so thirty days it was, no alcohol. I began on January 1. It would be easy to count that way, I told myself.

I was shifty. I dodged outings, parties, family gatherings. I left church events early. I told Jesse but no one else. He was supportive, but others promptly started asking if I was pregnant.

To my surprise, not drinking became a wonderful secret, something I was doing solely for myself. It was good for other people, no doubt. But this was for me. I cut myself some slack, rewarding myself with little cookies, going to bed early, small gifts to celebrate my budding sobriety. I kept my head down, I went quiet, a ninja.

Thirty days passed. I told Laurie; I told Tripp. They got it. Laurie because she loves me, and Tripp because he was now sixteen years sober.

I started sleeping better, no longer waking up sweating at three in the morning, no longer cranky, dry-mouthed, and generally resentful when the kids woke me up at sunrise. My body felt looser, felt free.

Grief and alcohol don't mix well, I began to realize more fully. Being sober might actually make it easier for me to survive and to heal.

10

PARENTING THREE

ᑫ∀ᖇᴇᴎ⊥IᴎᏟ ⊥ᕼᖇᴇᴇ

Dead Tree

The next time I saw Fritz's tree, two summers out, there was no question. It was dead, a standing pile of sticks; it had been dead for months.

The only leaves on the tree were the persistent ones that had held on, dry from the summer before. I didn't want to cut it down. But I didn't want anyone else to fell it, either; the job was mine to do.

The summer before, I had only been willing to cut away its dead branches. We'd been back visiting camp from Berkeley, a year after moving away from the lake, and I'd found some rusty old clippers in the shop and walked down to the tree, pruning away the dry and barren parts. It had budded again after that, despite the struggle of its first year, and thin, fragile new leaves shook in the breeze. The branches I'd cut away then had buds, too, but these never unfurled into leaves.

I tried to be hopeful then, but even pruned back, the tree struggled.

247

When we returned to visit the lake again later that summer, many of those new leaves were dead and dry, still fluttering but useless. The camp staff had been watering it diligently, but it did not help. Even as it hung on through another season, I could tell this memorial tree, planted for my dead son, was dying.

Now another summer later, I eyed the dead tree all week during our visit. I dragged my feet. We talked about planting another one, and Stuart, the camp director, said he'd install a drip system with a timer.

"All right," I told Jesse and Alice and Sam, finally. "It's time. We have to do this."

Jesse found a bow saw up in the shop, but I took it from him when we met at the tree.

"I want to," I said, unconvinced by the certainty in my own words. I did not *want* to, of course; the thought tied my stomach in knots.

I lowered the blade to the trunk and held it flat, just above the dirt. I pulled one stroke, the metal glancing off the silvery bark. The tree's smoothness had given way to tough ridges as it had dried out. I winced. Clenching my teeth, I pushed the saw back, slicing in, then again and again, until the weight of the tree began pinching the toothy blade. Fat tears rolled down my cheeks, making trails through the dust that my labor had kicked up.

I stood and staggered away, leaving the saw clamped inside the tree.

"You want me to take a turn at it?" Jesse asked.

"No," I called out, softly. "I just need a minute."

Alice and Sam played in the dirt while glancing furtively in my direction. I crouched down in the dry grass, sobbing, my face in my hands. A wallowing gasp emerged from my lips, the kind of sound I made giving birth.

I stood again, staring out at the lake, steadying myself by the light dancing across its surface. I returned to the saw, grasping it again with both hands, pulling and pushing, hard.

The tree was tall, but not very thick, just over two inches in diameter at its thickest. It hadn't lived long; it didn't take long to cut it down. The aspen fell toward the lake, bouncing gently. Even its dry branches still had some give to them, a kind of springiness in their death. I stood, presiding silently over this dead tree laid out in the sun, the tree that was supposed to stand in for my dead son.

And then I got to work again, picking up the clippers, removing the branches one by one until the trunk was stripped bare. Jesse watched, helping the kids, unquestioning.

"How long can the pieces be and still fit in the car?" I asked, finally.

"We're taking this home?" he responded, a smile sneaking onto his face.

"Of course we are." I expected he thought I was crazy, saving things like this. I didn't care. "I'm going to make something with it. I don't know what yet. But we're taking it home."

We had a Prius. It was already stuffed, but we would have to figure it out. Jesse seemed to sense this was not worth fighting, and he went to see what was possible. I sawed the trunk in half. It would fit. We switched gears, digging up the root ball to make space for a new tree. It was small, surprisingly so. The roots had never fanned out, we saw, never gone deep. It was nearly the same size as when we had planted it two and a half years earlier—no wonder it hadn't survived. Saving the root ball seemed excessive, though, even for me. We chucked it over the edge of the bluff.

The next morning, Stuart and I drove to the nursery in Carson City. The camp had paid for the first tree, and he was determined to get a free replacement—this man was as frugal as he was charmingly bold.

"Yes," he said plainly when an employee offered help. "We're here to see about replacing a memorial tree. It never thrived."

The nursery had a one-year guarantee on its trees. The worker probed a little and quickly pronounced that it must have come to us sick, even though it looked just fine at first. "Those trees can hide it well," he explained. "It sounds like it never really had a chance."

This sounded all too familiar. An invisibly sick tree for my invisibly sick boy. How very fitting.

An aspen specialist happened to be on-site that day; he walked us through the collection, helping us to see which were the strongest, the most likely to thrive at the lake. I picked a smaller one that already had three trunks weaving together. We don't survive anything alone, I thought to myself. Maybe more trunks will help.

This time, Alice helped dig out the hole while Sam played in the mud. They were joyful, playful, alive. The tree was lovely, its leaves already happily quaking.

"Where are Fritz's ashes?" Alice asked suddenly.

I blinked. She had been so verbal when he died that it was hard to remember how young she had been. Of course those memories were fleeting. Of course she would have to keep relearning the story.

Jesse stepped in. "They're buried here," he said, motioning to a patch of ground some four feet from the tree's hole, a little off to the side, just before the grass began to creep in.

I looked at him, hard. "No," I said slowly. "Actually, they are right here." I walked forward, placing my hand on the ground two feet east of the tree. Straight ahead to the tree and to the shore.

"Really?" Jesse asked.

"Yes." I said, stunned. "His ashes are buried *here*."

"And some are up at Spooner Lake," Jesse tagged on, his voice light, sounding like he was trying to make pleasant conversation with our almost five-year-old.

I looked at him, confused. I felt betrayed. "No, they are not. They are all here."

He turned, caught by the tightness in my voice. "Really?"

"Jesse," I started, taking a deep breath to keep from yelling, "I know where our son's ashes are buried." I meted out my words with all the authority I could muster. "We talked briefly about spreading some at Spooner, but we decided to bury them all here." Another deep breath. "Maybe you turned the conversation into a memory."

I was furious yet also sad. So much of grieving felt like solitary work, an undertaking I was responsible for accomplishing alone. It was as if there were an interior hermitage—an exile—where I was to live and work and eventually survive. I tried to tell myself that it wasn't true, that Jesse and I were in this together. That we would grieve alongside each other, even if we grieved differently. But that he did not know precisely where our son was buried? The weight of responsibility pressed down on me, unmistakable, demanding, unrelenting. It was my job to remember Fritz always, my duty as his mother.

I longed for other companions, mothers especially, who had lived through the loss of an infant. But I was a white, middle-class, well-educated American, and such people were hard to come by in my circles. I knew that across all of history, until very recently, parents simply lost children, that what I was living had been the norm. I had done some reading and knew that in the United States, in the 1870s, the infant mortality rate was about 195 deaths per 1,000 live births annually, compared to 5.82 deaths per 1,000 live births in 2014. Twenty percent of infants died before their first birthday back in the 1870s—not even counting all the children lost to common diseases. With American women having on average seven or eight children in that era, statistically, *every* woman lost a child. And I knew that in many parts of the world—indeed, in many parts of my own country, just not the parts I lived in—it was still commonplace to lose a child. Yet it often seemed that I bore my grief alone. I knew there were support groups out there, and I knew a few women who had also lost children, but none of this had translated into a sense of companionship in the grief. Not even in my own family, not yet.

I wondered, especially in the midst of my anger, how Jesse and I might share the grief more down the line. Wondered if it didn't have to be so lonely, if I could bring myself to give more of the grief over to him, how I could reach out to trust him with it. It seemed like a necessary direction yet also distant, full of hurdles.

But, with the hole dug and waiting, here was one next step we could take together: we planted the new tree, its own sort of mnemonic device. It would help us remember that Fritz was here, show us what remained, point us toward life returning. I would try to follow its lead.

But Where?

How do you introduce your son to his dead brother? What would you say? Where would you begin?

"Where are Fritz's ashes? Where are they in the ground? This is his tree?" Sam asked me, again and again.

Another year had passed, and it was now 2017. Sam was two years and five months old, and we were at the camp visiting Lake Tahoe again. He was only a little older than Alice had been after Fritz died, when she began asking these questions ad infinitum. Now it was Sam's turn to try to make sense of how someone could be here, yet not—how Fritz could hold such a central place in our lives and family but still be invisible.

We walked to the tree, to Fritz's second tree. So far, it was surviving. Sam had already jumped into bigger questions.

"What does Fritz eat? Am I alive?"

We rehearsed the strange litany again. "He didn't eat food," I reminded him. "He was only a baby. He nursed, he drank milk."

"Why?" Always, ever, the why.

"Because he was only a baby," I answered. "He didn't live long enough to eat other food."

"What does he eat now?"

"Well, nothing," I started, then backtracked. "Actually, I don't know." Even I was confused. "Our bodies don't need food after we die. Our bodies stop working. His body is just ashes now; it doesn't use food. But there are some stories about having really great food with God after we die, too, so maybe?"

"Where is he? Where are his ashes?"

He had asked this so many times already. I took a deep breath. My body remembered all this, the relentless dance of questions from Alice.

It was circular, questions chasing their own tails. It was not so much an information-gathering quest as it was an effort to make meaning out of what was fundamentally unknowable, trying also to forge a connection to his brother.

"They're right here," I told him, pointing again to the ground. "We dug a hole here, about this deep, maybe two and a half feet." I marked the depth with my hands, marveling at how little it was. "We used a shovel and piled the dirt over there, just to the side of this little clearing on the bluff."

The sun, doubled as it reflected up off the lake, was bright enough in our eyes that we had to squint.

"Everyone was here, Sam."

"Everyone?"

"Everyone came. Nana, and Dan and Annie and Charlotte, and Tripp, and Phil." Everyone—this constituted his world.

"Elias?" His friend, our neighbor, younger than him?

"No," I explained. "Elias hadn't been born yet."

At two and a half, Sam hadn't been told about *chronos*—the kind of time we know and mark here in this life, the kind that moves like an arrow, orderly, reliable, chronological—and *kairos*—the kind of time that folds in on itself, mysterious and creative and well beyond us, the kind of time that belongs to God.

"And with them all here, we—I—poured his ashes into this hole, into the ground. And then we took fistfuls of dirt from that pile, and put them into the hole, on top of his ashes, until it was filled in. We did it all together."

He stared at the level, dusty ground, the hole made invisible.

"But where is he now?"

Jesus, kid. Right, I thought, *where* was bigger than his ashes, the little that remained.

I fumbled, offering again that he was in our hearts, that we loved him, that he was with God. That the rain that had fallen had carried some of his ashes on already—into the trees, into the lake, somewhere else, onward, somewhere bigger than just here, right now.

It was a totally unsatisfactory answer. For him, and for me. He kept asking me, trying to wrap his young mind around it. I kept asking, too, I suppose. Where was the son I barely knew? Where was the soul who tore part of my heart out of my chest, cleaving to it while stealing it away? I didn't know.

"Why?" Sam asked again, eager, hopeful.

Milk and Dust

Sam was weaned. Finally and so soon, both. Two and a half years had been plenty for me, and finishing had been bittersweet. And stopping was also glorious, liberating, expansive.

It was the end of an era. Almost six years of nearly continuous breast-feeding—for my three babes, plus pumping for nine others, the twins in Carmel, twins in Novato, one not yet born in Bloomington. Pumping for Nathaniel and Ruthie, for the baby whose attempted abortion was unsuccessful in Dumas Bay, Washington, then each morning for Elias. I was able to give milk to so many others, and I was so done. My breasts were tiny now, smaller than they were before I started nursing. They drooped empty, clinging close to my body. And still, they were ready to give more, still not dry—even after weeks of cutting back, weeks of just at bedtime, and now a week of no nursing at all.

We returned to the lake one July weekend for a camp wedding. I'd known the bride since she was five, before she was even old enough to be a camper back in Indiana. All weekend long, in the midst of wild reunions and celebrations and sabbath time, I felt drawn to make a strange offering at Fritz's tree, at the place of his burial. I thought about going out early in the morning, before others woke. I was getting ready to, on Saturday, having heard Jesse rising with the kids, graciously letting me slumber on. He got them dressed, all in a hush, with me peeking through mostly closed eyes to appreciate the gift more. I heard them leave, the car starting up and backing away. I lay in bed, soaking in the quiet, and after resting a while longer, rose. I dressed and found coffee, contemplating the compulsion stirring in me.

And just then, I saw the car return, rolling over the packed gravel, back to our cabin. Jesse and the kids had ventured to a nearby playground, but it was too cold to stay without the sun yet up above the ridgeline. My opportunity had evaporated.

That night, after the wedding and dinner and dancing and cheesecake made by the bride herself, I trudged back to the cabin with Alice, exhausted. I helped her to bed, dozing off with her in the cave of her lower bunk. I considered returning to Fritz's tree later that night, after the music was done, under the half-moon and the endless stars, but I could not make my body move. I fell hard asleep, waking only to hold Alice in the wee hours after she woke from a nightmare.

Sunday morning came without much rest, but with a wonderfully slow pace. Alice and I shared tea and coffee, wove friendship bracelets, and eventually began packing the cabin up. Folks gathered to share a lazy breakfast outside, and it was on toward nine o'clock when I realized with some delight that it was Sunday and I was still in my pajamas. I watched cars begin to roll into the church parking lot as I sat sipping coffee, still without real designs for the day.

We decided to go kayaking one more time, wriggling into still-damp swimsuits and slathering ourselves with sunscreen. Jesse and I paddled the kids out to a kind of island, an outcropping of monumental boulders, all piled mysteriously on top of one another. We clambered about, and Jesse and I jumped off the higher ones into the water, to the kids' delight. We climbed to the top to soak up the sun and take in the whole lake. But we couldn't stay. We needed to eat, and we needed to hit the road, drive back—this was no longer fully our home.

We paddled to shore and carefully navigated up the old stairs, some steps now washed out from recent flash flooding. I asked Jesse for a minute to rinse off—I would meet them soon, I said. Jesse and the kids continued up to find lunch.

I stepped into the outdoor shower, happy to find lavishly warm water and good pressure—an upgrade from years past. I rinsed off slowly, looking out over the top of the cedar planks, out across the lake. I dried, and began up the sandy path, past the aspen groves. I came to Fritz's tree and stopped. With one beach towel around my shoulders, I spread another on the ground, just in front of where we buried his ashes. I sat down, cross-legged, breathing in the smell of sun on the sage, listening to the almost imperceptible rustle of the tree's quaking leaves. And then I leaned forward, pulling my left breast out from my bathing suit, and grasped it, squeezing tight until milk came. A little bit, a few thin streams, making big drops, falling into the dust. I put it back behind my suit, brought out my right breast, and again pulled the milk forward until it spilled out on the ground, just briefly, drops.

I sat there, steady, stunned. People kept asking me what it was like to have weaned, to have my body back, for it be my own again.

Ah, but it isn't really, is it? It isn't ever my own. It never was. It is gift, and it is futility. I sat in the dust and thought of all the ways I had been taught to prepare, ways to help my baby be healthy, thrive, develop a good immune system. I remembered the earnestness with which I approached breastfeeding, not shaming parents who used formula, but grateful that I could avoid it for my own babies. And now I sat on the dusty ground, above my son's ashes and tiny fragmented bones, crushed, mingled with the soil. Once more, I pulled each breast out in turn. I heard dear friends-turned-family laughing and playing on the beach and in the water down below, reveling in the beauty, in one another. Sheltered by the privacy of huge pine trees, I squeezed, I pulled, gripping until great streams erupted. Those wildly tiny, thread-thin streams, which can somehow become so much, came shooting out in different directions. I squeezed hard, until each breast hurt, pulling the last of my milk out, spilling it onto the ground, until no more would come. It disappeared down into the dust.

I sat in wonderment at my utter lack of control in it all. My life, my offering, from my very being, spilled into the dust and ashes. Why did the ancients make sacrifices, give up offerings, pour out libations of wine and oil and goodness? Why do people still offer drinks to the dead, who clearly have no use for them? I had never felt moved by such a ritual, even less now that

I was ritually avoiding all alcohol, yet I was compelled to offer the last of my milk to my dead son, offer it to my God, offer it to the dry earth. There was beauty resting in the knowledge that it would do no good, that it would change nothing. It was an offering without end or even reason. It was where I needed to finish. My last milk would go down into the dust.

I breathed in deeply again, grateful to have made this unexpected sacrifice, even in the midst of bustling camp life. "Thank you," I uttered, and I meant it.

I rose, I turned, ready to find the rest of my family.

Dry Bones Retreating

It was our third trip to the lake that summer, just a month after the wedding. I returned to Logan Shoals, to my trail, to my private retreat along the lake. I wasn't sure if I would even be able to run, having bashed and likely broken my little toe a few days earlier. But I couldn't come to the lake, come this close to my trail, and stay away. This was the place I'd begun to heal. I wasn't done.

Being mid-August, the parking lot was packed. Big groups of families and whole caravans of tourists swarmed around the established path to the official scenic vistas. A bride and groom stood off to the side, trying to get photos taken with just the two of them in the frame. Their limo waited, idling, blocking others in, the usual Tahoe summer madhouse.

I jumped the split-rail fence at the far end of the parking lot, well away from the fray. Looking over my shoulder, I crept down the hill, hoping no one would see me. I wanted this place to myself.

Soon the towering granite boulders blocked the sound of the crowds. I dropped lower, my feet sliding on the warm pine duff. A chipmunk darted out of my way, a Stellar's jay making a racket overhead. But I was alone with them, no people in sight. I landed down on the wide trail, unfolding before me in both directions. The lake was a lavish turquoise. I tested my toe, jogging a few paces, then pushing harder. It wasn't pleasant, but it would hold. Running didn't seem to make it worse.

I headed north, running up the hill with some trepidation, hugging the curves of the lake. I ran through the dry creek bed, still springing side to side out of habit. I arrived at the most treacherous part of the trail, totally smooth and without dangerous footing, but rife with memories. I could barely see what was once Ezekiel's valley of dry bones littering the trail. So much had changed in the three and a half years since that first winter, when all I could see was death.

Instead of that dry and lifeless spread of bone shards, the ridge of the hill was bright with the noon sun, heat radiating off the baking sand. Small, pale yellow butterflies flitted about, a vibrant, living cliché. Huge green bushes overwhelmed the trail, forcing me to dodge their many arms, reaching in from both sides. The branches were heavy with bright red berries. Berries, I thought. Not bones here, but *berries*! How far we had come. I pushed up to the rusty gate and ran down again, all along the lake, the length of the trail, then turned to run back up once more.

It was on the second lap that I looked more closely and saw that the red fruits decorating the bushes were not berries—they were rose hips. They hung thickly on the massive wild rosebushes. I stopped to examine them, amazed, pricking my skin as I ran my fingers across them. I crested the hill once more, filled with awe. As I ran back down, weaving along the dry sand of the creek bed, tracing water long gone through this gauntlet of roses, it came to me that it was Mary's feast day. This very day. Her day. Surrounded by rose hips—the fruit. I began praying fervently and was caught by surprise as parts of the Hail Mary came rushing to my lips—the bits at first incomplete and out of order, but slowly organizing themselves, making themselves right. I had never spent much time with the prayer, not since memorizing it as a funny gift for a dear college friend, a devout Roman Catholic, some dozen years earlier. But the words were with me, they were in me.

Hail Mary, full of grace,

the Lord is with you.

Blessed are you among women,

and blessed is the fruit of your womb, Jesus.

And then came the resounding truth, a proclamation—I heard it from Mary and from the lake and from all the surrounding creation—that blessed is the fruit of *my* womb, too. Blessed is the crucified fruit of Mary's womb. And all of us. All of us women who have born grief from our wombs. Not cursed, but blessed.

"Hail Mary," I called out through the hot sun on the solitary trail. "Come to me, Mary, full of grace. Blessed is the fruit of your womb, Jesus, and blessed are you among women. Mother of God, pray for me, a sinner, now and at the hour of my death."

I ran, tracing the lake, following Mary.

The words were jumbled, maybe, but they felt true. The form of Mary's presence, the form of her goodness and breath, sailed on ahead, up the trail. There was wisdom in this place, if I could only see it, if I could only follow her.

Through the Door

Sam had been asking us more and more. It came all of a sudden. Just as his language began to take off, now at about two and a half, so too came his questions about his missing brother. He had seen the tree, and he saw the photographs all around the apartment. He was hearing us talk about Fritz, sometimes. It didn't make sense to him.

And so we relived the early days after Fritz's death, the time when Alice, the same age Sam was now, needed the story incessantly, hour after hour, day after day. Her need for the story had been insatiable. Sam followed suit.

Mostly, though, his questions came at bedtime.

"Mommy," he started, staring up at the dark ceiling, "tell me about when Fritz died."

He interrupted me though, midstory, with more questions.

"Mommy, where is Fritz now? Why did he die? When will I die?"

Like Alice at this age, he couldn't yet pronounce his *r*'s. *Fawitz* this, *Fawitz* that, where is *Fawitz*? Two syllables. No brother.

I tried to answer honestly. I wanted him to know his brother, insofar as that was possible. I wanted this subject to be fair game. But why, dear God, I asked, must all this *always* come at bedtime?

Sam was finally silent for a while. I wondered, hopefully, if he might be slowing down. I was ready for him to fall asleep; I was tired of being the grown-up here. The pause stretched on, but it seemed like he was thinking, not resting.

Then, loudly, excitedly, pointing fervently: "Mommy, do you think Fritz is going to run through that door right now? Is he?"

I curled my body around this young, hopeful boy, this being who did not yet comprehend death or loss or separation, not really. He only wanted to get to know his brother. This brother, Fritz, the babe Sam would never meet, could still burst through the door at any moment, upending bedtime.

I had so much to teach Sam, though I wished I didn't have to. I wanted to chase down his expectant trust, follow it, give my own self over to that trust, too.

Four

January 9, 2018. On this morning, still in the dark, Sam crawled into bed with me and asked, "How do we get to love?"

I wasn't sure if he was wondering about the route to arrive at love, or how it is that we are so lucky as to be allowed to love—each a good question.

I tried to answer him, but the conversation turned quickly to roosters and volcanoes.

I headed out for a run after breakfast, but only a brief one, and it had to be close to home and filled with walking and stretching, as I'd been wrestling plantar fasciitis in recent months. There was no expansive wilderness to lean on this day, except within. I still felt cavernous, with no map. I made it only as far as our neighborhood park four blocks away before I stopped to stretch on a bridge, the rain-swollen creek rushing below. I lifted my foot against the iron railing, pushing hard into it, straightening the length of my leg. I exhaled. For the first time in recent memory, I saw my breath. My breath! This wild air that moves all but imperceptibly, unnoticed and nearly forgotten until it is gone.

It had been four years now, today, since Fritz ceased to breathe. What I would have given to see his breath blown over a cold creek.

Even with the run, even four years on, and with all I'd learned and survived, that day haunted me, gutted me, sank me, its images flashing before my eyes, as I continuously relived it.

The unutterable truth was that on days like today, I did feel like it was my fault. It didn't matter that we had taken Fritz to all the ultrasounds, none of which revealed anything they felt the need to follow up on with higher-level machines and more scrutiny. In addition to the midwife, we had taken him to an MD for a well-baby check when he was two days old; the doctor and nurses alike agreed he was enormous and healthy. Still, I was responsible for the things that I had left undone. I wished that after the urgent care visit I had fought, argued, gone to another doctor, to the ER, called 911 when maybe there was still time. Paid more attention as I sang him to sleep that night. Done something else, *anything* else, before it was so completely too late. But I didn't. I did so very little. I wasn't a fighter for him. This was the story that wound its way around me, suffocating me, enticing me in, trying to convince me that it was truth.

When I worked at it, I could usually get my mind back to a steadier place, making better sense of it, arriving at some intellectual peace. Most of the time I could settle there now, letting it be as it was. But on days like this one, after four long years without my son, I wondered if I could ever forgive myself, really. It might just be a burden I would carry, one that was particularly heavy on days like this.

I didn't know what God thought of how I'd cared—or not—for my baby's life, this most precious gift. Was it my sin that let my son die? It was not a question most people would want to engage, but it surfaced for me, nagging. *Was* it my fault? Could I have stopped it if I had tried harder, believed more? The creeping suggestion came, too, that I'd failed at my single most important job as his mother: to keep him alive. My action and inaction separated him from us, and me from so much. Was this not sin?

Whatever may have been true, the swirling mess of my thoughts tormented me. Deep in my bones, insidious shards of blame and guilt and regret and shame stabbed at me.

Some part of me wanted to ask for the Rite of Reconciliation—what's more commonly called confession—but I doubted if anyone would do it. I suspected Phil would try to talk me out of it, try to convince me that it wasn't my fault, that there was nothing to confess, save my faltering, limited humanness, same as every other soul. I would probably do the same, if someone came to me with this request.

I just wished I could put it all down.

Even in my anguish, there was the temptation to think that I had this by now, I was tough, I would be fine. The terrain was familiar, but it was no less menacing. The sight of that breathless baby would never leave me. A friend who is wise and rather qualified on such matters, having buried her own daughter, reminded me later in the day of the things that I preach and then promptly forget: that there was more than enough love, that it was true that it was still awful, that it was okay to ask.

And so I tried to reach for my dear ones this day. I told them that Fritz's death still broke me. I told them I still needed their love. And I tried to remember to say thank you, even if it came out feebly.

Bag of Booze

I had hemmed and hawed for some time before finally texting Emily, one of my co-workers, asking if I could give her a bag of booze. I knew she had noticed I'd stopped drinking, but we hadn't discussed it. I was scared to make her the offer, but she seemed like the right person for the unusual request.

She said yes. I brought the bag to work one quiet afternoon. I popped my head in her door but saw that someone else was in her office, too.

"I have the bag for you," I said, "and thanks."

I carried the big tote bag into my own office, the bottles rattling against each other—some half empty, some mostly full, some unopened. The remnants. I was amused that it had taken me so long, but I wasn't entirely surprised. I mean, what if I didn't actually quit in the end? What a waste, to give all that alcohol away, only to have to buy it again! It didn't feel risky to still have some at home, it didn't pose a particular temptation. It had been satisfying to watch the bottles gather more and more dust as the first thirty days turned into months, which then rolled by into a year, and on into my sober future.

Now it struck me as momentous to give it all away. And yet, what an odd thing: "Here, friend, would you do me the favor of taking all this delicious, expensive stuff that otherwise might slowly kill me?"

Why offer something potentially death-dealing for me as a gift to another, especially one I held dear? Why would I wish that on my friend? It was part of being honest, though. I knew that Emily was fine, and that ridding myself of the booze was right for me.

She ducked in to take the bag later that afternoon. "Hey, Liz, this is a big deal," she said. "This is a really vulnerable thing to share."

"Yes. It is," I replied, somewhat protected from her by my desk, a makeshift fortress of stacks of books, a standing-desk contraption, flotsam and jetsam. Except it was clear I didn't need protection. Emily had had my back this whole time. There was a softening, somewhere, in that space between us.

"It is a really big deal," I concurred. "I feel prouder of this than anything I've done in . . . a very long time."

I was still learning how to explain my shift to becoming a nondrinker—that was where the real vulnerability lay. I offered Emily a new way in, one I hadn't named out loud to another person yet. I reiterated what she already knew—that I have shit for genes—and I preempted what I suspected was everyone's question: "No, there wasn't a crisis, no DUI, no rock bottom." But then I owned it in a new way: "My off-switch is faulty, kinda broken actually, and unreliable."

Emily nodded, kindly and—this part surprised me—with an openness that carried respect. She didn't seem to think that *I* was broken just because my off-switch was. If anything, her response seemed to indicate that she saw that I was more whole for recognizing that it was busted and then changing course.

Holy shit: It blew my mind that in owning up to what was broken within me, I became more whole. That in living within my own limitations, others might see me more fully. I realized that all these years—these decades—I had received the story that drunks were deplorable people. That being an alcoholic was an identity to hide, one you should buy your way out of with fancy gifts, one we did not discuss.

The vulnerability I felt in handing Emily my bag of old booze—my now unnecessary, even unappealing booze—was rooted in the fear that, by telling her I was broken, I would be forking over my dignity as well.

Why, then, was she standing tall, shoulders loose, beaming at me? Why was there love in her eyes?

My mind flashed to one of my mom's worst binges, insofar as there was a scale for her binges. I was seventeen or eighteen, still in high school, and I was fed up. I had used up my patience, my strategic co-dependence, my compassion—my well was bone-dry. My mom was drunk again, had been for days. I got up and left the house still in the dark, the dawn light creeping in over the country hills as I drove the lonely winding road into town and to the YMCA. This happened before she was up: I dived into the pool or circled the track or found my way in the weight room—whatever could make me feel more alive than the doom that filled our house. I returned at dinnertime or later, having finished school and rugby practice, and she was already out cold again, drunk, gone in her room. Had she made it to work? I did not know. I had reached the point of being done with it.

And so on the next day—it must have been the weekend now, the sun streaming in through the windows—I tried to rouse her. I tried to force her up, as if that could make her sober. In my naïve anger, I wrestled the covers from her, trying to drive home my message. It was the middle of the day; it was time to be awake, time to live. Still drunk, missing clothes, she sat up. Forlornly, pathetically, she argued with me in a tired tug-of-war, trying to pull the covers back from my strong hold and steadier footing. She didn't want to leave that numb place, she must have felt physically ill, but this time we argued with words, too.

"Get up! You have to get up!" I yanked the covers, hard.

"Give me my dignity! You have to give me back my dignity!" she returned, angry.

I dropped the covers on the bed, giving up and walking away. *Dignity?* Nothing I did made a difference.

Still, it had lodged—this visceral sense that dignity exited when struggle with alcohol arrived. That one who had a broken off-switch forfeited dignity in exchange for self-awareness, that it was an embarrassment. I recognized how the logic didn't hold. It was not the judgment I would render on another, ever, but it was stuck somewhere deep in reference to me. I was my mother's daughter, after all, the fruit of her womb. If she had lost her dignity through drinking, and if alcohol was my problem as well, then—the faulty logic lied—my dignity was lost, too.

And yet. And yet here was this friend standing before me, her fiery hair tousled, her piles of work paused. She stopped and honored me, respected me, handed me my own dignity in her response. Or maybe it was already there, and she was just pointing it out.

Emily texted me that evening, after we were home, following up: "I really appreciate you, Liz Tichenor."

That was all. She upended my inherited worldview, my family's legacy. Living into my brokenness, eyes wide open, I was becoming whole.

Raw Light of Good Friday

Each year, All Souls offers a Holy Week service for children on Good Friday. Most of the services that week are hard for parents to bring their kids to— they're scheduled either too early in the morning or during school or after bedtime. This service of ours is sort of a mash-up, making our way through all the days of Holy Week in an hour, our attempt to welcome the kids into the mystery, into the waiting, into the reality of how painful the story of the crucifixion is. It flies in the face of all the bunnies and chocolate, which is exactly our intention.

The year before, I had constructed a new way to tell the ancient story, pulling together wooden storytelling pieces from our Sunday School classrooms and filling a two-foot-tall basket with them. Families gathered late in the afternoon on Good Friday. I had already spent four hours in worship that day, and was exhausted. We sat on the floor at the front of the sanctuary, forgoing the pews. These three- and four- and five-year-olds needed to be close so that they could see—and feel—the story being told.

I began helping them to get ready. "Today we're going to share a really big story," I started, showing them the huge basket. "It's a long story, and a sad one, but it's a really important story."

Sam, newly three years old, jumped to his feet, waving his hand fervently in the air. I stopped. "This is the story of when Fritz died!" he exclaimed, very proud that *he* already knew what we were talking about.

I slowly blinked. I faltered.

"Oh," I started, inhaling sharply. These conversations are rarely easy with my children. They are much more difficult in front of an audience.

"Actually, Sam, the story we're going to hear today is about when Jesus died."

I waited a moment, wondering if that would be sufficient, or if he would push back with more questions. He sat still. I collected myself, continuing.

Internally, though, I wasn't sure if I wanted to laugh or cry or do both at the same time. It was pretty funny that this preacher's kid didn't know the difference between Jesus and his own dead brother. It was also beautiful and heartbreaking, how he mixed them up, how he knew instinctively that they were connected.

The story was told, feet were washed, a cross was adorned and venerated with rose petals and modeling clay.

We had time for a quick dinner at home, soup reheated, before I returned to my office to finish learning by heart the sermon that I'd preach during the evening service.

Sam's assertion hung in the air around me. I had decided earlier in the week to preach about Mary that night, to exhort the congregation to connect with her, honor her, learn from her. I knew it wouldn't be easy, as all this was so close to home for me, for us, so close that my preschooler couldn't seem to keep it straight.

I paced in my office, trying desperately to commit my words to memory, to get this truth more deeply lodged in my body. I wasn't sure if I had it. About a year earlier, I had begun the practice of preaching without a manuscript, which was exhilarating and, at least from my side, felt more compelling. It was also nerve-racking when I wasn't sure if I really had it down.

I walked upstairs to put my robe on, with just five minutes to spare. I was still rattled. The acolytes and clergy gathered in the hallway, about to begin the solemn entrance into the sanctuary.

"You ready?" Phil asked. I shook my head.

"I don't have it in me, Phil." I hadn't done this before, giving up on a sermon at the last minute. "I have to print it out. I'll meet you in there."

He nodded, understanding. "Do what you need to do."

I ran up the half flight of stairs to grab my keys from the sacristy, then down the stairs to the basement, to our offices, my cassock and flowing surplice trailing behind me. I whipped open my computer, flustered, frantically reformatting the sermon and sending it to print. I ran back up, trying not to trip on my blood-red stole, jumping two steps at a time, feeling my mother's muscle memory in my own body. She always did that, two at a time, no matter where she was going. I snuck into the sacristy, tried to calm my breath to listen. It was still the first reading. I waited for it to finish, then quietly walked out and took my seat in front of the people.

My heart beat fast, shaking me further. Soon I went with the rest of the altar party to join the congregation, sitting in the front pew, listening to five readers proclaim the Passion Gospel, the story of Jesus's trial and death.

I thought I was maintaining composure, steeling myself. My friend Caroline, the lay leader that night, was sitting at my side. She reached out, taking my left hand. Tears brimmed in my eyes and began rolling down my cheeks. I wondered how she could tell. She held on. My mind drifted, remembering a walk she and I had taken in the winter a few weeks after Fritz died. We circled Spooner Lake, crunching through old, dry snow.

"I've been trying to imagine what you've been going through," Caroline had said then. "I don't know what it's like, but I'm trying to imagine, and it's awful."

I remembered looking at her through the cold, shocked. She was willing to go there, to try to put herself there—here, where I was. No one had articulated that to me, it had just been one long chorus, round after round of *I cannot imagine.*

The sound of the organ pulled me back to the present. Verses of a hymn were interspersed throughout the Gospel. "Were you there when they crucified my Lord?" we sang, slowly, mournfully. These words, familiar since my youth, now snagged in my throat. The tears came faster.

I joined Sam's confusion, unsure as to whether we were telling the story of Jesus's death or Fritz's, all of it blurring together again. The story continued. I had forgotten to put Kleenex in my pocket and shook my head. My mom? She'd have never have been so careless, as she was a crier, too, especially during hymns. I wiped my eyes with the flowing sleeve of my white surplice instead, and took a deep breath.

Phil, sitting on my right, reached to take my right hand. It was more than I could bear, having these two friends see me, join me, stay with me. My shoulders heaved, my tears flowing quickly now. I held on tight, grateful. The story continued. There would not be respite this night. I loosed my hands to blow my nose into my sleeve. It was disgusting. I was amused, and also strangely settled: this was just where I should be that night. Undone, weeping, clutching my friends' hands, very literally dripping with grief.

But I still had to preach.

I let go of their hands near the end of the Gospel. I had drawn their strength. Now I needed to steady myself, get ready to find my voice again. I wiped my face, the tears still coming, but more slowly. Eye shadow streaked across my wet sleeves from where I'd rubbed my eyes, the fabric now more ashen than starched white.

As I rose and walked up the steps, my feet were more sure than my heart was. I held on to the bright pine of the ambo—smaller than a pulpit, but more graceful than a lectern, it's the place where people read the lessons from scripture, and also where the response comes, in the preaching. Some say the name comes from the Greek, meaning "to go up, to elevate," just as the people of old went up mountains to listen to God. Others say it comes from the Latin, in which *ambo* means "both"—this place for both receiving and responding. It seemed clear I would be doing both tonight, and I grasped the wooden sides, grateful that it was enough to hold me upright.

I looked out into the darkened sanctuary, first at Phil's kind eyes, then at Caroline's, each still there with me. I was still blinking, fast. I opened my mouth, unsure of what sound would emerge. I heard my voice begin, but it sounded to me like it was coming from far away; I was not sure whose body I inhabited anymore.

> Mary is there with her son. Her feet are planted on the barren earth, even as her body trembles. She cannot pry her eyes off her son. She cannot look away from the cross on which he hangs. Mary's body is gripped with shock. Her mouth hangs open as she breathes in the sordid reality that is unfolding. She can't convince her mouth to form words. Everything has gone so horribly wrong.

I felt her body, overlaid with mine—or was I in hers? I traced our way through her story, through their story. How they ended up here, at the cross, on this night. And then I asked my parishioners to do what Caroline had done for me. I asked them to imagine, as imagining is the root of compassion, I said. This is the root of it: *com-passion*, suffering with. We are called to enter into the suffering of another.

I stepped back into Mary's body, not knowing where I was going, really, just speaking now. The paper in front of me had faded away.

> Mary knows this body intimately. She grew this body. She birthed him, she nursed him, feeding him of her own body. She sang and told stories and scrubbed him. Mary brought healing to this body before he became a healer in his own right. She bore the incarnation. Mary bore the body that now hangs, slowly giving up breath.

I was telling her story even as I was telling mine. Sam was right.

With Mary, I listened to Jesus, telling these witnesses, this family, that they belonged to one another. Even from the cross, he creates new kin. He was speaking to us, too.

The sanctuary had grown brighter as I preached, a raw light cutting through the dark. A primal glow stood among us, holding me steady on my feet, carrying me.

I was loud now, my voice raw as the light. Still it was emerging from beyond me, somewhere deep, somewhere other. On this night, the words were not my own.

> Mary bears the unbearable. This is her witness as the God-bearer. We are called to do the same, to bear the unbearable, with and for each other. We have to trust that we do not bear the suffering alone. Listen to the truth Jesus speaks, in the midst of all pain: behold, we belong to one another.

I closed my mouth, staring out at this gathered body for another long moment, before walking slowly down the steps, back to the pew, back to my place between these two good souls who had held my hands. They received me—breathing me into the silence, holding me there in their presence—and I felt how profoundly I belonged to them.

I realized I had been wrong, though, thinking back to my frantic scurry just before the service began. Maybe it was wise to have the manuscript in front of me, but I did have the story in me. I do. This story is who I am. It is Jesus's story, and Fritz's. It is Mary's story, it is mine, how we belong to each other and must face death together.

That night I slept hard, back in my own body, completely spent from the anguish of the day.

Holy Saturday was quiet, spacious, and long. I was busy learning my sermon for the Easter Vigil that night, a hairpin turn in my soul from the night before. I took a break for lunch and was standing in the kitchen when I heard Sam pipe up in the next room, this time quizzing Jesse.

"So it's tomorrow that Fritz comes back to life, right?"

I couldn't make out Jesse's response. I was just grateful that he was the one answering today, helping Sam weave his way through all this talk of death and new life. I didn't know how I was going to answer, knowing he'd be asking me too, and soon.

Preaching Vigil

It was now 2018, and we had made it through two years since I carried the silver box of the broken Son, since I had met Ruthie at our altar rail, grown on Fritz's milk. We'd kept living and had returned again to the Great Vigil. It was a downbeat, my point of rooting myself in the faith, going deeper into the truth where I placed my trust, year by year. Tonight it was my job, once again, to proclaim resurrection. This shaky thing, so hard to pin down, was mine to lift up. The weight of death still crushed me. I still felt the pain I'd preached the night before—Mary's anguish, and mine, and that of so many others. The compassion was real, too, but did not erase the pain.

The week before this Holy Saturday, Phil and I had driven in his roaring diesel truck to a feed store on the outskirts of the Bay Area. We walked in, both in collar, out of place among the peeping chicks and tack and salt licks.

"We'd like to see your options for stock tanks," Phil said plainly to the checker.

Perplexed, the checker radioed to another employee, then sent us around back. Soon we were rolling out different stock tanks from the side of a barn, testing them, kneeling down inside to see how we would fit. We had decided that this was the year we would do immersion baptisms. We just had to figure out how.

"Could we rent it?" Phil asked.

"No, that contaminates it for the livestock that would eat from it next," said the employee.

"Hmm, okay, what budget line would this come from?" Phil mused.

"Memorial gifts?" I suggested, which often covered new things for worship. "If we keep using it, it would soon be cheaper than renting one, anyway."

We hoisted the middle-sized aluminum tank into the bed of his truck. At nearly six feet in diameter, it would have to sit up on one of the wheel wells, sticking diagonally out of the truck. The feed-store guy went to work with twine, tying it in to keep us all safe on the freeway home. It was a laughable sight. We checked the rearview mirrors constantly, worried it might come loose.

Now at the vigil, the stock tank had become a font, filled with water in the darkened church, lit only by candlelight. It was surrounded by plants that folks had loaned us to help make the rough shine of the aluminum more beautiful. The silver metal glimmered under the dark water, visible even from the other end of the sanctuary.

The night was a blur of story and song, of adults splashing down into the water, all the way under, baptized. Of calling the saints present, again, to come rejoice with us. Of the church, filled at last, late in the night, with bells and light and alleluias. I stepped to the ambo to preach, exhausted, overwhelmed, riding the wave of the night.

I could not lie to them. I could not preach the light without naming the darkness, too. I returned to what I knew best, to the only way I could hope to know that the Resurrection was true: the ways I'd mapped a path through the darkness.

I told them about my twenty-ninth birthday, when those brave and kind and foolish friends came crashing, splashing into the frigid lake with me, simply because I asked them to. I remembered aloud the darkness of that day. Fritz's tree planted, his ashes ready to be picked up, all the souls already gathering, ready to help me bury him.

I told them about the life I heard as I emerged from the water, the sound of laughter, of raucous bodies racing for towels, shaking off like dogs. I told them how I realized that, against all odds, the laughter was my own. Life was happening within me, even as the unbearable unfolded all around me. This life could not be stopped.

As I finished my sermon, I realized with relief that I believed these words I spoke:

> This way of resurrection is scandalous. This hope seems like such
> a far reach. It did then for Mary and the disciples. It does now.

But here's what I will give witness to, on this night: God meets us in that hope. God is present there at the tomb, even before we can recognize this Risen One. It is a scandalous act to hope. And again and again, against all odds, God meets us there in the depths of darkness. God comes to us, under the crash of waves, calling our name. God hears our hope, pulling us from the waters and into new life.

I trusted these words, I realized, standing there, proclaiming them. This grace had happened to me; it was happening to me still. Even those facing the unbearable could be resurrected. We were being brought back to life, right now.

The Mantel

Two days after Easter, Jesse, Alice, Sam, and I packed up and flew to Dallas to see my brother and to meet his new baby. My nephew wasn't so new anymore, already five and a half months old, but our spending time together was new. John and I hadn't really done that as adults. There'd been a few family gatherings here and there, but he'd been gone for most of our twenties. Not quite two years older than I, John joined the National Guard before he graduated from high school and was sent into Iraq at the beginning of the war in 2003. He was later recruited for the Army Rangers and spent three more tours overseas, spanning the better part of a decade. We were only peripherally in touch, and as much as I loved him, it was hard to know what we had in common anymore. Our shared childhood adventures seemed like a very distant past.

But I wanted to try, especially with my nephew now on the scene. I wanted him to grow up knowing John's family, too. With our mom gone, our side of the family had really dwindled. And so we went, and I wondered what I would find.

Our little family parked in the cul-de-sac, and I looked up at my brother's large brick house, a sweeping archway over the front door. John was already opening it, coming out to welcome us, his German shepherds scooting past him to see what was happening. It was a gorgeous home and, by our Berkeley standards, huge. Jesse and I were used to apartments, tight quarters, no yards. We unloaded, came in, began to settle. It felt immediately and strangely familiar. John gave the kids a tour; I followed, curious, perplexed.

It hit me: his home was filled with our mom's furniture. With her art. With everything we'd left in her house to stage it. Joyful, awe-filled tears lighted in the corners of my eyes.

I had always assumed that he had taken nothing but our grandfather's stuffed duck, though I'd never brought it up again. But no, his home was centered around what our mother had left. The long dining room table with high-backed black leather chairs. Next to it, like a buffet table, the dresser we'd had for as long as I could remember, the one she'd repainted again and again.

"I hid inside this," I told Alice, pointing, grinning, almost giddy.

She cocked her head, incredulous.

"Right in here, behind these doors." I showed her the space in the bottom of the dresser, the same contact paper there, now faded.

Our mom's books sat on their shelves—novels, autobiographies, travel books—and there was our family's tattered dictionary from the days before computers.

Over the dining room table hung a painting that had been in our mom's office: three men on horseback, by an American artist, whimsical. I had never really liked it much, but she had loved it. I was glad to see it here now, presiding over the dining room.

The living room, too: a green couch, now frayed from the dogs. It had filled the tiny living room of her home, that last new house. I had held Alice on it, then a baby, weeping, reading my mother's journal, reading the closest thing we would have to a suicide note. I'd nursed Alice there on its deep pillows, stealing relief from her clutching me, letting me cling to her in return.

But it was all here, in Dallas. I couldn't believe it. I was so completely comforted to be here among it all.

John and I had not talked much about our mother, not since the end, when he took the brunt of it, trying to get her into rehab, then dealing with all the bureaucratic work left by a dead parent who left no will. We were supposed to focus on the positive, he'd said; I remembered that much.

It took a couple of days before I could mention it, sort of sideways, glancing. "I didn't realize you had taken mom's furniture," I said quietly, offhand.

"Yup," he replied.

"I'm really glad you did," I said, and I was. There was so much more I wanted to say, but I decided that was enough for now.

Each day we were there, I stared from the couch at a small cedar box sitting on the mantel. At my mom's funeral, her ashes had been in a huge marble urn, so heavy I struggled to carry it. I stared at this box, wondering. I wasn't sure I wanted to have that conversation yet. Things were going so well—did I really want to bring up the fact that we still hadn't chosen a place to bury our mother? But I wanted to know. I lay in bed at night, wondering if I could take some of the ashes home with me, just quietly, just to have a little bit of her close.

I crept back downstairs one night and padded into the silent living room. I reached up to the mantel, rising on my tiptoes, and took down the box. It was no more than three by five inches, but it was heavy. I turned it to one side, and then to the other. I could feel the ash and bone sliding back and forth inside, thick, heavy, inert.

But the box was sealed shut, some sort of yellowed silicone caulk wrapping the edge, filling the crack where it could otherwise open. I sighed, thwarted, disappointed.

And still. For the first time in more than five years, here was what remained of my mother. I was grateful to be near that ash, close to her bone, in the presence of what remained. It was a relief to sit, to simply exist within range of the body that made me.

11

LAST VISIONS

ᒥ∀ƧⱢ ∧IƧIO∩Ƨ

Into the Fires

Last night, the fires burned. All across California they raged, they raged also in my dreams.

We were in some sort of cabin, traveling. It was unfamiliar terrain, and the fires were getting too close, danger setting in. We had to get out, get home—and fast. It was night.

It was the *we* of the dream that caught me most by surprise. It was my mom and me, just the two of us. It was surprising mainly because it felt so normal, obvious. We were driving out in a ramshackle old pickup truck, seeking refuge, surviving the chaos and madness together.

It was pitch-black and smoky, the fire roaring over the road, the road itself on fire, but this flaming path was the only way forward. We realized, my mom and I, that I had to aim straight into the fire if we were going to make it out. I held tight to the wheel and I drove. My mother navigated.

Smoke filled every space, clouding our windows, masking the dark woods that covered us. Still, we could breathe easily in our little cab.

There was no extra light to guide our way—no streetlights, no headlights—only the glow of the menacing fire, beckoning us toward its center. I pressed my foot hard into the floor, gunning the engine, lurching forward. Careening around the dark curves, I kept my eyes locked on the fire even as it streamed by us, reaching in, flames licking all around us.

My mom was steady. In life, she had always been a wild passenger, squealing and flapping her hands at what seemed to her like near misses, but not tonight. Here in the fire, she was perfectly calm.

It was just so dark, this night, and yet so fiery. A cavernous furnace, building ever thicker walls of flame around us.

We plunged deeper, my mom and I. We pushed through, on and on, until we'd eventually outrun the immediate threat but could take the truck no farther. We left it by the side of the road, continuing together on foot, up rambling paths along hills and cliffs and water. The fire glowed behind us, still present but now more distant.

The dream jumped forward. We made it. We had arrived somewhere, at someone's home. We sat, resting on the screened-in porch, with a large and growing group of friends. We made introductions. It was only then that I remembered she was dead.

How can this be? I wondered. My mom had just accompanied me straight through this great ordeal, straight through the depths of the fire. How could it be that she was already dead, and had been for a long time?

I woke to real life in a start. I ached, starkly aware of having been with her body and with her soul. It had been ages since we had been together like that, even in a dream. It was now nearly six years since she'd died.

Her presence lingered as I became more awake—now Alice was climbing over me, now I was rising to make coffee, now Sam was stumbling out of his bedroom to demand my lap—yet my mother's presence hung about me.

She had walked with me again. She had seen me into the worst of the fires, and through to the other side. She was not fully gone from me.

"It never really ends, does it?" I had asked all those years ago, my belly swollen with Alice.

"No, it keeps on going," she had replied then, as she told me again now.

Resurrection in the Smoke

I have found that it is easier to trust resurrection, to practice it, when I am far away from death.

As we drove through the foothills from the Bay Area to Tahoe, winding up over the mountain pass, smoke settled in, gathering incrementally, turning from a vaguely cloudy haze to a thick wall, shielding all that lay beyond. Hot, dry California wildfires were burning all around. None were so close as to threaten us, but all were near enough to make us wheeze and cough. As we came down from the summit toward Tahoe, all the vista parking areas were empty. No tourists were bothering to stop—there was no first glimpse of the lake here at 7,000 feet. The kids whined in the back seat. I wanted to complain also. I *need* this lake to be gorgeous, I told myself. I *need* it to be blue.

It was blue, but only barely. I couldn't tell the water from the smoke and the sky until we were just beside it, forty feet from the shore on the last stretch of highway, but the tone of blue was ashen. It was dusky—the color newborns turn when they've stopped breathing but might still be able to start again. The water still rippled, but it only reflected the smoke, fine ash filling the air.

Arriving at camp, I wanted to cry, wanted to leave without even unloading the car. Everything was gray and bleak, the smoke shrouding the lake, hemming us in. There were no mountains rising on the other side, no sweeping, open sky. There was just this place, this ground right here, right in front of me.

I resisted the urge to ask Jesse if we could leave, just move on. I expected he would go along with it if I told him I was really miserable, if I told him I just couldn't take the smoke.

"I want you to feel good," he kept telling me.

I didn't know if it was possible here, not this time. I wondered if maybe I'd used up my share of resurrection, if maybe all the healing that could happen already had.

I hoped not, even as this fear nagged at me. I hoped more was yet possible. I bit my tongue. I'd try to make a go of it, even if I was mad, even if it felt like a waste to be back at this lake of cinders.

Before even unpacking, Sam led me to check on Fritz's tree. He remembered this time; he knew where it was and why it was there. All those countless rounds of telling him the story of his brother seemed to have helped, at least for now.

We stepped off the path, just before the young aspen. It was there. It was different. Trickles of water spilled into the ground from the drip hose, circling the trunk, water lines reaching out to the edges of the root ball down below. There were new shoots—more than the single small one that had poked up last year. Three, four—I counted five shoots emerging from the ground. But rising from their center was just one trunk. Was this the same tree? Had the last one died and Stuart quietly replaced it? It was about the right height, but I barely recognized it, absent its trinity of trunks. I circled again, puzzling. It looked healthy, at least, most of its quaking leaves still green even as the heat of the summer pounded down on it. I knelt, prying away soil from its base. I found one tiny stump, just next to the white trunk, then another, partially buried. Both had been sawed off, right at ground level. I wondered what happened—were they sick? Somehow injured? I felt guilty that I hadn't been the one to cut it back, but I suspected Stuart had been watching it, taking care of what it needed, and felt my guilt sliding into gratitude.

The two giant Jeffrey pines that used to shadow the tree were gone now, too. They had loomed tall even from their places rooted on the beach below, hedging in the view of the lake from Fritz's place, from his tree. Now it was wide open: just this spot, this tree, the lake. I couldn't see across to the other side, but at least I could still see the water from here.

We were sleeping outside, sort of. The only space available at camp this week was one of the tipis. It was an odd thing. I was uncomfortable with what struck me as the appropriation of Native culture, on Native lands, by a community of mostly white people. Yet these two tipis had made it possible for more kids to come to camp each summer, which I thought was a very good thing. With zoning and permitting on the lakeshore being such a lengthy, twisted challenge, tipis qualified as temporary structures, a quick way to increase capacity. It was always a dance here, trying to make room for everyone.

As evening fell, we settled in, rolling out sleeping bags on cots, arranging the kids' loveys and water bottles and other necessities within arm's reach. The sounds of campers singing around the campfire faded into those of the dark and crashing waves, and I was surprised by how glad I was to be here instead of in one of the cabins. This tipi was the closest I'd slept to Fritz since he died. I was just down the path from his tree, no more than thirty feet from where his ashes were buried. The smoky wind crawled in under the bottom of the canvas walls and climbed down through the open top to glide across my face. It was the same wind that had rustled the aspen leaves, swirled the dust of his grave. I could feel the earth holding me up here as I drifted toward sleep, the same earth that held what was left of him.

But I didn't fall asleep. I lay in bed, staring up. And I recognized a primal longing, deep in my gut: I wanted to sneak out and dig up some of Fritz's ashes. A piece of bone, maybe, something I could take with me. Would the sound of a shovel wake my family? Would there be enough light with the moon, right now waning, and hidden by all the smoke? Would I even be able to find the ashes? Was anything left of him? I didn't know the answers to any of these questions. They kept rolling into my mind, though, pulled behind the visceral urge to find my son, to take him back with me and keep him.

I woke early in the morning to the sound of raindrops on the canvas. Alice woke, too, both of us surprised, stepping gingerly to peer out of the tipi's opening. The rain stopped soon, and we returned to our beds, hoping for more sleep. It was light out, but the sun had not yet risen above the eastern ridge. I missed the cover of darkness. I missed its protection, the possibility it seemed to hold even for that thing that could not be, of holding some bit of my son again.

Do not cling to me, he had told her. *I am ascending.* These words rang in my mind again from that first encounter of the Resurrection. I hated them. *To my God and your God.* (John 20:17, ESV) That's where Jesus told Mary he was going, where he was rising. I couldn't seem to shake these words loose.

Now at dawn, I questioned the urge to unearth what remained of my son. I couldn't shed the longing to hold some part of him, no matter how slight, but for now I decided I would leave the ground intact.

Nothing was finished here. This was what the earth seemed to be telling me: the aspen, cut back but thriving; the tender new sage growing up from the sand above his ashes. The wind, too, told me that our resurrection was not yet finished, that we were still being pulled up, rising into the God we shared. I so wanted to trust this rising. I had come back to this place needing to find life, instead to be covered in ash, again. The haze of smoke left me struggling. I could see my grief here. My son's ashes seemed to hang in the very air I breathed. I had been fooled. I hadn't finished anything.

Any Trail

I stuck out the smoke for three days before I realized I was grateful to be at the lake, even as it was. That afternoon, Jesse and I dashed around the corner on the highway for a quick trail run at Logan Shoals. A friend had offered to keep Alice and Sam for a bit, and we jumped at the chance. It was sweltering, still 84 degrees, and dry, but the smoke had lifted some since the morning. A run seemed worth a try.

We parked in the empty turnout and hopped the fence, its top rail now lying on the ground, making it easy to clear. I could hardly find the secret path down to the trail, though, and I wound us haphazardly through the sage and underbrush and piles of oversized Jeffrey pinecones. We hit the wide trail at the bottom eventually, then turned north up the hill, as I always had.

Dry, loose dirt shifted with the sand underfoot. Lupines hung on their stems, but the blooms were dried up, the fanning teardrop leaves beginning to yellow around the edges. Rising higher on the trail, we saw a couple of small, faintly orange rose hips scattered here and there on the bushes. Mostly, though, they were just bushes—big, plain, poking, nondescript. There were no flowers, no fruit. It was odd, I thought—it had been August last year when I found Mary here, the bushes heavy with rose hips only fifty weeks ago, but now they were just bushes.

I ran up through the valley, where I remembered the shadow of death, where I could still see the bones in my mind's eye. There were none. Sticks, white ones even, but no bones, no shards.

My running was slow and labored. After wrestling myself free of plantar fasciitis over the last eight months, I found my more substantial shoes and my strength both clunky. I slapped the gate at the end of the trail and turned around, catching a glimpse of Jesse—bare feet, electric-blue gym shorts that he'd had as long as I'd known him, no shirt, but a wide-brimmed sun hat, the kind a river guide might wear. He might look goofy, but he had no interest in courting skin cancer. His bare feet only glanced the ground; his running was nearly silent as he followed me, carefully pushing off on the balls of his feet.

"You're welcome to go fast if you want to," I called back to him. "This is as fast as I can go today, but don't hold back."

For years, Jesse's default had been to let me lead when we ran together. He knew it helped me to relax, to feel a little less threatened by how fast and fit he always was.

We returned to the center point in the trail, and just beginning up the southern hill, he burst out, pumping past me and up the trail in a dead sprint. I continued plodding slowly, breathing steadily but feeling the altitude. I rounded one corner and then another, and then saw Jesse loping back to me, great slow strides, bouncing down the trail. He fell into place behind me again, silent for a few minutes before his watch beeped the end of a timed interval and he jetted off in front of me again. We each hugged the curves of the shore, winding past the lake. It didn't steal my breath like it had done that night, the dark night when Fritz died. It didn't paralyze me today, sinking me in adrenaline and despair. Today we were here. Today we just ran.

It was less smoky this afternoon, much improved even from the morning. The sky above was largely blue, and the lake was finally washed in a bright blue, choppy, speckled with whitecaps all across. This was the lake I knew best. The smoke remained farther out, though, veiling the mountains on the other side. The water simply evaporated into a gray wall of smoke, far off. I still couldn't see anything beyond.

No one carried me today. No mysterious wind lifted my feet to fly me forward. There were no visions, no miracles. The sandy dirt was radiating heat, and it was deep as I ran up the hills. For each step I took, I was sliding partway back down again.

But we were here. We were still together, Jesse and I, running slowly, in and out of sync. I kept going mostly forward, and he kept looping back to find me, the two of us still together on the same path.

Maybe I had been wrong, thinking there was no miracle today, no thin place with visions crashing through for me. Maybe today, that vision, that miracle, was us: running on a trail that could be any trail, together, both of us still breathing. It was more than I had expected at so many turns, that I would even make it this far. Perhaps I was wrong about being carried today, too—because everyone was carrying us, everyone had carried us—all along and to this point and on this day, too, they continued. Lifting us, guiding us, carrying us. Christ, and his Body, very much alive and risen, lending us strength and keeping us moving forward, living, alive again. They carried me still. I trusted they'd carry me always.

The Night Lake

The day was done. The trail run that Jesse and I had shared was settling into my tired muscles. Alice and Sam appeared to be asleep. What was left here of Fritz lay undisturbed, quiet streams of water still trickling all around his tree. I sat outside the tipi. It was just past dark, the tiniest glow still remaining in the sky, which was clear, at last, after days of smoke. I had seen the mountains, dark and silhouetted, at sunset, and I saw stars, now, and Mars rising bright over the ridge, frozen waters hidden in its warm glow.

The wind had calmed for now, the leaves on Fritz's tree only barely quaking. But the water on this lake, my lake, was alive in the night. Someone far out of sight held the other end of the black silk cloth, a miles-long bolt, shaking it into long ripples that washed up on the smooth rocks just below my three children, Jesse, and me. Light skittered faintly in each trough before another peak overtook it, tossing the light until it rose, over and again, piling onto each other but never flooding us here on shore. It seemed extravagant, and yet it was not too much.

Still, I sat, listened, watched. The waves crashed onto shore, singing, lapping, rolling just down below. They washed everything new. Tomorrow I would jump in again, first thing.

Acknowledgments

This book is born out of the generous love of community: you all have shown up in countless ways to make my living and my writing possible. Thank you.

Thank you, dear reader, for your courage to join me in this story. May you find strength to share your own as well, and may it be a blessing.

Thank you to the great many friends and family who have chosen to be present and who have loved us through it all—there are far more of you than fit in these pages, more than I can name or number, and I am grateful to you all.

Thank you, Jane Vandenburgh, endlessly: for believing in this book, for taking me under your wing with such spirit and grace, for reading so many drafts, and for guiding me through it all with love. Thank you, Jack Shoemaker, for your unwavering faith and encouragement, and for your tremendous care in bringing this book into the world. Thank you to the whole Counterpoint team, for your incredible creativity and hard work making this a reality. Thanks especially to Janet Renard for your brilliant copyediting, to Donna Cheng for the cover design, and to Jordan Koluch, Yukiko Tominaga, Carla Bruce-Eddings, Nicole Caputo, Megan Fishmann, Katie Boland: you all are magnificent and such a joy.

Thank you to the dear friends who read drafts of this book, and for your kindness as I wrote. Thank you, Jeannie Koops-Elson, for your companionship, your poetic help with the manuscript, your relentless pursuit of shared delight, and your willingness to brave the depths with me, again and again. Thank you, Sheryl Fullerton, for your keen eye and truth-telling. Thank you, Nikky Wood, for the steady downbeat of your confidence and your deep well of generosity for this book in all its iterations. Thank you, Laurie Walsh, for receiving it first and raw, and with such grace. Thank you for being my rock, my love. Thank you, Phil Brochard, for walking this way with me, on holy ground and in these pages, and for showing me where to hang my heart in this life.

Thank you, Judith Esmay, Lynne Sharp, Caroline McDowell, and Joellynn Monahan, for all your hours of listening and guiding me over the years, for teaching me to hear the call, and to respond. Thank you, Ana Hernández; thank you, Jamie Apgar; and thank you to the Taizé Community: your music makes it easier for me to believe. Thank you, Tom and Cheri Brackett, for taking us on and taking us in, for being sanctuary. Thank you, Ruth Payne, for teaching me to run and to rest. Thank you, Francine A'ness, for teaching me to write in the first place and for your beautiful love all these years.

Thank you, Beth Bojarski, for trusting me with Ella, for teaching me how to grieve, and for walking me through this land. Thank you, Jane Thomason and Laura Eberly, for teaching me about being kin, a truth woven through every bit of this, and for loving our kids so completely. Thank you, Emily Hansen Curran, for continually lending me your joyful reassurance, for your laughter and all the poems, and for being a righteous coach. Thank you, Tripp Hudgins, for your sass, your baked goods, and for showing me the way, one day at a time. Thank you, Lisa Tucker-Gray, for your bold and tender love in suggesting this is the best part of my life.

Thank you to our beloveds—Catherine Crandall, Erik Jacobson, Reed Loy, Linden Rayton, Phoebe MacRae, Karen Orrick, Carmen Wenger, John and Haley Bolin Shellito, Andy Shamel, Callie Swanlund—for your fearless love.

Thank you to the kin of Waycross, for bringing me into the fold, and to the kin of the Edge, for forming my faith over all those Wednesday nights and garlic fries.

Thank you to the wondrous hosts who welcomed us while I was writing: Sandi and Mike, the Campbells and all of Camp Galilee, Camp Stevens, and the Moosilauke Ravine Lodge. Thank you to the Djerassi Resident Artists Program for the gift of time and space, indeed, and thank you to the fabulous writers who have been such good company in that haven. Thank you, good people of All Souls for your spirit, your love, and for your very tangible support through the gift of sabbatical and in letting me set aside that musty old room downstairs in the parish house as a space to write.

Thank you to our family, near and far. Thank you to Annie and Cheri for stepping in to mother me. Thank you to Dan and Annie and Charlotte for weaving our lives together. Thank you, Dad, for the gift of language and laughter, both of which come so clearly from you. Thank you, Mike, for staying with me and for raising me up. Thank you, John, for brothering me, no matter how many miles separate us. Thank you, Carl, for being our adventure and our joy and, in the end, for being all heart.

Thank you, Jesse, Alice, and Sam, for your remarkable patience and boundless encouragement on every one of these days and for loving me and sticking with me, come what may.

And finally, thank you to my sweet mom and beloved son, who are somehow never far away, and to the Holy One who holds us all.

LIZ TICHENOR has put down roots in the Bay Area but is originally from New Hampshire and the Midwest. An Episcopal priest, she serves as rector at the Episcopal Church of the Resurrection, Pleasant Hill, California. Tichenor and her husband, Jesse, are raising two young children and continuing to explore the adventure of living, parenting, and serving in their community.